CLYDE WARRIOR

New Directions in Native American Studies
Colin G. Calloway and K. Tsianina Lomawaima, General Editors

CLYDE WARRIOR

Tradition, Community, and Red Power

By Paul R. McKenzie-Jones

University of Oklahoma Press : Norman

Portions of quotations that appear in this book first appeared in Paul R. McKenzie-Jones's "Evolving Voices of Dissent: The Workshops on American Indian Affairs, 1956–1972" and "'We Are among the Poor, the Powerless, the Inexperienced, and the Inarticulate': Clyde Warrior's Campaign for a 'Greater Indian America'" in *American Indian Quarterly* 38(1) and 34(2), published by the University of Nebraska Press.

Library of Congress Cataloging-in-Publication Data

McKenzie-Jones, Paul R., 1970–
  Clyde Warrior : tradition, community, and Red Power / by Paul R. McKenzie-Jones.
    pages cm. — (New directions in Native American studies)
    Includes bibliographical references and index.
  ISBN 978-0-8061-4705-5 (hardcover : alk. paper) 1. Warrior, Clyde, 1939–1968.
2. Ponca Indians—Biography. 3. Indian activists—United States—Biography.
4. National Indian Youth Council—History—20th century. 5. Indian youth—United States—Political activity—History—20th century. 6. Indians of North America—Politics and government—History—20th century. 7. Indians of North America—Civil rights—History—20th century. 8. Indians of North America—Government relations—History—20th century. 9. Ponca Tribe of Indians of Oklahoma—Social life and customs. 10. Oklahoma—Biography. I. Title.
  E99.P7M34 2015
  323.1197—dc23

2014039244

Clyde Warrior: Tradition, Community, and Red Power is Volume 10 in the New Directions in Native American Studies series.

The paper in this book meets the guidelines for permanence and durability of the Committee on Production Guidelines for Book Longevity of the Council on Library Resources, Inc. ∞

1 2 3 4 5 6 7 8 9 10

For my wife, Yvonne, and our children, Jordan and Lula

CONTENTS

ILLUSTRATIONS

Acknowledgments

As a graduate student in the University of Oklahoma history department in the spring of 2005, during a directed readings course on contemporary American Indian history, Clyde Warrior's name jumped out at me. In each of the texts, however, there was too little information about him to satisfy my curiosity. This curiosity spurred a master's thesis in 2006, a PhD dissertation in 2012, and now this book. There have been many edits and rewrites along the way, and each step has further educated me about the life and vision of Clyde Warrior, one of the most important yet underappreciated American Indian activists of the twentieth century.

To those who shared their memories of Warrior and took the time to retell them, I will be eternally grateful. Warrior's family, from his widow, Della (Otoe-Missouria), to his sisters, Charmain Billy, Darlene Harjo, Elizabeth Primeaux, and Vernice Willis, and his cousin Steve Pensoneau (all Ponca or Otoe), were especially gracious in sharing memories of a cherished family member. Without their memories I would never have understood exactly how intense Warrior's love of his Ponca culture was. Family friends Mona Reed and Thomasine Grass (both Ponca) also added to my understanding of Warrior's relationships within the Ponca Tribe of Oklahoma. Shirley Hill Witt (Mohawk), one of the last surviving founders of the National Indian Youth Council (NIYC), offered instruction as well as memory, and I will always gratefully remember her input and advice, especially with regard to issues of identity, culture, and collective responsibility within the NIYC framework. Fellow NIYC members Charlie Cambridge (Navajo) and Gerald Brown (Flathead) added to my understanding of how cultural identity played an integral role in Warrior's activism. Al Wahrhaftig crossed the bridge between instructor and friend to Warrior, and I thank him for his stories, especially the one about the Cherokee National Air Force. Close friends from Warrior's student days at the University of Oklahoma and the Workshops on American Indian Affairs added invaluable depth to my perception of Warrior, and for this I thank sisters-in-law Jeri Redcorn (Caddo) and Kathryn Red Corn (Osage), Garrick Bailey, and Tony Isaacs. I also wish to thank Frank Turley, whose memories of traveling the powwow circuit with Warrior were enlightening and entertaining. He and Mike Tucker also offered me invaluable firsthand knowledge of Warrior's role in the Poncas' Hethuska Society, as did John Lukavic, Gordon Roy (Ponca), and Jimmy Duncan (Iowa). This knowledge provided me with vital cultural insight into the connection between culture, identity, and activism. Further insight into the history of the modern Hethuska as well as the original society, and the links of Warrior and his family to both, were provided by Jimmy Duncan. Thanks also to Gus Palmer, Jr., (Kiowa) for his childhood memories of traveling from Oklahoma to Gallup, New Mexico, and back, listening to Warrior and his uncle Sylvester sing Ponca and other tribes' songs on the fifteen-hour journey. I must also thank Gus for his added support, advice, and humor as a family friend. Each and every one of the above remains a faithful friend to Warrior, and I am grateful that they trusted me with their memories. I would also like to thank Charmain, Darlene, and Frank especially, for treating me like family and "adopting" me, my wife, and my children in the "Indian Way."

There are several scholars whom I must thank. I don't think I will ever be able to repay them personally for their generosity with their time and knowledge, but I am determined to use them as examples of academic collegiality as I pursue my own academic career. The first is Warren Metcalf. His continued and unstinting support from thesis and dissertation supervisor and editor, to letter writer and general advocate is greatly appreciated. Clyde Ellis shared his vast knowledge of the early Oklahoma powwow circuit and the hobby-ist movement and passed on the contact numbers of several of the sources I thank above. Robert Warrior (Osage) allowed me access to his research files from *Like a Hurricane,* the Indian movement history he coauthored with Paul Chaat Smith, as well as copies of transcripts of interviews he conducted with Della Warrior and Hank Adams. Fred Hoxie allowed me to bounce ideas off him when we shared a shuttle bus to and from the National Archives while I was researching my PhD dissertation. Bradley Shreve shared his insight and understanding of the early years of the NIYC and several documents I had not uncovered, while also helping me far beyond the call of duty with editorial suggestions. My acquisitions editors, Alessandra Tamulevich and Tom Krause, were also a constant source of support and advice through the early stages of the publishing process. My copy editor Chris Dodge has done a sterling job in turning my English prose into American, while Emily Jerman Schuster seamlessly took over the editorial reins from Alessandra.

There are many archivists to whom I also owe thanks: staff at the Center for Southwest Studies at the University of New Mexico; the Special Collections and University Archives Department of Stanford University Libraries; the Wisconsin Historical Society; the National Archives; and the National Museum of the American Indian Archives. All deserve special mention for finding materials and occasionally mailing them from long distance when limited funding constrained my travel plans. I also thank the archivists at the University of Oklahoma's Western History Collections, the Newberry Library, and the special collections departments of the University of Chicago and Princeton University libraries, as well as the University of Illinois Library interlibrary loan staff and Heather Hawkins, a friend of a colleague who happened to be in Albuquerque when I needed to review the NIYC archives there.

Researching and writing a book requires a solid support network, and I was lucky enough to have one on both sides of the Atlantic. Back home, my sister Sharon, brother John, cousins Richard and Kate Parry, and good friends Chris and Janine Bull, Gill Collinson, Catherine and Sam Roberts, and many others were never more than a phone call or e-mail away, often not to talk about research but just to remind me of home and my ties to Liverpool. Without my parents' financial and emotional support, the trip across the Atlantic that enabled me to study at the University of Oklahoma and facilitated my research on Clyde Warrior would never have happened, and I will always thank them for dipping into their meager savings to pay for my plane ticket. On this side of the Atlantic, there are many other people to thank. Matt Despain has allowed me to vent and bounce ideas off him, and he has generally just been there when I've needed to escape for a while. He may be an unreliable timekeeper, but he's a damn fine squash player and an even better friend. John Rhea is another friend who has helped me to crystallize rough ideas through intellectual analysis, especially during the post-dissertation phase of my research, thinking, and writing. My in-laws have helped above and beyond the call of duty. In England we have a tradition of telling slanderous mother-in-law jokes. I can think of no one less deserving of this treatment than Sandy Tiger (Cherokee/Seminole). She and my father-in-law Marcy (Creek/ Seminole) have lent support, occasional sympathy, and often money, and they have flown at the drop of a hat for numerous family emergencies over the years. Above all, they welcomed me unconditionally into their family. At the latter stages of my writing, friends and colleagues in Urbana, Illinois, especially Kate Williams, Marisa Duarte, Nepia and Rangimarie Mahuika, Matt Sakiestewa Gilbert, Vince Diaz, and Tina DeLisle, listened patiently while I put forth ideas, and they offered some very helpful suggestions in how to interpret cultural issues.

My deepest gratitude is reserved for Yvonne Tiger (Creek/Seminole/Cherokee). We met on my first day as a transfer graduate student on the University of Oklahoma campus, and she has stood by my side ever since. To many we seem like an odd couple, the fullblood Oklahoma Indian, raised in Germany, and the working-class Scouser, but we are a team. In our nine years together we have survived two life-threatening pregnancies (more she than me), and we have made it through four master's degrees (two each), a PhD, and the writing of this book. Along the way, she has cajoled, critiqued, edited, and listened. She also produced the two most amazing children I have ever had the pleasure to meet. I have tried my best to be a husband and father first but have not always succeeded. Jordan's entire life has been spent with me behind a computer or away on research trips, to the point that he tells people that I teach "about Clyde Warrior." We often find him in his bedroom conducting his own research on his toy dinosaurs or flooding the bathroom with water experiments, as he too wants to be a 'fessor (albeit a scientific one). Lula was born toward the end of my PhD and like Jordan has known nothing but academia and the strains on family life that my occupation often brings. They both share a wonderful sense of humor and a fearless sense of adventure, which will serve them well in life. My family has intermittently driven me crazy, kept me sane, unnecessarily distracted me, and offered me the perfect pro-crastination excuses. Above all, they have made my life complete, and this book is dedicated to them, for their enduring patience in listening to complaints about deadlines, archival access, and fund-ing, and for listening patiently as I processed my research about Clyde Warrior into the analysis that follows.

INTRODUCTION

Clyde Warrior: Tradition, Community, and Red Power is the first published biography of one of the most sagacious and influential activists of the Red Power movement. Based on primary sources including the oral history of some of his closest friends and family, the text details the complexity of community, tradition, cultural immersion, and tribal identity that surrounded Warrior. It discusses how these issues combined to inform and influence him, his rhetoric, and his campaign for tribal cultural and political autonomy and self-determination. Warrior was the architect of Red Power as an ideology and a movement, an extremely influential leader of young American Indian activists in the 1960s. He was a tenacious campaigner whose rhetoric influenced federal Indian self-determination and education policies. He was an adept and insightful social observer who had the ability to inspire Indian people's hope and anger in equal measure as they fought for cultural relevancy in education, retention of traditional practices and languages, and tribal autonomy.

Warrior was raised in Oklahoma in a traditional Ponca household, wherein Ponca cultural motifs formed the bedrock of his worldview and his later interpretation of Red Power. As a young activist during the civil rights movement era, Warrior used this basis from which to push for tribal self-determination, first as president of the Southwest Regional Indian Youth Council (SRIYC) and later as founding member and ultimately president of the National

Indian Youth Council. Warrior was the first to introduce militant rhetoric into Indian affairs, as he condemned Anglo-Saxons as the "sewage of Europe," derided tribal leaders as "Uncle Tomahawks," and helped take the campaign against treaty abrogation to new levels through protest and direct action.[1] To Warrior, Red Power was the strength of a Native community to preserve its culture, traditions, and integrity while also striving to succeed in the contemporary world. Red Power was the right to speak one's own language, to practice traditions unique to one's own community, and to celebrate one's own culture without fear of reprisal or censure. Self-determination was the political, economic, and social means by which Indian nations could uphold the principles of Red Power as sovereign peoples.

Warrior and his cohorts were educated enough and canny enough to realize the power of using Cold War rhetoric and motifs, such as referencing the Mau Mau uprising in Kenya, to help and protect their own communities. Warrior spoke forthrightly of decolonization, but he was a cultural pluralist who recognized himself as both Ponca and American. He wished to free his Ponca community from the yoke of federal oversight and control, but, secure in his tribal identity, he never demanded his people's freedom from US citizenship. Instead he strove to find ways for the Ponca people to attain personal and communal economic, political, and social success, or at least equity, in the American system without sacrificing their cultural integrity. It was this insistence on cultural integrity that personified Red Power and laid the foundation for an even more militant generation that would follow and remake the ideology in its own image. Clyde Warrior's Red Power was a modern, articulate, and intertribal attempt to protect and preserve the myriad cultures, languages, and traditions of its proponents in a manner that contemporary civil rights and free speech advocates would recognize and celebrate.[2]

Too often in studies of American Indian activism, words such as "tradition" and "culture" are used without explanation or example. Many texts offer compelling accounts of the political issues at stake for later Red Power activists, but these typically fail to address tradition and culture in any depth. This shortcoming is problematic on several levels. It leaves the reader to assume what constitutes tradition for American Indians of different cultures. It ignores the many different traditions, cultures, and identities within Indian Country, and in doing so helps perpetuate the myth of pan-Indian cultural homogeneity. It also tends to place activists' rhetoric and actions in a singularly reactive position against federal government policy. In short, there is ample discussion of what the activists have fought against, but there is scant explanation of what exactly the activists are fighting *for*, beyond political and economic self-determination.

Any history or ethnobiography of American Indians needs to be projected through the prism of cultural relevancy. A discussion of Clyde Warrior's cultural framework and his social identity is absolutely necessary to place his words and their meanings in a proper context. While this book frames Ponca history within the context of Indian-white relations, it also attempts to portray Warrior's tribal culture, and his participation in it, within the more faithful framework of the internal social structures of the tribe. In his essay "Ethics in Writing American Indian History," Donald Fixico insisted that cultural relevancy should be foremost in the mind of writers of Native history. Any such history, he said, should use "introspective analysis of how Indians perceive history with regard to tribal language, values, kinship relations, infrastructure, societal norms, tribal beliefs, and worldview."[3] Each of these issues is covered in this book. For example, with regard to kinship relations, the term "sister" has been used to denote the relationships between Warrior and Charmain Billy, Darlene Harjo, and Elizabeth Pensoneau, as brother and sister are the relational values through which they identified each other. In western societal norms, they are actually Warrior's first cousins. Similarly, the terms "full-blood" and "mixed-blood" are used in the context that Warrior and his cohorts used, not because I think they are correct. I use "American Indian" and occasionally "Indian," rather than "Native American," because these are the terms that Warrior used most often. This is also why I use "tribes" more often than "nations" or "peoples." Fixico also warned that the "ethical scholar" must remain respectful of "sensitive knowledge" about tribal ways and not publish information about certain rituals."[4] I too am committed to this respect when it comes to portraying tribal ceremonies and traditions. All cultural information included is with the permission of informants. Any request that information remain "off the record" has been honored.

Cultural relevancy doesn't rest solely within the realms of tradition and culture in the telling of Warrior's story. It is also, through the creation of model school programs focused upon cultural immersion, one of Warrior's greatest legacies. Warrior and his National Indian Youth Council cohorts identified and implemented programs to pursue one of the most crucial aspects of self-determination, the right for tribes to educate their children in a culturally relevant manner that embraced and celebrated each community's worldview.[5] Toward the end of his life, Warrior crossed educational, racial, and social boundaries to advocate for the tribal peoples of the United States, recognizing and championing the unique history, tradition, and identity of each of these nations. It was this dedication to the preservation of distinct tribal cultures that led former NIYC colleague Hank Adams (Assiniboine) to describe Warrior as a cultural carrier, forging intertribal unions that were previously unheard of and forcing federal officials to pass laws to protect the right of each of these tribes to preserve its own community's future.

In most discussions of Red Power, Warrior is a marginalized figure, dead before the real action begins. Here and there a paragraph discusses his prescience in foretelling the backlash against the system by angry young Indians, the American Indian Movement (AIM), and those who occupied Alcatraz Island. Few historians have fully acknowledged Warrior's influence on these Indians, who were building upon foundations that Warrior and his cohorts had laid. For too many years, Warrior's alcoholism and early death have overshadowed his intellect and achievements. His death from liver failure shortly before his twenty-ninth birthday was indeed tragic, but this should not detract from the ferocity of his speeches, the veracity of his words, his absolute conviction of the validity of his heritage and identity, or his loyalty to his community. Recognition and further analysis are due for a man who helped create and direct a movement that changed the face of American Indian activism in the twentieth century.

Recent books by Daniel M. Cobb and Bradley Shreve have moved to correct this omission. Both correctly reposition Red Power as beginning with the activism of the NIYC rather than the later American Indian Movement. Cobb's *Native Activism in Cold War America* (2008) portrays Warrior and his NIYC cohorts as leading the fight against perceived inconsistencies in the War on Poverty programs of President Lyndon B. Johnson. Cobb's is the first major attempt to reposition the origins of Red Power from the activists of the Alcatraz occupation to an earlier cadre of American Indian youth. Shreve's *Red Power Rising* (2011) shows how the men and women of the NIYC strove to change the face of American Indian activism and change the pace and tone of the rhetoric used. It is the first book since Stan Steiner's *The New Indians* (1968) to capture the vibrancy and urgency of the early Red Power advocates as they introduced direct action as a tactic and strove to form a proactive, rather than reactive, movement for Indian rights. Warrior appears more prominently in *Red Power Rising* than in any other monograph about the Red Power era.

While he did not act alone—recognition needs to be shared with fellow NIYC officers and activists such as Mel Thom, Shirley Hill Witt, Karen Rickard, Hank Adams, and Herb Blatchford, to name a few—Warrior carried an aura that drew people to him. He used this aura, born of his unshakeable self-identity, to drive and cajole people toward his aims. These included culturally relevant education for American Indian schoolchildren and the right of tribal communities to devise and adapt their own social, cultural, and economic development programs. He sought cultural and political self-determination and campaigned long and hard for Indian voices to be heard. By the time he died, the commissioner of Indian affairs was listening, and tribal self-determination policies were being discussed in the White House. Many Indians of Warrior's generation still tell his widow Della how much his words inspired them. Warrior's influence in shaping these polices and gaining educational advances for American Indian children should no longer be ignored.[6]

Clyde Warrior was both a pioneer and a traditionalist. While he moved freely between two worlds, he often had the uncanny knack of upsetting people on either side of the cultural divide with his assessment of Indian-government affairs and tribal communities. Scholars have focused on two of Warrior's essays and speeches,

"Which One Are You? Five Types of American Indian" and "We Are Not Free," using these to highlight Warrior's outspokenness. Such a narrow sample of Warrior's words does him an injustice, however. In October 1969, Stan Steiner wrote to Della Warrior in tribute of her late husband. He suggested, "Someday when the time, the mood is right, one of us should put his words together in a book, or write a book in his words."[7] Neither of them ever completed the task, and that nobody else has attempted it is surprising, given Warrior's position as eloquent speaker and ideological leader of the early Red Power movement. This book is intended to give Warrior's voice a new and wider audience.

CLYDE WARRIOR

PROLOGUE

A Ponca History

An awareness of Ponca history is essential to understanding who Clyde Warrior was as a person and why he led the fight for tribal sovereignty as powerfully as he did. That awareness also reveals the cultural worldview from which he constructed Red Power as an ideology and a movement. The Poncas were originally one of five groups of the Dhegiha division of the Siouan family, which included the Omaha, Osage, Kansa, and Quapaw tribes. These groups had almost identical languages.[1] The tribe's geographic origins are unclear, with some scholars placing them east of the Mississippi River in the Ohio River Valley before migration starting in the sixteenth century led them to what is now Nebraska via the Black Hills, while others trace them back to the Red River near Lake Winnipeg. The tribe settled along the Niobrara River around 1790.

Traditional Ponca spirituality is based on the belief in a single creator, Wakánda, who imbued plants, objects, and people with Xúbe, or supernatural power. This is a variation of a common Plains tribe belief that humans are equal recipients of the creator's power, rather than superior to every other living thing, including the earth itself. According to Shawnee/Iowa teacher Jimmy Duncan, Xúbe is gathered and stored in medicine packets and sacred bundles, with the packets worn or carried about the person and the larger bundles ceremonially stored in a dry, safe place. The bundle itself is known as WaXúbe.[2]

The tribe divided into a clan system, with hereditary clan chiefs and a second set of lesser chiefs beneath them, agreeing upon a principal chief who was the nominal head of the tribe. Records vary as to the exact number of clans within the tribe, but the most commonly recognized number is seven, used by the tribe in contemporary times even though the system is in decline. Besides the clan system the tribe had several martial and spiritual societies, the most prestigious of which was the Hethuska warrior society. There were also several women's societies within the tribe, one of which performed the scalp dances, or Wí-watšì, with which to honor their warriors. Despite the presence of martial societies, it was essentially a peaceful nation, forced to action only in response to incursions.[3]

The Poncas first encountered whites in 1789, when they began dealing with fur trader Jean Baptiste Monier, a Spanish national of French descent.[4] A series of treaties of "peace and friendship" with the United States in 1817 saw the Ponca homelands steadily decrease in size until 1878, when the US government removed the tribe from their lands along the Niobrara River in Nebraska to Indian Territory. By April 1878, after several attempts by the federal government to relocate them in other parts of Indian Territory, almost three hundred Poncas had been forcibly relocated from Nebraska to the fork in the Arkansas and Salt Fork Rivers that became known as White Eagle, a journey of about six hundred miles. The remaining tribal members followed when government funds became available for their removal in July that year.[5] While the Poncas eventually embraced northeastern Oklahoma as their home, the forced removal remained a painful, indelible memory that defined the people's perception of the federal government. It would be a point of reference for much of Warrior's rhetoric during his years as an advocate for tribal self-determination.

Once the majority of the Poncas were reunited, except for those few families who had fled Indian Territory to quietly return north, a feast was planned to commemorate the establishment of the tribe's new homeland. Following a Plains Indian tradition, the Ponca Hethuska Society invited neighboring tribes to the celebration. The tribes who accepted the invitation, the Omahas, Kaws, Osages, Pawnees, and Otoe-Missouria people, all shared similar Plains Indian traditions of introduction and neighborly acceptance. These tribes were also considered the most traditional, unassimilated

Indians in western Indian Territory.[6] The celebration, held in a clearing now known as the South Arena, became an annual homecoming tradition and eventually the modern Ponca intertribal powwow, where Warrior honed his skills as a dancer.[7]

The longest running intertribal powwow in Oklahoma, the Ponca Powwow is held every August at White Eagle, in the North Arena, which is surrounded by bleachers constructed in 1928. The South Arena is still used for smaller, more ceremonial and personal dances. White Eagle is the name the Ponca adopted for their community in 1896 after congressionally approved funding allowed the tribe to purchase the land outright in 1881. The name honors hereditary chief White Eagle, who in 1877 had helped choose land for the new tribal homeland. The funding approval was granted after events sparked by the attempt of another of the clan chiefs, Standing Bear, or Ma-chu-nah-zha, to return home to Nebraska. The events would also have far greater repercussions for the legal status of American Indians throughout the United States.[8]

In December 1878, Chief Standing Bear's son, Bear Shield, died of malaria. Having already lost his daughter Prairie Flower on the tribe's forced trek from Nebraska, he vowed to bury his son in the traditional Ponca burial grounds back in Nebraska. On January 2, 1879, Standing Bear, with his wife and thirty men, women, and children of his band, began the journey home. Upon the group's arrival at the Omaha Reservation, General George Crook was ordered to arrest them so that they could be forced back to Indian Territory. A court case that followed, *United States ex rel. Standing Bear v. Crook*, began on May 1, 1879, and immediately made national headlines, including the front pages of the *New York Times* and *Chicago Tribune*.[9]

Prior to the case, Standing Bear had admitted that "he was not liked and respected by all Ponca chiefs."[10] He acknowledged that the tribe was now split into two distinct camps. The first comprised the traditionalists, who strove to retain the tribe's customs. The second, including himself, comprised assimilationists, who wished to educate their children in non-Native schools. He claimed that their ambition was to become more self-sufficient along Office of Indian Affairs guidelines, no matter the expense to their cultural traditions.[11] The division between traditionalists and assimilationists, which some saw as allegiance either to the Ponca Nation or the United States, became deeply rooted and would persist over many generations. The tribe would still be divided along these lines when Clyde Warrior turned to activism in the 1960s. Warrior commented upon these tribal factions and their conflicting influence and aspirations—tribal community versus individual uplift—in essays he composed at the Workshops on American Indian Affairs in 1961.[12]

In 1880, in response to the Standing Bear case and ensuing Senate hearings on Ponca removal, Ponca chief Standing Buffalo, Clyde Warrior's paternal great-grandfather, wrote two letters to Secretary of State Carl Schurz rescinding the tribe's claim to its Nebraska homelands. In May he informed Schurz that after three years of waiting to return home, the Poncas were "tired" and had "abandoned all hope." The chief now claimed that compensation for "damages committed by the Sioux" would enable them to remain in Indian Territory instead of returning to the Niobrara. In October he informed Schurz that "the land was good" and they just "wanted the white people to leave them alone."[13] In the December hearings, Principal Chief White Eagle testified that all of the tribe's other "principal men" had agreed to the contents of the letter before it was sent. As for Standing Bear and the other absent Poncas, White Eagle told Schurz that "we hope to take them back, but they walk according to their own hearts."[14]

The General Allotment Act of 1887 (the Dawes Act), authorized the federal government to survey communal tribal lands and divided them into private allotments for individual Indians. By 1892, the Jerome Commission, created in 1889 by President Benjamin Harrison and sent to organize allotment of Cherokee and other tribal land in eastern Indian Territory, had achieved relative success in convincing the majority of tribes to accept allotment. The most intransigent opponents were the Poncas. The tribal leaders consistently refused to turn out to meetings in sufficient numbers to produce a legally recognized "council," and the remaining chiefs from the forced removal of fourteen years earlier were particularly unhelpful. Standing Buffalo insisted that he was now too old to hold any influence over the tribe. White Eagle's son, Horse Chief, reminded commissioners that unlike many tribes in the region, the

Poncas actually owned their land and it was "theirs to do with as they wished."[15] He declared that the tribe would not sell its land to the government even if offered seven dollars an acre. White Eagle himself said that he had taken an allotment but could not condone the sale of surplus land unless the entire tribe took allotments and consented to a sale.[16]

Negotiations with the Poncas continued into the summer of 1893. By this time White Eagle assured the commissioners that any surplus land after allotment would need to be retained to provide for the next generation of Poncas "yet to be born," and he closed down any suggestion that there might be room for negotiation over sale of surplus land. Standing Buffalo, backing his chief, raised the ghost of removal and the land lost in Nebraska, telling commissioner David Jerome that "now I am down here like a fox that has no hole." In a move that, decades later, Warrior would condemn as highly illegal, Jerome responded that despite the legal sale of the land the government had "retained title" and could do as it wished with the land, and that the commission would remain in the area until the Poncas agreed to sell it.[17]

At the final meeting between the commissioners and the Poncas on June 6, 1893, Warrior's great-grandfather Standing Buffalo insisted that while white ways might be "superior," the Poncas could not adopt them. He also suspected, quite correctly, that if the Poncas did take allotments and lease out their lands, their white tenants would cheat them. The commissioners returned to Washington without a signed agreement. Although many of the tribe had taken personal allotments, they had not agreed to sell the surplus lands. While the loss of the Ponca lands was a defeat for the government, it had bought more than enough from the other tribes in the area to open the land up to white settlers. In September 1893, settlers lined up to claim new 160-acre homesteads in the area known as the Cherokee Outlet, a vast tract of land that surrounded the Poncas to the north, south, and east.[18]

In 1904 Congress finally recognized defeat over the surplus Ponca land and authorized its allotment to any Ponca children born since 1894.[19] The Ponca victory had far more beneficial repercussions for their Otoe-Missouria neighbors, who were emboldened by the success of the Ponca strategy and refused point blank to enter into discussions. The 1904 act of Congress allowed the tribe to divide its entire land base among its own members, unencumbered from federal interference. Despite this success, Ponca land soon began slipping out of the tribe's control. The passage of the "Dead Indian Act" of 1902, an appropriations act for the "current and contingent expenses of the Indian Department," established a system whereby the heirs of a deceased allottee could sell the land without approval from the secretary of the interior.[20] Meanwhile, a series of hot, dry summers curtailed Ponca farmers' crops, and Indian agents reported increasing drunkenness and despondency. The "Dead Indian Act" provided an opportunity for financial security and people began to sell their allotments.

In 1906, the Burke Act gave the secretary of the interior the authority to arbitrarily circumvent the land sale restrictions of the General Allotment Act. In 1907, the same year that Indian Territory and Oklahoma Territory were incorporated into the state of Oklahoma, the "Noncompetent Indian Act" granted further authority to the secretary to overrule the "noncompetent" status that retained millions of acres of allotments in federal trust status due to the respective allottees' inability to speak, read, or write English. The secretary could now waive this ruling at his own discretion.[21] These three acts of 1904, 1906, and 1907 enabled a total 26,120 acres of Ponca land to be sold. Much of this was purchased by the Miller Brothers, who in 1905 began the Miller Brothers' 101 Ranch and Real Wild West Show.[22] The remaining 75,249 acres were divided between 628 tribal members, except for 524 acres set aside for the tribal cemetery (situated on high ground overlooking the community as per Ponca tradition), agency buildings, and a boarding school, at which the children were forbidden from speaking Ponca.[23] The Clyde Warrior Memorial Building now occupies the old school site.

Those Poncas who remained at White Eagle and the surrounding area fought hard to retain their tribe's cultural identity and traditions. Each winter they set up camps on the Arkansas River, away from their main settlements.[24] A remnant from their past as a nomadic hunter nation, the camps provided shelter and a place for community after men returned from annual summer bison hunts. Prior to relocating to White Eagle and living under restrictions that saw hunting and other cultural practices banned, warriors were sent out to seek a suitable location for the camps as soon as the annual summer Sun Dance ceremony was over. Primary locations were those where shelter might be taken from the bitterly cold Plains winters. Traditionally at the winter camps, tribal historians would take a head count and record the stories of deeds achieved throughout the year, putting these stories in songs, pictographs, and the beadwork for which the Poncas were famous. In later years in White Eagle, these camps of temporary round houses were primarily a communal exercise enabling people to maintain one of their oldest traditions, swap songs and stories, and teach new generations the tribe's history.[25]

In 1909 the Miller Brothers created the 101 Ranch Oil Company, with Ernest W. Marland, to search for oil on their land. In 1911 Marland struck oil on Ponca land leased from Willie Cries-For-War for a thousand dollars a year. The company now known as ConocoPhillips became the Marland Oil Company, and in 1918 a giant refinery was built on the banks of the Arkansas River to process the crude oil that Marland was drilling, now from other leased Ponca and nearby Tonkawa Indian land. The development of the refinery and the Ponca and Tonkawa oilfields caused massive environmental destruction, with the Arkansas quickly becoming highly contaminated with toxic oil waste.[26] The pollution forced the tribe to abandon their practice of winter camping, which resulted in an irreversible change in Ponca culture, by 1915. The loss of the winter camps meant not only disruption of the cyclical nature of tribal life, but that life was now restricted to the vicinity of White Eagle. There was also psychological trauma associated with loss of traditions and customs exclusive to the winter camps, including months of logistical and ceremonial preparation. By this time, the Ponca had already lost the Sun Dance, which had been declared illegal for all tribes under the Courts of Indian Offenses in 1883. Adding to these woes, many homes, including the Collins family farm where Warrior was raised, used water from wells that tapped directly into the now polluted Arkansas and Salt Fork River watersheds.[27]

The Poncas also struggled to maintain the traditions of the Hethuska Society, which would undergo periods of dormancy throughout the years until Warrior's "uncle" Sylvester Warrior, his father Lamont's cousin, revitalized the society in 1958. While the reservation and allotment eras had rendered the martial aspect of the society relevant only for remembrance, the society's other duties—to maintain the tribe's spirituality and to look after the elders, widows, and orphans—continued.[28] Rather ironically, Hethuska-inspired martial societies thrived in neighboring tribes. One of the foremost acts of intertribal respect among Plains nations was the process of gifting songs, dances, and society rights, and since arrival in Indian Territory, Ponca leaders had passed the right to the Hethuska ceremonial to several other tribes, including the Osage, Kansa, Sac and Fox, and Comanche people.

The first diffusion of the Hethuska was to the Osage people in appreciation for their help tending to Ponca elderly and infirm while the Poncas acclimatized to their new environment in Indian Territory. In the gifting of the Hethuska, representatives of the recipient tribes received a drum, specific ceremonial songs, and instructions to form a society within their tribes that represented their own cultural values. As Sylvester Warrior, *nuda'ho"ga* (head man) of the Ponca society in the 1960s and 1970s, later explained, "We passed on the social aspect and retained the spiritual Ponca side [for] ourselves." The respective tribes were expected to add their own spiritual meaning to the songs and societies. This distinction between social and spiritual formed the bedrock of Clyde Warrior's worldview.[29] The society weathered three federal dance bans in 1881, 1893, and 1921 under the Court of Indian Offenses, economic hardship, and declining membership through attrition and the death of its oldest members, but its songs remained with family members to be passed down through the generations. Rather than federal oversight, the main contributor to the early-twentieth-century decline of the Hethuska was a rise in Peyotism and Christianity among the Poncas and the subsequent rejection of their traditional faith. Originally a ceremonial religion of Mexican Indians, Peyotism had spread north in the late 1880s. Recognizing the strength of the two "new" religions and combining them, two Ponca men, Frank Eagle and Louis McDonald, helped found the Native American Church in 1918, with Eagle being elected the church's first president.[30]

The warrior aspect of the Hethuska Society, dormant under federal restrictions and army supervision since removal from Nebraska, was briefly revived during World War I, as young Ponca warriors were inducted into the US military. However, by the end of the war, many Poncas had become converted Christians and disavowed the society. Some of these war veterans created the first American Indian chapter of the American Legion in 1918, naming it Buffalo Post 38 in honor of Bob Buffalohead, a Ponca soldier who had been killed in action.[31] Remarkably, these veterans were not US citizens. The federal government granted citizenship to Indian veterans of World War I a year later, and citizenship for all American Indians finally arrived in 1924 when Congress passed the Indian Citizenship Act.

The Ponca veterans did, however, adopt many of the songs and dances of the Hethuska, adopting a secular approach devoid of the traditional spirituality, which they now found elsewhere. Buffalo Post 38 also formed the "Ladies Auxiliary" that supported the veterans by performing scalp dances and soldier dances in their honor. Many of the original warrior songs of the Hethuska were changed to accommodate new enemies. For instance, one song challenging Spotted Tail to war was changed to include the word "kaiser," in reference to the German leader. The dances of the Hethuska were not restricted to the American Legion, and the burgeoning southern plains powwow circuit, which spread from the Ponca homecoming ceremony, provided an excellent outlet for Ponca singers and dancers, who were recognized among the other tribes as being among the most skillful in Indian Country.[32] It is widely acknowledged that Ponca dancer Gus McDonald created the Fancy War Dance in a 1926 contest between him and two dancers from the Kiowa and Cheyenne nations. The flamboyance, artistry, and sheer athleticism of his dance saw McDonald leave the other two dancers behind, as he incorporated cartwheels and back flips into his repertoire. He was crowned the first Fancy War Dance world champion, a title that Clyde Warrior would later hold three times.[33]

The title of world champion sat well with the Poncas, and their annual powwow became a popular destination for many Indian dancers intent upon challenging McDonald. Throngs of tourists also swarmed to White Eagle each year to view the spectacle. In 1928, the Ponca Indian agent finally granted the tribe's wishes for a dance arena and solicited funds for the creation of one. However, the commissioner of Indian affairs, Charles Burke, author of the 1906 Burke Act and a third federal dance ban ("Circular 1665"), objected and demanded an explanation. The agent responded that the arena would ensure that the Poncas stayed home rather than spending "about half their time attending dances on the Osage reservation."[34] The Osage Inloshka Society had grown in strength as the Ponca Hethuska had dwindled, but in recognition of the society's origins as a gift from the Poncas, the Osages always treated them as honored guests at their dances.[35]

In 1936, two years before Warrior was born, Congress passed the Oklahoma Indian Welfare Act (OIWA), which created a system whereby tribes could create governing councils designed as business councils. The OIWA set aside a revolving credit fund for tribal economic development and halted the allotment process. The OIWA specifically targeted the Five Tribes—the Cherokee, Choctaw, Chickasaw, Creek, and Seminole peoples who had been removed to Oklahoma from the Southeast in the 1830s—and their neighbors. Ostensibly designed to assist tribes economically and protect their cultural, religious, and linguistic rights, the OIWA also introduced what Warrior later described as a "system of peonage" that distinguished between the larger tribes such as the Cherokees and the smaller ones that were deemed more traditional by federal administrators.[36] Rather than drive the economic expansion of the smaller tribes, the OIWA unwittingly created a situation where many of these tribes felt incompetent, and communities withdrew into themselves. The Poncas were such a community and refused to adopt a tribal business committee whose structure bore no resemblance to traditional tribal governance by consensus. By 1950, in the face of potential federal termination as congressional leaders looked for suitable tribes with whom to relinquish the trust relationship, tribal leaders felt compelled to adopt such a governmental structure to preserve their culture and identity.[37]

The Ponca Business Committee, as it was formed in 1950 under the OIWA, focused upon three core tenets as its code of ethics: "Be good to the people; be good to orphans; and be good to the needy."[38] The tribal seal, created at the same time, depicted three tepees, each representing one of these tenets, behind the Poncas' sacred ceremonial pipe.

Thus it was into a conflicted situation that Clyde Warrior was born. Ponca nationalism and traditionalism continued despite cultural loss. Ponca people survived despite poverty, dispossession, collective self-doubt, and schisms between traditionalists and assimilationists, thanks, above all, to an absolute commitment to the community by those who held tradition and identity dear. This cultural and historical inheritance would ultimately define Warrior's ideology of Red Power and underpin his campaign for tribal self-determination.

CHAPTER 1

A PONCA UPBRINGING

"My world was that of my tribe."

In Indian Country, the questions "who are you?" and "where are you from?" often require a more complex answer than merely stating one's name and place of birth. The enquirer usually expects to hear one's name, clan, tribe, and parental and grandparental history. In the pre-reservation era, when the names of renowned warriors and leaders carried great power and afforded family members respect, such an introduction was often a diplomatic necessity. Then and now, lineage, community, and history are intrinsically linked to identity and self-awareness. When addressing youth councils or testifying before Congress, Clyde Warrior usually introduced himself as "a full-blood Ponca Indian from Oklahoma." In more formal cultural or ceremonial settings, he deferred to the traditional protocol of name and familial history described above.[1]

Clyde Merton Warrior was born into the Ponca Tribe of Oklahoma on August 31, 1939. He was the eldest child of Gloria Collins and the only child of her relationship with Lamont Warrior, although both Gloria and Lamont had several children with other partners. Clyde's maternal grandparents were William Collins, Sr., and Metha Collins (née Gives Water). His paternal grandparents were Rolla Oo-hay-ga-he (Making a Path) and Maude Warrior Mon-zhay-gay-tee. In Ponca society, clan membership is patrilineal. Warrior, through his father, was Thí xí'da (Blood) Clan and a direct descendant of Chief Standing Buffalo (Ta-tan-ka-na-jim). Warrior was descended from hereditary chiefs on both sides of his lineage. William Collins, Sr., was a direct descendant of Chief Big Elk (Ompa Donga) through the Wa'xé hé hé'bé (Half Breed) Clan. He also had Irish ancestry on his mother's side, which made him one-sixteenth Irish, or fifteen-sixteenths Ponca/Iowa, as near to full-blood as most American Indians, even in traditional communities like that of the Poncas, could claim by the twentieth century. His Ponca name, given him by his maternal grandfather, was Ma' He Ska (White Knife).[2]

Warrior's maternal grandparents, in keeping with a Ponca tradition still widely practiced at the time, raised him from birth.[3] His mother eventually moved to Enid, Oklahoma, and raised six children there with an Otoe-Missouria husband, after having three more Ponca children, sons Stanley and Colin Snake, and a daughter, Barbara, who was also raised by her grandparents. Although Gloria and Clyde remained close throughout his life, he rarely visited her in Enid, but he was remembered as always being open and loving to his extended Otoe siblings, Charlie, Vernice, Glenda, Susan, Holly, and Levi, when he saw them at the annual Ponca encampment (powwow).[4] Through his grandparents, Warrior was fully immersed in Ponca language, traditions, and customs, which included learning the history of his tribe. This immersion ensured that as he entered adulthood he would have an incredibly strong sense of self, with many friends and colleagues commenting on how easily he mixed with the world around him, white and Indian. Ponca history instilled a determined nationalism within the people—and the reputation of this nationalism was strong even among other tribes in Indian Country. It was a quality that Warrior inherited and wore naturally—and that many of his friends and colleagues remarked upon in Warrior's adult life as an Indian civil rights activist.[5]

Warrior's emergence as the architect of Red Power and as an advocate of tribal sovereignty and cultural self-determination was influenced as much by the Poncas' strong cultural identity as by the brief yet traumatic history of his people's relationship with American settler culture and the federal government. While that history shaped the Poncas and their interaction with the world outside of White Eagle and the surrounding Ponca communities, Warrior's upbringing forged his cultural identity and worldview.

Before his emergence as an activist, that Ponca worldview shaped Warrior as a person. His complete immersion in language, traditions, ceremonies, and songs informed his knowledge of what it meant to be Ponca.[6] In turn, "being Ponca" underscored his later understanding of the issues facing tribal communities across the country as he shaped Red Power as a movement and an ideology. Warrior's Ponca worldview influenced his intertribal, rather than pan-Indian, approach to Indian affairs. This meant that tribal identity took precedence over Indianness at every turn, and Warrior often commented upon the distinction. Warrior viewed Red Power as the distinct and unique cultural identities and heritages inherent within tribal nations throughout the United States. Red Power was not just something to fight for; it was something to protect and preserve.[7]

Warrior was raised by his maternal grandparents on the Collins family farm, a working farm situated in Bois D'Arc, a Ponca community approximately two miles due west of the Ponca tribal complex at White Eagle.[8] The family grew corn, green beans, onions, and tomatoes, and raised cows, hogs, and chickens.[9] As Metha Collins, Warrior's grandmother, required a wheelchair for mobility in her later life, the younger children of the family were responsible for many of the lighter manual tasks around the farm, such as gathering eggs or drawing water from the well. What food the farm did not provide, such as rabbit or fish, they hunted, living off the land as much as they could.[10] Having attended the Ponca school at White Eagle until he entered junior high school at twelve years old, Warrior's cultural contacts were almost exclusively Ponca. Any external influences came from neighboring tribal communities and elders with whom his grandparents mixed.

Despite living apart from the tribal complex, the family maintained strong ties to the White Eagle community. Warrior described being "raised by my grandparents in a typical American Indian home, poverty stricken . . . my world was that of my tribe and I (took) part in all gatherings, organization, and functions of my tribe."[11] Part of Warrior's upbringing was learning to understand the pipe religion and spiritual significance of tobacco as the plant that connected the creator to the earth, a belief that was still strong

The Collins family farm where Warrior grew up, now unused and overgrown.

in some elements of Ponca society. For followers of the traditional spirituality, it was usually a private affair. In the late 1950s Warrior's friend Frank Turley casually remarked to Warrior, as he saw Grandpa Bill light some tobacco, that he had never realized that Clyde's grandpa smoked. Warrior, laughing, retorted, "[H]e's praying, you idiot."[12] According to James Howard, the Ponca tribal pipe, which was also the sacred pipe of the Hethuska Society, was in the property of Mrs. Grace Warrior (née Standing Buffalo) as recently as 1954. By the time of the society's revival in 1958, however, Grace was alleged to have sold the pipe to a collector. Jimmy Duncan remembered that Clyde Warrior spent his life searching unsuccessfully for the pipe in an attempt to return it to the tribe.[13]

Many afternoons after school Warrior would sit at the feet of his grandfather, listening to discussions of tribal politics, gossip, and stories and songs shared with friends. Elders from other tribes, including the Otoe, Osage, Tonkawa, and Kiowa nations, were regular visitors to the Collins kitchen. It was here that Warrior learned respect for, and insight into, tribal cultures other than his own, and he came to know the crucial role of tribal elders in maintaining and preserving those cultures. He also learned the arts of listening—to his elders—and talking, and he gained a strong sense of social responsibility in a traditional setting.

As it was spent raised in a traditional household, Warrior's childhood was filled with song. By the age of four he could join in and even lead the many songs he heard his grandparents sing. Singing was such an integral part of the Collins home that most mornings began with Grandpa Bill singing Ponca prayers and war songs as he prepared breakfast or coffee at the kitchen's large pot-bellied stove.[14] Bill and Metha Collins were drum makers who began selling their drums in 1928, and Warrior did not simply watch his grandparents in the long, arduous, culturally uplifting process of making the traditional drums—he joined them. The process was far more than simple manual labor and construction. Clyde's immersion in this process gave him a respect for, and attachment to, Ponca traditions and culture beyond that of many of his generation.

For many American Indians, across all tribes, the drum is much more than simply a musical instrument. It is a significant and spiritual symbol of the earth's power. The drumbeat holds a variety of meanings, ranging from thunder to the heartbeat of the earth itself. As such, many people across Indian Country view the drum as a living, breathing entity. In powwow and ceremonial situations the drum is central. Without it there would be no ceremony. Therefore a great deal of respect and honor is paid to drum makers. The traditional creation of a drum begins with skinning cattle. The age of the animal is significant, with Warrior's grandfather insisting that it must be "over two years old or the hide will be thin."[15] Warrior's sister Betty Pensoneau recounted having to negotiate her way through cattle carcasses and drying hides whenever she was on the farm. Warrior and his grandparents would strip the fur from each hide, which was then repeatedly washed in cold soapy water before being left to partially dry in the sun, returning to it when it was slightly damp rather than saturated. While the hide was drying, Warrior and his grandparents would strengthen the midsection of a large wooden barrel with an iron "wheel rim," which they inserted and fastened inside. They would then cover the barrel with bark from an ash tree. Once the hide was almost dry they would cut it in two and then stretch a piece over each end of the barrel. Once the hide was stretched, Warrior or his grandparents would cut a series of slits into the drum skins and then lace dried sinew from the same animal through the slits to tie the two drum skins together. They would then tighten the threaded sinew until the skins were taut enough to make the musical tone of a "tuned" drum rather than the dull thud of an "out of tune" one. They would then leave the drum out in the sun for the skin to dry completely, occasionally tightening the lacing to ensure that the skin remained taut as it dried. The process was the same whether the Collinses were making small hand drums or larger "powwow drums." Each drum would take Warrior and his grandparents several days to complete. Toward the end of the process, Grandma Metha would, as she described, "put several songs in the drum when I lace it." Grandpa Bill, meanwhile, would "lift it and beat a song into it when it [was] finished." These songs were important because they established a form of "medicine" inside the drum that created a sense of what Bill called "good feeling, a feeling of health and prosperity."[16] Having grown up in this environment, Warrior became a skilled singer and drummer by a very young age, perhaps inevitably.

Warrior's grandparents also taught him the difference between social and ceremonial meanings of the songs and the drum. There was a distinction between social and ceremonial practices that generations of Plains Indians had observed as they shared songs and dances between tribes as methods of diplomacy, an intertribal diffusion that laid the foundations for the evolution of the powwow. Many academics argue that this cultural diffusion ultimately created a homogenous pan-Indian culture. Those involved in the process saw it differently, however. For example, Warrior's uncle Sylvester insisted that the Poncas had clearly defined the difference between spiritual and social when they gave their Hethuska ceremonies to neighboring tribes. It was a distinction that Warrior himself would carry forward as a young adult as he delineated clear cultural differences between not just the Indian and non-Indian worlds, but also between differing tribal worldviews within the framework of Indianness. His grandparents raised him to be aware of the economic necessity of catering to the tastes of non-Indians by creating different styles of drum for sale. For tourists and non-Indians, the Collinses painted the drum skins with a picture of an Indian chief in full headdress. There was no such decoration on drums intended for Indians, though, as "Indians care only for the sound. They don't want paint that may flake off after many beatings."[17]

The Collinses sold their drums all across Indian Country. This included the annual Gallup Ceremonial in Gallup, New Mexico (where there was always an abundance of tourist traffic), the Miller Brothers Ranch 101 Real Wild West Show store in Ponca City, and on the southern plains powwow circuit in and around Oklahoma. Both the Gallup Ceremonial and the powwow circuit heavily influenced Warrior. The first dated back to 1920, when Indian superintendent Samuel Stacker conceived the event. The Indian Ceremonial, as it was first called, took place at Crownpoint, New Mexico, in 1920 before moving to Gallup in 1922. Here the organizing committee, under the control of the Gallup Chamber of Commerce, adopted a grander title: Gallup Intertribal Ceremonial Exhibition. The event was first organized to showcase the dances of Navajo and neighboring tribes, and, instead of receiving monetary payment, "all Indians attending were furnished food, hay and oats for their horses, with camping space on the ceremonial grounds."[18] By 1929, the food available to Indian dancers and artists included a daily free barbecue. It was noted that "55 goats, five beeves and 700 loaves of bread" were eaten during the three-day event.[19]

In the 1930s the Gallup Ceremonial expanded its exhibits and gradually recruited dancers from the Plains as well as California and New York tribes. Warrior accompanied his grandparents on their trips to New Mexico and quickly became aware of the many cultural distinctions between the various nations that attended the Ceremonial. He observed the Pottawatomi Eagle Dance, Apache Fire Dance, Hopi Katzina Dance, Taos Surrender Dance, and Zuni Butterfly Dance, and saw descendants of Aztecs wearing long headdresses, pheasant feathers, and peacock feathers.[20] Ceremonial programs gave a brief history of each dance and the significance to the particular tribe that performed it.

The vast intertribal gathering exerted a considerable influence on Warrior throughout his life. The trips to Gallup, which usually included his uncle Sylvester, who on these occasions sang with a Kiowa drum accompanying Kiowa dancers, educated Warrior in the myriad songs and dances and languages of Indian nations. At the "49s," social gatherings that followed each day's dancing, Indians from many nations would mix and share songs and dances, teaching and learning from each other. No small amount of alcohol was consumed as old friends caught up with each other, romances were kindled, and stories swapped. The experience enhanced Warrior's cultural understanding of Indianness within the context of the sheer diversity of ceremony, tradition, and performance throughout Indian Country. This cultural awareness and sensitivity, rather than Indian/white relationships or the suffocating racism he was surrounded by in Ponca City, dominated his worldview.[21]

The southern plains powwow circuit, in contrast to Gallup, evolved in two separate stages. The first started with a Ponca intertribal dance in 1878 and an intertribal feast commemorating the survival of Poncas in the forced removal from their homelands in Nebraska to Indian Territory. Following a Plains Indian tradition, the Ponca Hethuska Society, invited neighboring tribes to the celebration. Eventually going beyond Ponca-organized intertribal events, a southern plains powwow circuit grew and spread in the 1920s.[22]

The second stage of the circuit's growth occurred in the wake of World War II, as many Plains tribes felt the necessity to revive age-old but long dormant warrior traditions to honor those among them who had enlisted in the US military. The revival of warrior societies and ceremonial dances had a domino effect, creating greater interest and demand for a more social and inclusive form of cultural expression, which the powwow filled. As powwows grew in popularity, a generalized "war dance" was replaced by specific contest categories. Each of the male categories were derived from traditional Plains Indian military society ceremonial dances, and the most popular categories were Straight Dance or Southern Traditional, Grass Dance, and Fancy Dance. At this time the Chicken Dance and Northern Traditional were exclusively performed at northern plains powwows. The distinction between northern and southern plains traditional dances traced back to the Poncas' arrival in Indian Territory, with the southern regalia resembling post-bustle Hethuska regalia, which had been shared as the Poncas gifted the rights to their ceremony across the region. The commonality of Straight Dance regalia—including the otter sash/drop reciprocally gifted to the Poncas by the Osages—and songs harked back to the Ponca diffusion of the social aspect of the Hethuska Society to other tribes.[23]

As educational and enthralling as Gallup was to Warrior, he felt much more at home on the southern plains powwow circuit. Even though the Poncas had no ceremonial societies themselves after the 1920s, Ponca singers were a regular presence on the circuit and their talent was widely respected. The Ponca Powwow was also a highly popular event on the Oklahoma powwow calendar. It was a five-day celebration of war dancing, with dances that closely followed the traditions of the Hethuska ceremonial dances. Warrior's grandfather, Bill Collins, had been a member of the Hethuska Society before it disbanded in 1929, and he had taught Warrior many of its songs and dances. This was a traditional practice among Plains Indians as a way of keeping their ceremonies and traditions alive, even if they appeared to be in decline or lost to future generations. As well as the traditional Hethuska dancing, which transferred to the Straight Dance powwow category, Grandpa Bill also taught Warrior the Fancy Dance moves that he himself had learned from Gus McDonald, a close family friend, and the original Fancy Dance world champion, as well as the traditional feather-pulling contest that the Poncas had shared with the Sioux during the pre-reservation era.[24] The contest was an annual event that marked "a day of grace or peace" between the two nations. A four-inch feather was placed in the ground and dancers from both tribes would position themselves either side of it. Issues were resolved in favor of the tribe whose dancer managed to remove the feather from the floor with his teeth while in full motion and ensuring that his arms did not touch the floor.[25] Warrior's uncle Sylvester was also a skilled singer and drummer, and Warrior benefited from his advice and expertise, as well as that of Owen Walkingsky.

Whether sitting at his grandfather's feet or visiting the Gallup Ceremonial, Warrior absorbed many different types of songs, and his college roommate Tony Isaacs credited Warrior with an uncanny, sensitive, and "very intuitive" ability to "feel" songs.[26] This foundation—learning the cultural necessity of songs, social and ceremonial, to Indian peoples and identity—formed the basis of his activism in years to come.[27] Warrior learned when a song could be used for both social and spiritual or ceremonial purposes, and he created a vast, internal database of songs from many different tribes that he could recall at a moment's notice. The powwow circuit was a natural extension of Warrior's cultural comfort zone and introduced him to the Plains tradition of intertribal recognition of shared contexts and meanings within songs and dances. By the time he was just four years old, his grandfather had "paid" his entry into the dance arena with a gift to the drum (as the singers and drummers are collectively known), the request of a particular family song, and a giveaway for respected friends and Gives Water Service Club members.[28]

Warrior was already a fluid dancer and skillful singer in his young teenage years, with an affinity for the songs and dances of other tribes that many of his friends and peers would comment upon. Isaacs depicted Warrior as "the only Indian that I had ever met that whistled Indian songs."[29] This affinity would serve him well, because, as fluid and skillful as a dancer might be, there are other vital aspects to any Fancy Dance. A dancer's feet need to touch the ground upon every honor beat, and he must be able to stop dead in his tracks the second the song ends.[30] Neither of these requirements is easy given the tempo at which Fancy Dance songs are sung.

Warrior's Ponca heritage undoubtedly helped him develop his dancing skills, and the Ponca singers held the reputation as the best Fancy Dance singers in Indian Country. Gus Palmer, Jr., remembered them as being the best, saying, "They're fast, and they're in the ruffle dance, they call it. It's the real fast one, where they roll around. You get down and shimmy all over. And then when the drum goes, you go, but you don't know when it's going to stop."[31] The ruffle dance—or trick dance, as it is also known—is musically idiosyncratic, stopping and starting at irregular intervals, and it was a Ponca invention. Dancers who master the ruffle dance are supremely talented, as it takes enormous concentration to focus on high-speed footwork and unexpected drumbeats. In 1954, at the age of sixteen, Warrior was crowned world champion Fancy Dancer at the annual Ponca Powwow. This was a title he would win twice more, including a 1956 dance-off with Vance Buffalohead. In later years he switched to the Straight Dance category.[32]

It is essential to understand the complexity of the intertribal, rather than pan-Indian, relationships within the powwow circuit in order to fully appreciate the influence of inter-tribalism upon Warrior's activism. As already mentioned, Poncas gave Hethuska traditions to the Osages, Kansa, Sac and Fox, and Comanche people as a mark of respect and honor.[33] This diffusion across the southern plains formed the template for the southern powwow circuit, with many of the dances appearing very similar across tribal boundaries. This similarity of songs and regalia was a factor in academics labeling the celebration pan-Indian, predicting that this would lead to complete assimilation into American society.[34]

Even in dormancy, the Hethuska Society still informed many aspects of Ponca life, and the home and powwows were not the only places where Warrior received a cultural education. In 1945, Grandma Metha, from the Gives Water family, organized the Gives Water Service Club in recognition of the Poncas who had served in World War II. For Metha, the word "service" carried a double meaning: honoring veterans but also referring to service to those in the tribe who needed help. Her intention in forming the club was to gather baskets for single mothers and other needy people in the community, and she requested donations of food, clothing, or anything else that was useful. She also formalized the "free feed," based on the Gives Water tradition of feeding whomever stopped by, when "people would come out to the Gives Water family arbor just to be fed."[35]

In the 1960s, Albert Waters, Metha's uncle and a Gives Water family member, occupied the clan's ceremonial land. Waters, who headed the Ponca singers, constructed the arbor under which the Service Club gathered for an annual dance. It was traditions such as this that Warrior insisted were necessary for tribal communities

Warrior being presented with the Ponca Powwow Fancy Dance World Championship (McDonald Family) trophy in 1956 by Rochelle McDonald, granddaughter of Gus McDonald. (Courtesy of the *Ponca City News*.)

to carry forward to retain their cultural integrity. Many Gives Waters ancestors had been prominent Hethuska Society members in the past, and the tribal ethos of always helping others sat naturally with them. Indeed, many of the veterans' songs, war songs and round dance songs the Service Club performed were based upon traditional Hethuska songs. This continued to be the case after the society's revival in 1958. Regalia for the dance was, and still is, the same Hethuska-style regalia that became known as Straight Dance regalia in the powwow world. As at the powwows, women dancers are required to wear a shawl, over the shoulders or draped across an arm, before entering the arbor.[36]

Each day of the dance began with Metha addressing the gathered crowd and leading a procession into the arena. In later years she was pushed in her wheelchair. Aside from warrior and veterans' songs, the drum sang "specials" in honor of specific veterans. Specials, which are common at southern plains powwows, usually consist of a family or clan song being sung by the drum while the honored one returns the gesture by conducting a "giveaway." The person hosting the special gives away groceries and blankets, harking back to pre-reservation commitments to provide each other with food and shelter. Between 1883 and 1934 the Courts of Indian Offenses had deemed giveaways illegal, with the federal government considering such apparently wanton disregard for property a prime example of Indian "savagery." Each member of the Gives Water family, including Warrior, attended the dances and helped with honoring the veterans through feasts, dances, and other activities that were required.[37] The Gives Water Service Club continues to be a prominent and respected organization in Ponca culture, hosting gatherings every Memorial Day and sponsoring charitable dances throughout the year.

The annual Ponca dance was especially important to Warrior because of the connection to Metha, his maternal grandmother. As a Gives Water, a widely respected dancer and singer, and later a tail dancer for the Hethuska Society, and as a dedicated follower and proponent of tradition, Warrior saw it as his duty and honor to attend each year. This commitment also exemplified his attitude toward the continuity of tradition and community as the basis for a successful tribal future. Although he was of a generation too young to be involved in many of the older traditions, he understood their value enough to grasp the importance of *ga-hi-ga* and *wa-shu-she*. Translated into English, these concepts roughly mean "carrying the people on my back," which epitomizes the Gives Water ethos, and "to make bravery a part of your being." Warrior's campaign

Warrior (*holding trophy*), next to Rochelle McDonald, with powwow chairman Francis Eagle (*hat*), and Fancy Dance third-place winner Nick Webster (*left*) and second-place winner Vance Buffalohead (*center*) in 1956. (Courtesy of the *Ponca City News*.)

for self-determination encapsulated both of these concepts and re-flected the depth of his cultural immersion.[38] Such was the respect he was afforded by fellow traditionalists that he was made wel-come at the drum whenever he was home, and while he constantly impressed his friends and family with his vast knowledge of other tribes' songs, he was always most at home with his Ponca songs, dances, and prayers. So vast is the number of Ponca songs available that it is a common tribal boast that they can "sing for four days and four nights without singing the same song."[39] The honoring rejuve-nated him and brought him back to the bosom of his family, where, according to his widow Della, "he was always happiest."[40]

In addition to powwows (including the Gallup Ceremonial) and the Gives Water dances, Warrior's childhood also included regular visits to the Indian Village at Quapaw, Oklahoma. Located on US

Route 66, this was a massive trading post that sold regalia, fabric, beads, and drums, catering to Indians and tourists alike. His grand-parents sold drums there, and occasionally Warrior danced for tourists in his Fancy Dance regalia, an image of which was immor-talized on a postcard. It was here that he met Bill Center, a trader and hobbyist from Pawhuska who had extensive contacts with the California hobbyist movement of non-Natives who dressed as Indians and copied their dances. Center later told people that he had first seen Warrior "running on the roofs of the cabins, jumping from one roof to another, and hollering and carrying on like a wild young man." He saw Warrior dance later in the afternoon and gave the fifteen-year-old boy some cash in appreciation of his talent.[41] He also bought some of Warrior's grandparents' drums to sell in California and at his trading post in Old Town, Albuquerque.

The relationship between the Collinses and Center went much deeper than business, and Center took Warrior under his wing, acting as a surrogate father with the blessing of Bill and Metha. Sources vary as to Warrior's relationship with his biological father, from seeing his father absent for the most of Warrior's life to say-ing they had a good relationship.[42] It is similar with his mother: al-though she and Warrior are described as being close, she is largely absent from conversations about Warrior and his childhood. As surrogate father, Center often took Warrior with him on trips to California and exposed him to a vastly different world from Okla-homa. On his first visit to Los Angeles, Warrior went down to the shore by himself and "sang to the ocean," so awestruck was he by the sight and the power of the vast expanse of water. It was also in California that Warrior began an unusual and enduring friendship with a number of hobbyists.[43]

The hobbyist movement evolved from the early-twentieth-century Indian lore enthusiasts described by Clyde Ellis in "More Real Than the Indians Themselves." By the 1960s hobbyists were usually former Boy Scouts who had witnessed Sioux ceremonial dancing during Scout-led rites of passage and decided to "adopt" Indian practices in adulthood. For many Indians, hobbyists are un-welcome "cultural tourists" who play at being Indian, with no real appreciation for the true nature or meaning of song and dance to

Indian cultures.[44] Warrior, however, was impressed by how much the California hobbyists attempted to respect the traditions of the songs and ceremonies they copied. He was welcoming and open to anyone who displayed a genuine interest in learning about his heritage. He trusted the hobbyists because they never adopted the paternalistic attitude that Indian songs and dances were dying out and needed to be saved. Instead, they immersed themselves respectfully in the Indian powwow world and became friends with Warrior and other Indians rather than ghoulish observers. Due to Warrior's willingness to share with them, the hobbyists' interest changed from their usual fare of Sioux and Northern Plains songs to Ponca culture, songs, and dances. Frank Turley, a hobbyist Center employed to teach children to sing and dance, and his friend Jim Steiner, began to accompany Warrior back and forth on his trips between California and Bois D'Arc.

Turley remembered, "the three of us would be driving around, beating on the dashboard and singing." They would also swap stories, including one of Warrior's first stint as a seasonal worker in Disneyland, employed to paddle tourists around in canoes. Warrior spent two summers working at Disneyland to earn enough money to stay in California. He spent the first summer "playing Indian" as a tourist guide and the second doing manual work around the amusement park. On one occasion a precocious child insisted that everything in Disneyland was make believe and that Warrior was therefore "not a real Indian." No matter how hard he tried, Warrior was unable to convince the boy that he was a real Indian. Warrior used to laugh a lot, Turley recalled, at the memory of being called a fake Indian.[45]

Warrior's friendship with the hobbyists displayed his absolute self-confidence in his identity and culture. Turley described Warrior as having a large "coterie of friends from different tribes that would sing and dance together whenever possible." Warrior also introduced Turley and friends such as Tony Isaacs to the 49, where he would always be at the drum, singing songs he had picked up from the powwow circuit and the Gallup Ceremonial, as well as the Ponca songs he had been raised with. Warrior and his uncle Sylvester had met Isaacs at a California powwow in 1958. Many of the hobbyists saw Warrior as an "ambassador" due to his friendly charm and magnetism, especially because he would take time to talk with those of them interested in Ponca music and traditions.[46] Turley and Isaacs appreciated that Warrior was willing to share, especially because, as Turley described, "so many of the Ponca songs are word songs"—that is, not simply consisting of vocables. "He would help translate and that was really valuable for me. Because I wanted to learn." Mutual respect led to a friendship that would last the rest of Warrior's life.[47]

Isaacs described Warrior as very passionate and was thankful to him for teaching him a lot about Ponca songs and the ways of others Indians, with long chats into the night about various tribal, ceremonial, and social songs. He recalled that during visits to Boulder, Colorado, where Warrior attended summer student workshops, Warrior would have off-the-cuff singing contests with a Winnebago named Andy Thundercloud, wherein they would try to out-sing each other, dueling back and forth with Ponca and Winnebago songs. Isaacs, a skilled musicologist, was also struck by how, as passionate as Warrior was about Ponca songs, he was also instinctively and intuitively receptive to all tribal songs. He was astonished one evening as he and Warrior listened to a recording of Sioux songs. Halfway through the recording, Warrior told him, "Listen, they're crying," as he could hear pain in the song and the inflections of the voices. Although the song was being sung in Lakota, Warrior could hear the lament in their voices and was astonished by the skill of the singers. He instructed Isaacs to listen, saying, "You know they're crying. . . . It's amazing what you can do with a bunch of yo's and heys." Through conversations such as this, Warrior taught Isaacs a great deal about how to listen and interpret the many nuances and idiosyncrasies that make each war, stomp, ceremonial, or powwow song unique. He would later utilize this in a long and successful career as the owner and creative driving forced behind a recording and distribution company, Indian House Records.[48]

Warrior's friendship with Isaacs and Turley extended beyond cultural sharing, and he often took them home to the Collins family farm, where they were welcomed as part of the family. One such visit was at Thanksgiving in 1964. Isaacs described Warrior striding into the house with his two guests in tow and announcing, "look Grandma, I brought Pilgrims."[49] Warrior's sister Charmain Billy recalled people rushing to the farm to hear Warrior's stories, yelling "Clyde is back! Clyde is back!" and greeting him like an adventurer returning from far-flung lands.[50] Because of the number of people present, the dinner table was too small for the occasion, and the meal was set out on a large canvas sheet spread across the floor. With everybody seated around it in a circle, Warrior's sister Darlene blushed as she recalled being teased as the food was passed around, with her brother nudging her and saying "hurry up, darlin'—darlin' Darlene."[51]

Warrior's open attitude toward the hobbyists was in sharp contrast to that of many Oklahoma Indians, who deeply mistrusted their motives. The openness came about because of his childhood experiences around tourists and his attending a public school, Ponca City High School. At the time he resented being one of a handful of young Indians forced to attend "white school" rather than Chilocco, the Indian school north of Ponca City where most of his Ponca friends went. The experience of attending a predominantly white school eventually gave him insight into everyday American culture and societal structures. As an adult, he would always be grateful that he had not been sent to Chilocco. Ponca City High School was not an easy experience for him, however. He later remembered, "During my high school life, I really experienced no association with the dominant society."[52] In other words, though he attended school with white students daily, he rarely mixed socially with them. On a social, cultural, and economic level, they were from different worlds. He later admitted "I used to hate white people and hated them with good reason. I went around hating them for years." But, he added, "I realized that it wasn't the white people I hated, it was the bureaucracy, the institutions they created, the education, the system."[53] Warrior was surrounded by white students in a town renowned at the time for its racist attitudes, especially toward the Poncas—and to such an extent that when he walked to and from school, Warrior carried a bat for self-protection.

White Ponca City residents' anti-Indian racism focused upon the Ponca community, some say out of resentment of the town's name. Della Warrior, Clyde's widow, grew up in the Otoe-Missouria community just south of White Eagle. She recalled applying for a job in Ponca City as a young woman and the employment counselor noting on her application that she was neat, clean, and pretty, before commenting, "You're not from around here are you? You're not like the rest of these Indians"—though she still didn't get the job.[54] Similarly, Warrior's friend Kathryn Red Corn (Osage), who met them both at the University of Oklahoma and roomed with Della, remembered the shock on Warrior's face when he discovered the she and her Osage friends were served openly and welcomed warmly at Dean's Barbeque, a local restaurant.[55] The establishment had a blanket ban on serving Ponca Indians. There were also common tales of Ponca children as young as nine or ten being strip-searched on the street under accusation of shoplifting.[56]

The communal and individual poverty of the Ponca people was exacerbated by the fact that the only facility that would have openly employed them was the oil refinery, but Poncas refused to work there due to long-standing disputes over leasing and mineral rights and pollution of the Arkansas and Salt Fork Rivers. Poncas were often subject to the same sort of segregation as African Americans suffered in the Jim Crow South. Many garages in town would have "white" entrances and "Negro/Ponca" ones. Those restaurants that would serve them operated "white" counters and separate "Negro/Ponca" ones.[57] Such was the pervading atmosphere of the town in which Warrior attended a predominantly white high school. As he lived "off reservation," the choice of where Warrior was educated fell out of the realm of Bureau of Indian Affairs (BIA) authority and lay with his grandparents. Perhaps influenced by their own bitter experiences at boarding schools, they deemed the local public school the lesser of the two evils when it came to offering Warrior an education. Despite segregation elsewhere in the city, Indian schoolchildren were required to attend the white schools rather than African American ones.

Warrior initially refused to learn English or accept any instruction from his teachers. He later described how, as late as eighth grade, "I thought that English was a bunch of nonsense. I would scream, almost scream, that my language was sufficient enough for me to be understood, that there was absolutely no reason why I should bother learning English." Once he began to learn the language, however, he became a voracious reader and enrolled in the school's Library Club for his final three grades as a student. Socially, he found that money, or the lack of it, played as much a part in being accepted by his white peers as race and language. He recalled that as a Ponca, "you knew you didn't fit. Economically you didn't fit, socially you didn't fit." The situation was occasionally so restrictive that he sometimes gave up: "There wasn't a year that I didn't quit school at least twice."[58]

Warrior remembered participating in functions "to the greatest extent of which I was permitted—which was not much due to the dominant attitude and also my background of limited resources."[59] He did find respite, and some acceptance, in music, as a tuba-playing member of the school's "Big Blue" band. He played in the January 1957 Rose Bowl Parade in Pasadena, California, after band members raised $13,500 to pay their way. His cousin Steve Pensoneau described the entire family huddling round a television and hearing his aunts yell out "there's Clyde!" as the cameras briefly panned past Warrior.[60]

Attending a predominantly white high school taught Warrior methods of survival and interaction that served him well later in life. The experience also showed him, although it would be years before he could articulate it, that the educational requirements of the American system clashed dramatically with the worldviews of American Indian students. Despite this intellectual and cultural clash, the experience gave him knowledge of modernity in the United States. This knowledge and experience later allowed him to frame his rhetoric on terms that both sides of the racial divide could understand.[61]

This rhetoric came later, though, with the maturity of adulthood. As a teen he retreated into traditionalism and the retention of his Ponca culture and worldview. In 1958, he assisted his uncle Sylvester and Owen Walkingsky in the revitalization of the Hethuska Society. He was nineteen years old at the time. Until this point, Poncas had contented themselves with singing at the Hethuska derivatives of the Osage Inloshka Society (still faithfully performed in the towns of Pawhuska, Hominy, and Gray Horse, Oklahoma),

Warrior (*right*) places third in Ponca Powwow Fancy Dance World Championship in 1957; pictured with winner Ted Moore (*left*) and runner-up Cecil Louwalk (*center*). (Courtesy of the *Ponca City News*.)

the Pawnee Ruska, and the Otoe Inloshka. The process of reviving the Hethuska began with Sylvester Warrior's experiences as a marine in World War II, when he witnessed Indians of other tribes perform their ceremonial dances in the Pacific. Seeing Apache soldiers perform their Devil Dance, Pottawatomis perform the Eagle Dance, and Hopis perform the Hoop Dance, and experiencing Navajo Mountain Chants and Kiowa and Comanche War Dances made Sylvester Warrior anxious to reconnect with his own familial, clan, and tribal traditions. The dances he witnessed were true ceremonial dances rather than the social versions displayed for tourists that he and Clyde had observed at the Gallup Ceremonial. The more intense performance made him determined to reinvigorate the Poncas' most revered ceremonial society and dances. The Hethuska Society quickly became an integral part of Warrior's identity and worldview.[62]

Sylvester Warrior was raised by his mother, Standing Buffalo's daughter, but his paternal grandfather was also a great influence on his life and cultural upbringing. Big Kansas (Konze to"ga), one of the Ponca chiefs who had traveled to Washington with White Eagle and Standing Bear in the 1880s, taught Sylvester the same Hethuska songs that Grandpa Bill taught Clyde. His mother also passed on to Sylvester the two personal songs that had been given to Standing Buffalo during his life. This background was fundamental to Sylvester as he tried to piece together as much information as he could about the original society, its rules, etiquette, and cultural values to the Ponca people.[63]

Sylvester's ambition, he promised, was to "provide inspiration for younger Poncas to keep our Ponca ways," but he found unexpected resistance from many of the older generation, including those who had been members of the original Hethuska Society.[64] To this generation, the Hethuska was a "memory of times that could not be brought back."[65] To Grace Warrior's generation, many of whom had converted to the Native American Church, the Hethuska represented an old religion that had been cast off. To many of Sylvester's and especially Clyde's generation, most of whom had experienced the rigidity of boarding school life, the Hethuska was ancient tribal history. Sylvester's brother Amos, for one, told him to let the society remain "a victim of history."[66]

Likewise many Ponca elders were reluctant to share the spirituality behind ceremonial rituals with Sylvester because felt they were not authorized to share. Such was the resistance from the older generation that Sylvester relied on the 1911 epic history *The Omaha Tribe*, written by Alice L. Fletcher and Francis LaFlesche, to learn the internal structures of the Hethuska Society. Drawing from the history of the society in the period when the two Omaha and Ponca tribes existed as a single entity, when it was known as Hethu'shka, Sylvester gathered enough information to re-establish the society. A small number of older society members were also willing to share information with him, enough for him to re-create a purely Ponca

Warrior in Hethuska regalia.
(Courtesy of the *Ponca City News*.)

Hethuska. Before he could formally do so, however, he needed the permission of those elders who had been members of the original organization, some of the most revered and respected Ponca elders. Using the traditional protocols for requesting authority, Sylvester, Owen Walkingsky, and Clyde Warrior sought individual meetings with Ernest Blueback, Henry Snake, Woolsey Walkingsky, Simon Eagle, Jim Poorhouse, David Buffalohead, and Bill Collins, Sr.[67]

Each meeting took place over a period of four days and involved taking gifts of food and Pendleton blankets to the elders. On the fourth day, if the gifts had been accepted, they were allowed to ask about the Hethuska and its rituals. Once this process had been undergone, protocol demanded that a feast be organized, at which any tribal member who attended "accepted and sanctioned the request of the sponsor" to reorganize the society. Sylvester, Warrior, and Walkingsky held fourteen feasts to ensure the support of a majority of elders and clans within the tribe. A final hurdle to overcome was the hesitation of some elders over Sylvester's qualifications to be the *Nuda'ho"ga* (head man). Although a marine veteran of World War II, Sylvester had never seen combat, which concerned several elders. The Hethuska had, after all, originally been a military society, and the idea of the society leader having never actively engaged an enemy was disturbing. Eventually, several combat veterans lent their support to Sylvester's case, and he was given permission, albeit not unanimous, to revive the organization. Betty Littlechief, as the oldest surviving Hethuska member, added a stipulation—the new society must be called Hethuska Ishagè, meaning "this Hethuska is like the old way but it isn't the same thing."[68]

In September 1958, at the Gives Water Dance Arbor, Sylvester sponsored the first Hethuska Society dance since 1929. He appointed Albert Waters as *Xú'ka-hoN-ga* (head singer), a role that had not existed in the original society, and Lamont Brown and Joe Rush, the latter a member of the original society, formed the backbone of the drum. Owen Walkingsky and Clyde Warrior were the first two *SiN'-de*, or tail dancers, while Abe Conklin was the *wanoshe*, or whip man. In pre-reservation times, the tail dancers were society members who carried the crooked staffs, or coup sticks, some as long as eight feet, which were formerly used to strike the enemy. The crooked end of the staff was used to scoop wounded warriors from the battlefield and carry them to safety. The sticks were also used to poke fallen enemies to ensure that they were dead. The tail dancers were the last warriors to leave the battlefield, thus protecting the rear of the war party.[69] To be appointed to such a role at the age of nineteen showed the respect with which Warrior's dancing was held among his people. Warrior also included a whistle as part of his regalia. Whistles are often used by dancers, not restricted to tail dancers, but what made Warrior's whistle significant is that not only was it a gift from his grandfather but also, according to Shawnee/Iowa anthropologist and educator Jimmy Duncan, "the last Ponca whistle from the original Hethuska."[70]

Modern tail dancers are chosen because they are "either outstanding dancers or because they or their families provided outstanding service to the organization."[71] Warrior was well qualified on both fronts. Once chosen, dancers act as role models for the younger society members and as representatives for the society as a whole. The coup sticks are now short, beaded sticks about three feet long, known as tail sticks. In ceremonial gatherings, tail dancers dance on the repeated final, or tail, verse of a song, to represent the original duties of their office. Some tail dancers, of which Warrior was one, will kick their foot at the final beat of the tail verse, signifying the act of kicking a fallen enemy to ensure he is dead. In recognition of the honor of Warrior's selection as tail dancer, and to pay Warrior's way into the society, Grandpa Bill provided a roasted hog for a feast. Outside of the Hethuska, Warrior's singing skills were also recognized, as he enjoyed an open invitation to join the Ponca singers whenever he had the opportunity. His grandparents were permanent members of the drum, with Metha forming part of the circle of women singers who would sit behind the men.[72]

The revival of the Hethuska Society by Warrior and his uncle coincided with a surge of similar cultural revitalization across Indian Country. In southwestern Oklahoma, the Kiowas revived two of their societies. On July 4, 1957, the Kiowa Gourd Dance Clan officially reformed after a 1955 exhibition of gourd dancing was particularly well received at the American Indian Exposition in Anadarko. The revival sparked a wave of gourd dancing across the southern plains as many more tribes followed the Kiowa lead. In 1958, two months after the first Hethuska meeting in twenty-nine years, Gus Palmer, Sr., a good friend of Grandpa Bill, revived the Kiowa's most prestigious warrior society, the Black Legs. Palmer did this to honor his brother Lyndreth, who had posthumously received the Bronze Star in recognition of his bravery during bombing expeditions during World War II. The symbolic crooked staff of the society bears forty-two eagle feathers, one for each mission Lyndreth Palmer successfully carried out. In respect for the spiritual and social gravitas of the original society, Palmer altered the name to its present version: Black Leggings Society. Further afield, in the areas close to the Poncas' former homelands in Nebraska, traditionalists in several Sioux nations were reviving the self-piercing rituals of the annual Sun Dance.[73]

Each of these revivals spoke to the pride and honor with which the tribes, all of whom also held powwows, attached to their traditions. They also offered compelling evidence against anthropologist James Howard's theory of collective pan-Indianism usurping tribalism as the banner of identity in Indian Country as, he claimed, Indian people teetered on the brink of full assimilation into the American mainstream. The theory of pan-Indianism and the perceived rejection of tribal identity fit well into the Cold War "liberal

Warrior in action, Fancy Dance. (Courtesy of the
Ponca City News.)

consensus" and America's culture of conformity. The fear of the
"other" drove a desire for conformity in a society anxious about
communism and threats from afar. People rallied around the perceived perfection of American identity and the necessity for all
minorities to be absorbed within it. In Indian Country the imposition of the desire for minority conformity was most obvious in the
government's termination policy(targeting specific tribes for the
relinquishment of the federal trust relationship) and the Urban Relocation Program. The cultural revitalization of the Hethuska and
other societies flew in the face of the liberal consensus and both
government policies.[74]

By early adulthood, Warrior had grown into a striking, muscular,
athletic man, better known for his charisma and positive outlook
than any militant viewpoints. He was viewed by many as the most

graceful Indian dancer of his generation and known for his vast knowledge of many different tribal songs and cultures. Warrior's curriculum vitae noted that he had placed in powwow contests in Oklahoma, New Mexico, Arizona, California, Wyoming, and even Illinois (Chicago).[75] His athleticism and fitness can partly be attributed to the Ponca game of Shinny or Tabégasí, in which Warrior was as agile and swift as he was fluid in the dance arena. This fast, furious, and often violent ball game involves players of two teams attempting to drive a ball onto a single six-foot goalpost using short, curved, ash sticks. Each game is gradually made more difficult, as the ball, made from horsehair, is decreased in size each time a goal is scored. The first team to four goals is declared the winner.[76]

Culturally, Warrior's childhood was a perfect example of tribal traditionalism fighting to survive and remain relevant in the twentieth century against a backdrop of myriad external influences and interference. His knowledge of being Ponca was informed primarily by the examples set by his grandparents and the surrounding communities of elders and equally culturally immersed Poncas. It was, however, also informed by the perceptions and treatment of outsiders such as white schoolteachers, religious leaders, and Ponca City residents. Their stereotypes and racism forced Warrior and many in his community to embrace their culture and identity even closer, even as they were being told that this identity was worthless. At this point in his life, however, Warrior was not equipped to articulate the necessity of community, of cultural immersion, traditionalism, and retention as a means of survival or as an emblem of pride and identity, even if he knew these things instinctively. Despite his intelligence and the solid grounding of his grandparents and the rest of his family, Warrior was, as most people are, intellectually immature as he entered early adulthood. His educational choices after high school were significant factors in his evolution from exceptionally talented singer and dancer to leader and architect of the Red Power movement.[77]

CHAPTER 2

LAYING THE FOUNDATIONS
OF A MOVEMENT

"The sewage of Europe does not run through these veins."

Warrior's college attendance came as a growing number of American Indian youth groups and student organizations were developing on campuses across the United States. His connections with Indian students across the country expanded his cultural and political worldview through increased awareness of Indian affairs, and contributed significantly to his emergence as a leader. Intellectually, Warrior was introduced to anthropological concepts of societal structures and issues such as internal colonialism, and he would enjoy a more sympathetic attitude to American Indian history than he had encountered in high school. As he absorbed and processed the information he gleaned from youth councils, workshops, and conferences, he also began to adapt it to expand his worldview.[1]

Warrior's grandparents continued as an abiding influence on his intellectual development, and encouraged him to go to college, but such a step was far from easy for American Indians in Oklahoma. Della Warrior, who had been accepted by both the University of Oklahoma and Kansas State University but blocked by the BIA from attending either, described, "The Bureau [of Indian Affairs] just kind of frowned on that and insisted that we should go to the junior college and stay at the boarding school." No doubt aware of the large percentage of American Indian students who failed to adjust to college life, "they really believed that [attending] the smaller institutions would be better . . . so wherever there was a college near a boarding school, then students were encouraged to go there."[2]

Accordingly, in the fall of 1960 Warrior enrolled at Cameron State Agricultural College in Lawton, Oklahoma. There he found the atmosphere easier to adjust to than high school, undoubtedly eased by a larger presence of American Indian students than the handful attending Ponca City High School. The residential aspect—boarding with fellow young adult Indians—also helped.

Once at Cameron, Warrior made the ultimately life-changing decision to join the Ittanaha Indian Club. Again he was following examples set by his grandparents, who had instilled a sense of service to the world beyond Bois D'Arc and White Eagle. Warrior's grandmother, Metha Collins, had served as a member of Chilocco's Minnehaha Club and vice president of the local YWCA, and she was also first sergeant at Chilocco during World War I.[3] The Ittanaha, which comes from the Choctaw for "council fires," was originally a cross-campus club for all Oklahoma Indian students in higher education. In the 1950s, it had amended its rules, now accepting only Cameron students. Membership in the Ittanaha would take Warrior and his cohorts to meetings and conferences across the Southwest.[4] Providing a sense of community among Indian college students, intertribal clubs such as the Ittanaha reflected a tradition of discussion and consensus among men and women of American Indian nations that predated even the US colonial era. For Warrior, it was an opportunity to compare the poverty and lack of resources of his Ponca community with the economic situation in other nations. Many of the students enrolled in the clubs were previously unaware that the vast majority of reservation Indians across the United States shared the social and cultural depravation of their particular homeland. As they came to recognize shared circumstances, a growing number of culturally aware young Indians involved in groups such as the Ittanaha became bolder, unafraid to voice the discontent and anger they felt at the contemporary and historic dispossession of their people.[5]

The Ittanaha Indian Club had such an intellectual impact upon Warrior that he soon encouraged Indian students at his old high school in Ponca City to start their own club. Mona Reed (Ponca), a friend of his younger cousins, described Warrior telling her that the name of the club was important and that she needed to think about

Warrior (*far left*) and other Ittanaha club members (*left to right*) Richard T. Hernasy, James Pedro, James T. Owens, Myles. R. Stevenson, and Harold G. Kihega, from the 1960 Cameron Junior College yearbook. (Courtesy of Cameron University Archives.)

what she wanted from it before naming it. When she replied that she and the other Indian students wanted a group that would encourage members to graduate from high school and attend college, he suggested the name Oo-Kee-He (Able to Accomplish) Club.[6]

In his first year of college, Warrior quickly earned a reputation as something of a radical on the youth council circuit, despite his relatively short membership. This circuit included the Sequoyah Club at the University of Oklahoma (OU), which was the oldest university-affiliated American Indian student group in the country, founded in 1914. The Sequoyah Club enjoyed a reputation for its serious and dedicated members and served as the nexus for the smaller Indian clubs across the state. It was at a Sequoyah Club meeting that Warrior met Browning Pipestem (Otoe), an OU student and Sequoyah member, and the two quickly became close friends. Pipestem later recalled that many students felt uncomfortable with Warrior's forthright approach, wherein he would "take that negative image of Indians and shove it down people's throats." However, even more students began to engage with the plainspoken Ponca's rhetoric.[7] On April 28 and 29, 1961, the Sequoyah Club hosted a Southwest Regional Indian Youth Council (SRIYC) conference, the "Workshops for College Sessions," which offered Warrior a chance, via the SRIYC annual presidential election, to share his burgeoning ideas on American Indian affairs. The conference was also where he met Mel Thom, with whom he later cofounded the National Indian Youth Council. Thom, who at that time was president of the Tribe of Many Feathers Club at Brigham Young University, was leading a panel on "the changing relations between tribal and federal governments."[8] Pipestem and Thom would remain two of Warrior's closest friends and confidants over the following years.

The SRIYC, originally named the Santa Fe Indian Youth Council, had grown out of an annual conference held in collaboration with the Kiva Club of Indian students at the University of New Mexico. As with the Ittanaha Club, the Kiva Club recognized traditional motifs in its name, a kiva being a Pueblo ceremonial room. One of the attendees of the first conference, in Santa Fe in 1954, was a young Navajo student named Herb Blatchford, who later was instrumental in the founding of the National Indian Youth Council and another of Warrior's confidants. That 1954 conference promoted college education as an attainable goal for Indian students of the local pueblos, especially those of the Santa Fe Indian School. By 1958, the organization had evolved into the SRIYC and now included student groups from Arizona State University and high school and college students from Colorado and Utah, and it expanded again in 1961 to incorporate the Oklahoma student organizations.[9]

The Southwest Association on Indian Affairs (SAIA) funded sponsorship of the SRIYC under the direct control of Charles E. Minton, the executive secretary of the SAIA. A former lawyer from Missouri, Minton had moved to New Mexico to work with Indians in a position in the Works Progress Administration in the 1930s. He worked his way up through the state bureaucracy, eventually becoming executive director of the New Mexico Commission on

Warrior (*fourth from right*) in the 1961 Cameron Junior College yearbook; *front row*: James Pedro, Robert Poolaw, Cecil Marie, Irene Goombi, Stuart Tonemah, Emerson Eckiwardy; *back row*: William Blind, Cecil Eriacho, Charlie Billie, Warrior, W. J. Becker. (Courtesy of Cameron University Archives.)

Indian Affairs before taking up his post with the SAIA. He proclaimed three objectives of the SRIYC: "to stimulate Indian youth to acquire . . . skills that would . . . be of service to the tribes and communities; to expand their circle of Indian acquaintance . . . and to acquire an understanding of the varied and complex problems in Indian affairs, so they will work together . . . to improve conditions among Indian people."[10]

Publicly Minton welcomed the expansion of the conference from the Southwest as a chance to get "acquainted with Indian students from Oklahoma and [see] how different conditions there are from New Mexico and Arizona."[11] Privately he was concerned about such an emerging "controversial" figure as Clyde Warrior standing for the annual presidency of the SRIYC. Prior to the 1961 conference in Norman, Oklahoma, Minton turned to Warrior's friend Gerald Brown (Flathead) and talked him into standing against Warrior.

Brown eventually acquiesced to Minton's request and diligently prepared a thirty-minute speech outlining the issues and causes he thought the council should pursue.[12] After Brown made his case to the assembled youth caucus, Warrior leaped to the stage, rolled up his sleeves, and raised his arms. "I am a full-blood Ponca Indian," he proclaimed. "This is all I have to offer. The sewage of Europe does not run through these veins." These visceral words comprised his entire campaign speech.[13] Warrior was so immersed in, and attuned to, his Ponca heritage and identity that he instinctively rejected the government's assimilationist tactics of blood quantum and did not count his meager quota of Irish blood as being significant. It was also irrelevant to the bellicose rhetoric of a young idealist. In three short sentences Warrior tapped into the frustration, anger, and resentment of many of his fellow students toward the dominant white society, even if the forcefulness of his language shocked some in the room.

Minton's fears were realized as Warrior won the election in a landslide. Warrior remained close friends with his reluctant opponent, who later confessed to feeling relieved that Warrior had won, having been pressed into running for election in the first place.[14] As simple and direct as Warrior's speech was, it was also a highly significant moment in American Indian protest. It was the first time in generations that such direct, condemnatory, and anticolonial language had been uttered publicly by an American Indian toward the hegemonic American settler culture. While it did not immediately change the face of American Indian protest and activism, the speech set Warrior and many of his cohorts on a trajectory toward even more militant language and tactics. In that small meeting room on an Oklahoma college campus, Warrior signposted a new direction in the way American Indians campaigned for their rights, away from negotiation and lobbying and toward militant protest and direct action.

Attendance of regional youth council meetings was just one of several paths of intellectual growth that Warrior traveled during the early 1960s. Halfway through the summer of 1961, still buoyed by his victory in Norman, Warrior told his friend Frank Turley that he would not be heading out onto the powwow circuit with him after their trip to Warrior's home in Bois D'Arc. This was such staggering news that Turley initially thought Warrior was teasing him. Warrior, however, said he was going to southern Colorado to attend an educational workshop and leadership training.[15] Fully aware that Turley was broke and relying on companions for food and transport, Warrior told Abe Conklin, Hethuska whip man and future Nuda'ho"ga, to drop Turley at the Collins farm later in the summer, promising to meet Turley there to resume powwowing when he was done with his workshop.

The Workshops on American Indian Affairs held at Boulder, Colorado, that summer, had been created in 1956 by Dr. Sol Tax of the Department of Anthropology at the University of Chicago. Aided by his graduate students Robert "Bob" Thomas and Al Wahrhaftig, Tax conceived the workshops as a practical extension of his concept of "action anthropology." Tax was as certain of the workshops' importance for American Indian education as Minton was confident in the youth councils. Fellow anthropologist Robert Rietz and sociologists Murray and Rosalie Wax joined them in this experiment. As Wahrhaftig explains, "Action anthropology held that by intervening in a community in such a way that new alternatives can be created without co-opting the power to incorporate only such alternatives as are perceived by its members to be beneficial, anthropologists can observe 'values in action': they can simultaneously study and help."[16]

By 1961, when Warrior enrolled in the workshops, D'Arcy Mc-Nickle (Flathead) had assumed control of them. McNickle was a seasoned campaigner for American Indian rights as a founding member of the National Congress of American Indians (NCAI). He was also a philosopher, anthropologist, novelist, and historian, and he wished to create a more humanistic approach to education at the workshops than the previous administration had done. Over the following three years the workshops would undergo several major changes in teaching and thematic focus, and classes would become more focused on the perceived needs of the student rather than any reformist desires of faculty. Although the readings were often selected to emphasize comparison and contrast between whites and Indians and rural and urban, the treatment of Indian, or folk cultures, was far more sympathetic than students had experienced in high school. Texts such as William Hagan's newly published *American Indians* joined John Collier's *Indians of the Americas* in celebrating American Indian history. David Riesman's *The Lonely Crowd* offered a critique of the cultural isolationism of western culture, while Robert Redfield's concept of "folk society" was a firm foundation for Thomas and showed his strong belief in the "structuralist" vision of Indian communities as folk cultures. Although folk, or rural, communities had been seen as static and restricted by tradition, Riesman found them far more inclusive and communal than urban societies.[17]

McNickle's mission for the workshops was producing wise Indian leadership, and in keeping with this he decided that the students, including Warrior, would travel to Chicago for the first week of the 1961 workshops, to attend and participate in the American Indian Chicago Conference.[18] Rosalie Wax speculated that this arrangement boosted applications and attendance for the workshops in comparison to previous years. The Chicago conference, which ran June 13–21, had been planned by Sol Tax to gather as many tribal leaders together as possible to give a unified intertribal voice on the future direction of the federal trust relationship so that they could present a single set of demands to new president John F. Kennedy. Tax and his fellow organizers wished for Indian communities to control their own destinies but argued that this could only happen through consensus and a unified voice. McNickle meanwhile believed that this event would introduce his students to respected leaders such as Thomas Segundo (Papago/Tohono O'dham), whom he viewed as the type of traditional yet forward-looking leader he wished them to emulate. He wanted the students to observe these men and women as they created "a body of recommendations to guide Indian programs in the future," as a model for their own future behavior as tribal leaders.[19]

The students immersed themselves into the Chicago proceedings wholeheartedly. Warrior seconded a motion by Robert Burnette, president of the Rosebud Sioux Tribal Council, during the opening session, which called for certification of individual and tribal delegates for voting purposes. Burnette was convinced that without

Warrior (*third row in glasses*) with Mel Thom (Walker River Paiute) (*head down*) and Leo LeClair (Muckleshoot) (*third row in tie*) at the 1961 Chicago Conference, listening to D'Arcy McNickle (*at microphone*). (Courtesy of the Newberry Library.)

individual certification, "mixed-blood" tribal leaders would collaborate to push through their own agendas and dominate voting as tribal delegates. With individual certification, he was confident that the more traditional full-blood Indians in attendance would be heard and their issues addressed. This argument was a constant source of division and factionalism in the NCAI, and Burnette was determined to ensure that a voting bloc would not seize power at the conference. Warrior, having listened at the feet of his grandfather to complaints of tribal political corruption and incompetence throughout Oklahoma, was extremely skeptical of tribal politics and tribal politicians. He held similar views to Burnette on the perceived intentions of mixed-blood leaders, and viewed them as opportunistic politicians rather than traditional leaders. A few years later, after his own leadership qualities and ability to articulate his views evolved, he would expound upon the differences between traditional cultural knowledge and political leadership and the significance of this distinction in the tribal community. For now, though, he was content to support Burnette's attempt to protect the voice of more traditional Indians at the conference.[20]

Warrior also volunteered for the drafting committee that had final editorial control over the Declaration of Indian Purpose, which served as the unified voice that Tax had wanted. In the declaration, tribal delegates reiterated their inherent sovereignty rights as the original occupiers of the land and positioned themselves squarely behind the concept of self-determination. Warrior noticed however, a difference between the private exhortations of committee leaders and their public speeches on the conference floor. While the declaration was drafted behind closed doors, delegates' speeches took place under the watchful eye of BIA officials. Warrior later complained, "It was sickening to see American Indians just get up and tell obvious lies about how well the federal government was treating them, what fantastic and magnificent things the federal government were doing for us." Making a clear delineation between tribal leaders he mistrusted and the elders with whom he closely identified, he referred to the conference as a gathering of "tribal finks," declaring that it had been a bad meeting.[21] The contrast between the private and public behavior of the tribal leaders was also noticed by McNickle, who complained that the conference had descended into a situation where "in the absence of traditional channels for intertribal communication . . . at several critical moments the conference stood ready to dissolve."[22]

This petty and vindictive bickering was unlike any behavior Warrior had witnessed when tribal elders of various nations had gathered at his grandparents' farm or at Gallup and on the powwow circuit. In each of these situations, he had seen mutual respect, sharing of stories, dances, and memories. The actions of tribal leaders in Chicago confirmed the negative impression he had formed of politicians from the stories of his grandparents and their friends. So frustrated were Warrior and other young Indians, including fellow workshop students Karen Rickard (Tuscarora) and Bernadine Eschief (Shoshone Bannock) and fellow SRIYC members Mel Thom and Herb Blatchford, that they began having meetings of their own between sessions, drafting statements and resolutions.[23] Shirley Hill Witt (Mohawk), who met Warrior at Chicago, maintained that the conference "allowed us to recognize that we could be movers and shakers and work towards change. [Meanwhile] we watched the older generation engaged in their timeless competition for scarce resources."[24] Warrior later complained, however, that "every time we . . . stood up and worked within that structure, our own kind stood up and screamed at us, 'radicals!' 'Possibly Communists are infiltrating us! Ignore these young foolish kids. They really don't know what they are doing.'" He added, "I was pretty sorry of my own kind of people, [that] they had degenerated to such a level where they would do that."[25]

The frustration that Warrior later evinced produced a heady cocktail of alternative ideas and demands for action. At the suggestion of Herb Blatchford, twenty members of the youth caucus agreed to meet again at the August Gallup Ceremonial in New Mexico to discuss forming their own organization. This was not what McNickle had had in mind when he'd envisioned the students learning from their Chicago experience. It had taught them the type of leaders they wished *not* to become. Blatchford later extolled the resourcefulness of the workshop students and other interested young people who, concerned that the conference was going "out on a tangent" and away from its purpose, drew up an alternative statement. According to Blatchford, they were described by many as "the most unified group in the conference."[26]

The bond forged by the young Indians as they struggled to make their voices heard on the conference floor was strengthened as they socialized together after hours. Shirley Hill Witt remembered everybody gathering each evening for singing and dancing. She recalled the official conference powwow, in which Warrior placed second in the war dance behind Tom Eschief, as seeming to her to be too much for public display: "All right, all you Indians, go out and dance in circles for a while. We're going to put the cameras on, we're going to put lights up, and you do your colorful stuff!" Once the cameras were turned off and the entertainment over, however, they would begin their 49s. As well as being a formidable traditional singer and dancer, Warrior was also an entertaining and accomplished 49 singer. Usually associated with powwow culture, a 49 is a purely social dance, not a sacred one, and it takes place in an atmosphere of fun, where people get together informally.[27] 49s take place away from the powwow arena, as courtships, or "snagging," are often played out, songs are sung in English, and etiquette and tradition are absent: the focus is on enjoying oneself, making friends, and, quite often, drinking alcohol. The friendships forged this way after hours in Chicago would be maintained throughout their lives.

Back in Boulder afterward, the workshops similarly offered formal and informal social gatherings alongside the rigorous intellectual instruction. On July 1 the White Buffalo Council of Denver entertained the students with baseball and barbecue at the Lone Star Ranch, in Elizabeth, Colorado. There were also several uncomfortable informal gatherings of students and faculty where, as Bob Thomas later described it, the students were "expressionless and non-committal guests" who had concluded that their role at the party was to paint their academic future. Accordingly, when confronted by the instructors, a student "delivered a modest, but well organized address describing his [her] educational plans."[28]

Each weekend, briefly free of the constraints of early-morning starts and the intellectual demands of the faculty, many of the students would 49 in nearby fields. Several students complained about the socializing, especially the alcohol consumption, but the instructors never saw fit to impose a curfew on the after-hours activity. The students, however, imposed their own, of sorts. Della Warrior (née Hopper) described the students' self-imposed rule as a simple one: "if you couldn't get up the next morning and be at class at eight o'clock, then you shouldn't party."[29]

Thomas, for one, viewed joining the students in their social activities, which often included drinking late into the night, as an ideal way to gain their trust.[30] According to several sources, it was not until Thomas's late-night workshop drinking sessions that Warrior began drinking alcohol. Frank Turley was adamant that until that point, rather than alcohol, Warrior drank "about twenty Cokes a day." Whenever people teased him about it, "he would just shrug and go ahead and get another Coke."[31] The late-night drinking

Warrior (*top right corner*) with fellow Boulder workshop students, 1961; *from front, left to right, roughly in rows of four*: Marie Emery-Counsellor (Oglala Sioux), Wynema Burgess (Creek), Harriet Marmon (Laguna Pueblo), Gloria Emerson (Navajo), Karen Rickard (Tuscarora), Charles Emery (Cheyenne River Sioux), Bruce Wilkie (Makah), Dorrance Steele (Fort Peck Sioux), Leo LeClair (Muckleshoot), Emerson Eckiwardy (Comanche), Isaac Beaulieux (Ojibway, Saulteaux) Lois Steele (Assiniboine), Jacqueline Crow (Bad River Band of Chippewa), Katherine Saubel (Cahuilla), Brenda Gillette (Arikara–Gros Ventre), Mary Natani (Sioux), Cecelia Tallchief (Osage), Norma Bluebird (Oglala Sioux), Dave Warren (Chippewa-Tewa), Tom Clark (Detroit), Robert W. Rietz (director), Thomas Eshchief (Shoshone-Bannock), Bernadine Eschief (Shoshone-Bannock), Howard McKinley Jr. (Navajo), Richard Whitertree (Seneca-Cayuga), Robert Thomas (assistant director, Cherokee), Warrior (Ponca). (Courtesy of the Newberry Library.)

Warrior (*second row, fourth from right*) with fellow students at the 1962 Workshops on American Indian Affairs, Boulder, Colorado; *standing, left to right*: Dorothy Davids, Fran Poafpybitty, Michael Taylor, Jeri Cross, Clyde Warrior, Louise Tansy, Bruce Wilkie, Lenore Lamere; *front*: Gordon Keahbone, William Allen, Gerald Ignace, Gerald Brown. (Courtesy of the Newberry Library.)

sessions quickly developed into intellectual sparing matches between Warrior and Thomas, the two bouncing ideas and theories off each other, and they developed a friendship that went beyond teacher and student. The friendship would continue, along with occasional collaboration, until Warrior's untimely death in 1968.

As well as attending classes, dancing and singing 49s, and drinking late into the night with Bob Thomas, Warrior served as coeditor, with Bernadine Eschief, of the workshop newsletter, *The Indian Progress*. The mid-workshop newsletter, published on July 10, during week four, carried several ringing student endorsements of the conduct and vision of the young leaders present at the Chicago conference. Leo LeClair (Muckleshoot) was grateful for the opportunity to attend the conference, which he said had helped him understand some current and historical problems in Indian affairs, and Bruce Wilkie (Makah) was proud that "for the first time in recorded history American Indians assembled, representing all parts of the country to form a common front to define the things in which they all believe."[32]

In the following issue, however, Warrior and Eschief's editorial comment painted an entirely different picture, and they pleaded for a new style of leadership within Indian Country. Reflecting the frustration that had led to the agreement to meet in Gallup, but without referring directly to events in Chicago, the pair declared, "Today the Indian people are without great leadership. Today the Indian people are in dire need of leadership." They went on to argue that Indians needed to provide this leadership from their own young people, beseeching, "Young people, we must, by the fact that we are born American Indians, be dedicated to our people. There is nothing else we should do except work for, with, and among our Indian people."[33]

Warrior intended to build upon the rhetoric of the joint editorial when he headed toward Gallup and the reunion with the rest of the Chicago youth caucus. Traveling with Tom and Bernadine Eschief, he visited the All American Indian Days powwow in Sheridan, Wyoming, along the way. Originally part of the Sheridan (Wyoming) Rodeo, it became a separate, Indian-controlled event in 1958, and it was one of the largest Indian celebrations of its day, often attracting upwards of four thousand Indian participants, not least due to its hosting of the Miss Indian America pageant. The detour was a successful one for Warrior, who took first place in the Fancy Dance contest, further enhancing his reputation as one of the foremost dancers of the era, and Tom Eschief placed third in the Straight Dance.[34]

Warrior was not unique among his cohort in depth of cultural immersion. All of the caucus members were equally comfortable within their individual tribal identities. The collective that met in Gallup August 10–13, 1961, to discuss plans and goals was very much an intertribal gathering of varying tribal worldviews rather than a pan-Indian collective as it has been labeled. The meeting aptly coincided with the fortieth anniversary of the Gallup Inter-tribal Ceremonial. A couple of months beforehand, SRIYC sponsor Charles Minton had expressed doubts about the viability of a nationally organized Indian youth council. Consequently, there were initial concerns at the Gallup meeting about Minton's potentially disruptive influence. Warrior assured people that Minton's main concern was that the SRIYC was covering too much ground, having only been intended for New Mexico and Arizona. This concern was partially born out of the frustration of several SRIYC members at the time and cost incurred traveling from New Mexico to Oklahoma for the 1961 annual meeting. Subsequently, Minton saw the development of separate regional councils as a good thing "as long as they do not get out of hand with this development." He argued, though, that it would be best for regional Indian youth councils to establish themselves and then wait for students to demand a national organization, rather than impose "forced development."[35] But the young Indians disagreed, convinced that they could use Minton's plan in reverse to organize the growth and management of regional councils.

Herb Blatchford had suggested the Gallup Ceremonial as a time and place to meet in part since he was director of the Gallup Indian Community Center and helped organize the Ceremonial. He was also presenting a paper on the future of Indian youth on the Saturday afternoon of the event. He convinced the other Ceremonial organizers to allow the caucus to meet in office space originally set aside for the conference portion of the week's events. At that time there was no contest powwow in the Ceremonial, with the event focusing on the exhibition of ceremonial dances from tribes across the nation. There were also exhibits and sales of locally made jewelry and art as well as lectures from anthropologists and other "experts." Despite their being no contest powwow, with only performers receiving payment, the Ceremonial was a regular detour from the powwow circuit as a way for dancers to meet up with old friends, observe other cultures, and 49 each evening once the tourists had left the grounds.[36]

Warrior was wary of the youth caucus falling into the pattern of political maneuvering so common in Indian Country and especially rife at the Chicago conference. He raised his misgivings about the intention and structure of the group and initially confessed that he didn't like the way it seemed to be going. He wondered, "[Are we] really going to help our people, or are we going out to seek status for ourselves?" He was also concerned that the group might do something disastrous.[37] Rather than be trained to be good Indian leaders in the established model favored by the NCAI, Warrior and his cohort favored changing the concept of leadership. They intended to foster and bring forth the vitality of youth, while leaning on the advice of culturally knowledgeable elders for support, rather than see their vitality institutionally compromised. Although Warrior has often been categorized as a central figure in the American Indian youth movement of the 1960s, he was extremely uncomfortable with the concept of such a movement. He complained that "National Indian Youth" sounded like one was talking about "little kids," while the youth caucus was acting like anything but that. Additionally, as the ideal was to lean upon the knowledge of tribal elders, he viewed it as a cultural movement, rather than specifically a youth movement. This ideal would eventually lead to fractured relationships between the fledgling National Indian Youth Council (NIYC), just beginning to be discussed in Gallup, and both the NCAI and workshop organizers, with Warrior often immersed in these conflicts.

One issue the group discussed was identity, with several caucus members pondering the idea of restricting membership to federally recognized Indians. Warrior, however, was loath for identity to be subsumed to federal control and rejected government recognition through "blood quantum." He advocated that any self-identified Indian be allowed membership, whether they were federally recognized or not, emphasizing his conviction that identity was defined by the self and that tribal and community membership were more significant that federal recognition. He also had a pragmatic rationale, saying, "We need the money, and theirs is as good as anyone else's." He sought both harmony and strength and believed that a wider membership would ensure greater results, saying, "We seem to have this continuity of force to band together, and out of this group we can develop some understanding."[38]

On the second day of the caucus meetings, Warrior displayed his leadership skills and reflected his own cultural traditions when, in a move that marked the official beginning of the NIYC, he made sure that males and females would have equal roles in the group. Due to the societal norms of the era, this was an internal system of equality hidden behind the external front of male "spokesmen" that were the public face of the organization. For the initial leadership of the National Indian Youth Council (NIYC), he nominated Mel Thom for president, Shirley Hill Witt for first vice president, and Joan Noble (Ute) as second vice president, with each choice unopposed. When Mary Natani (Ho-Chunk) and Thomas Eschief withdrew their names as contenders for general board positions, and Karen Rickard (Tuscarora) accepted such a position, the remaining names went into a hat at the suggestion of Witt. The names pulled out were those of Warrior, Bernadine Eschief, and Howard McKinley. Warrior then nominated Blatchford to serve as executive director, to which all agreed. Warrior also unofficially appointed himself the conscience of the group, and, reflecting his obligation as a Hethuska tail dancer to "inspire others to achieve something that benefits the whole group," he urged them not to "just forget about this" when they got home. This role as conscience was one he increasingly grew into over the following years as the movement gathered more members and growing visibility. Before offering to close proceedings with an invocation, he reminded everyone there, "This is going to be a tough year because we are building a foundation, and if we all get lax and let it go, then the whole organization will disintegrate. We are all part of this now."[39] The initial skeptic was now a firm believer in the movement, and he intended to fight tooth and nail to ensure its success as a bridge between elders and youth, past, present, and future generations, tradition and modernity.

Warrior continued to develop his leadership skills as president of the SRIYC, issuing a newsletter in October 1961 that discussed the Chicago conference and the formation of the NIYC. He maintained a busy conference attendance schedule during the 1961–62 academic year, in which he won an award as Cameron's outstanding Indian student. It was during this time that Warrior met Della Hopper, his future wife, who was now also enrolled at Cameron and a fellow Ittanaha Club member. Della later recalled not being overly impressed with Warrior when they met, saying, "Every morning we would get on the bus, and he would be singing or whistling or something, and I just thought it was really annoying."[40] Despite this inauspicious start—and his continued whistling of Ponca songs on the bus each morning—they slowly became friends over the ensuing months, and Warrior made Della aware of the Boulder workshops and the fledgling NIYC.

In December 1961, Warrior received a letter from SRIYC sponsor Charles Minton, who threatened to restructure the regions within which the organization would be funded. Having already conveyed Minton's concerns to the caucus forming the NIYC in Gallup in August, he nonetheless was worried enough about Minton's threat to write to Herb Blatchford expressing concern. Blatchford replied that Joan Noble had expressed similar concern over the future of Brigham Young University's Indian student group, Tribe of Many Feathers, the proposed host of the 1962 SRIYC conference. Blatchford sought to comfort them both with the news that Minton would stand down as director of Southwestern Association on Indian Affairs on December 31, at which point the board would decide what level of support they offered. He told them, "Mr. Minton has written this letter to keep you on your toes."[41] While relatively benign, this exercise in political brinksmanship was the first real challenge Warrior faced as a leader.

Warrior continued to develop his intellectual and leadership qualities at Cameron and as SRIYC president until April 1962. In July, the increasing respect that the NIYC was garnering became evident when the group received the gift of a drum from Marcelo Quintana of the Cochiti Pueblo. The gifting of a drum was an age-old tradition, especially among Pueblo and Plains Indians, in which the gift represented the recognition by the giver of the receiver's adherence to the "old ways." As such, this was a significant moment in the NIYC's first year, as it represented the high regard with which young traditional Indians already held them.[42]

The summer of 1962 was also significant for the continued evolution of Warrior's political ideology. First, he wanted to returned to the Boulder workshops, where he had received a disappointing final grade of D for his efforts the previous year. In February 1962

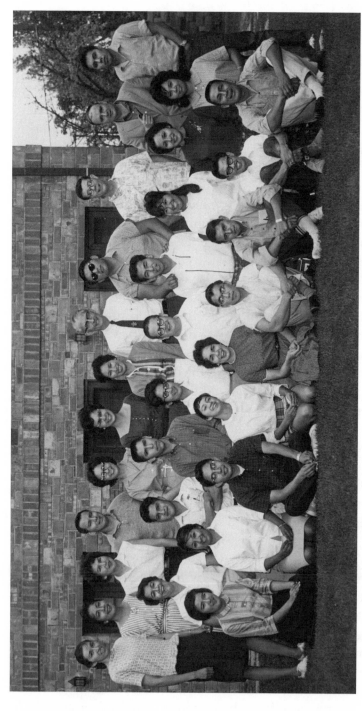

Warrior (*back row, far right*) with fellow Boulder students and teachers, 1962; *back row, left to right*: Lenore Lamere, Rita Goode, Louise Tansy, Bruce Wilkie, Janis Herman, Jeri Cross, Fran Poafpybitty, Robert Rietz (assistant director), Browning Pipestem, Michael Taylor, Robert Thomas (assistant director), Warrior; *middle row*: Dorothy Davids, Frank Duckapoo, David Roybal, Janet Arviso, Gerald Brown, Andrew Thundercloud, Veronica Homer, Angela Russell, Mary Padilla; *front row*: Kathryn Red Corn, Gloria Keliiaa, Gerald Ignace, Georgianna Webster, Sandra Johnson, William Allen, Gordon Keahbone, Michael Gorospe, James Pedro. (Courtesy of the Newberry Library.)

he had accepted D'Arcy McNickle's offer to serve on an advisory committee to the workshops to help in deciding what courses to include. Warrior conceded to McNickle that "last year I missed much due to my being blinded by youth" and requested permission to attend the workshops again. He pointed to his increasing intellectual development, saying, "I have grown up since then (I think) and I believe I could learn much more if I was to attend another session."[43] His request was granted, and, along with Bruce Wilkie, Warrior returned to the workshops in the summer of 1962. Before this, though, he and Eschief produced one more issue of *The Indian Progress.* It opened with a summary of the intentions of the workshops and an analysis of the 1961 model. The joint editors declared that, in the previous workshops, "everyone became aware of the needs, the lacks, [and] the problems of the Indian people. Everyone left with one thought in mind—to help in one way or another all the American Indian people on this continent." Tucked away in the middle of the newsletter, with no fanfare, was an announcement: "On August 11, 1961, the National Indian Youth Council was formally initiated." The list of officers included Warrior, Bernadine Eschief, and Karen Rickard from the class of 1961.[44]

When Warrior and Wilkie returned to Boulder in 1962, they and instructors found that much had changed. There were familiar faces for Warrior, however, who had now graduated with a two-year degree from Cameron. Aside from Wilkie, his friend Browning Pipestem also attended. The two shared a similar upbringing and outlook on life, having been raised just a few miles apart on the outskirts of Ponca City. Other friends and acquaintances there were Jeri Cross, Gerald Brown, Georgianna Webster, Angela Russell, and Fran Poafpybitty, whom he knew from the powwow circuit, regional youth councils, the NIYC, or Cameron. The abundance of familiar faces for so many of the students dramatically changed the dynamic of the workshops.[45] Also at this session Warrior had a brief yet intense relationship with the older Tillie Walker (Mandan). His romantic relationship with Della Hopper started two years later.[46]

The maturity that Warrior claimed he had gained between 1961 and 1962 was obvious in his essays that summer, which earned him an overall grade B for the workshops. Clearly influenced by friends

Warrior (*second from right*) taking a break from studies at the 1962 Boulder workshops; left to right: Louise Tansey, Fran Poafpybitty, Mary Padilla, Browning Pipestem (obscured), Warrior, Jeri Cross. (Courtesy of the Newberry Library.)

and events at Gallup and regional workshops in the intervening months, his burgeoning vision shone from the pages. In regard to whether or nor his tribe should "shape up," Warrior observed, "It is not natural for one group of people to tell another group of people what is right and what to do." For Warrior, the benefits of self-determination were manifold, and this belief became a cornerstone for him. He argued that once people accomplish projects independently and become self-sufficient, their pride as a collective people and as individuals will return. Subsequently, they then have a basis to help others, seeing that "we are as everyone else."[47] This idealism was based on his understanding of traditional Ponca methods of community organization that he wished to continue in a contemporary setting.

Warrior, second from right, and Boulder workshop friends in dance regalia, 1962. *From left:* Kathryn Red Corn, Tom Eschief, unidentified, David Roybal, Louise Tansy, Warrior, Bernadette Eschief. (Courtesy of the Newberry Library.)

Following the 1962 workshops in Boulder, Warrior enrolled in the University of Oklahoma for the 1962–63 academic year. There he took classes in history, anthropology, government, and Latin American history as well as attending the College of Education. These classes supplemented the anthropological background he had immersed himself in during the previous two summers. He also took a political science class in which he wrote a seventeen-page paper on his favorite US president: "Thomas Jefferson and Jeffersonian Democracy." Between and after classes, Warrior continued to increase his presence in intertribal American Indian political affairs. In December 1962 he displayed an increasingly forthright political ideology about the needs of American Indian communities in a letter to former NCAI executive director Helen Peterson (Lakota). He

Warrior (*back row, second from left*) with fellow Sequoyah Club members at the University of Oklahoma, 1964. *Bottom row, left to right*: Warrior's sister Charmain Pensoneau, Warrior's future wife Della Hopper (misprinted as "Cella" in original caption), Wynema Thornton, Sharron Sims, Mary Thornton, Norma Bearskin, Marilyn Watt. *Top row*: Franklin Chappabitty, Warrior, Alice Echo-Hawk, Anthony Brown, Keron Kickingbird, Victor Clement, Grosvenor Pollard, Thomas Todacheeney, Stuart Tonemah. (Courtesy of the University of Oklahoma Student Media.)

complained to Peterson that the current NCAI leadership was not "intelligent, devoted, responsible, [or] sincere," nor was the NCAI unified. He was convinced that without unity in the organization, Indians would not be able to affect lasting political, social, or even cultural change in their communities, saying that a tribe alone cannot do this. He expressed sadness that he could not see anyone capable of bringing about the unity of the various tribes as Tecumseh had done in the early nineteenth century. He expressed determination, however, for finding such a leader. Acknowledging the societal gender norms of the era, he wrote that: "We must start now to look for this man [who] is intelligent, devoted, responsible, and sincere for the welfare of his Indian people."[48] Warrior's grandparents had taught him that "a man doesn't look for people to lead but . . . the people look for a man to lead them."[49] That person, he wrote to Peterson, had to be "filled with the initiative, self-determination, and sacrifice" for Indian people and "will give his all" for them.[50] These were qualities that Warrior himself possessed but about which he would never boast.

Warrior's enrollment at OU also meaning leaving the Ittanaha Club for the Sequoyah Club, with which he had already worked. Continuing the political ascendency that began with his SRIYC presidency, Warrior was elected president of the Sequoyah Club in his first semester at OU. The vote demonstrated Warrior's increasing profile as a leading young Indian intellectual and provided him with a much larger platform from which to promote his ideas than the SRIYC platform had offered. The presidency of the club carried many responsibilities, and Warrior excelled at meeting these. One was to act as the occasional host of the *Indians for Indians Hour* radio show broadcast out of OU's student station, WNAD.[51]

Created in 1941 by Don Whistler (Sac and Fox) and attracting over seventy five thousand listeners in its heyday in the 1940s and 1950s, the show still carried a substantial number of followers when Warrior took to the air.[52] Warrior decided to use the radio broadcasts as a form of outreach, merging music and activism. The usual format for the radio show was for the presenter to briefly announce personal dedications sent in by the audience before introducing the music, which was themed each week. One week's broadcast would showcase an hour of Kiowa prayer songs or gourd dance songs, while the next week's might feature Ponca war songs or Apache fire dance songs. These would either be played recordings or songs performed live by visiting drums. Warrior's first broadcast followed this pattern, with him announcing local dances, powwows, ceremonials, tribal meetings, and social events before presenting different singers and songs from various tribes. His second broadcast was markedly different, however: he announced the upcoming annual Ittanaha Youth Conference to be held in Norman on April 19 and 20, 1963, spent some time in describing what it would cover, and urged listeners to attend.[53]

The Ittanaha Conference, an Ittanaha Club event hosted at OU so that more people might attend, was one of many such Indian conferences that were now operating out of university campuses across the Southwest, demonstrating the far-reaching effects of the SRIYC and NIYC. College attendance by American Indians had also grown in that time. In the late 1940s and early 1950s, there were so few Indians in higher education that no records were maintained. By 1963, though, according to Associate Commissioner of Indian Affairs James Officer, there were 3,141 Indians attending colleges or universities and 2,290 others enrolled in post–high school vocational schools.[54] While the growth in college attendance undoubtedly helped the surge in youth councils and conferences, the relationship was reciprocal. The youth councils were intended, from the viewpoint of sponsors such as Charles Minton in New Mexico, and B. D. Timmons in Oklahoma, to set an example to high school Indians: college was an attainable and achievable goal for young Indians. They were also, as were the Boulder workshops, intended to create wise Indian leadership in tribal communities. Wider leadership, such as with the NCAI, was envisioned by such administrators as something that the students might mature into after several years' experience of tribal politics.

Warrior's use of *Indians for Indians Hour* as a propaganda tool was a perfect example of the more direct approach favored by the NIYC. The intention was to draw the regional youth councils under its influence and foster discussions of such issues as colonialism, cultural retention and identity, and the preservation of treaty rights. Through the show he reached a number of young Indians far in excess of the three thousand college students across American college campuses that the regional youth councils served. This included many young rural Indians far removed from political action in the white world. On April 9, 1963, he urged his listeners, especially "those of you who have children in high school or college or know of Indian students in college," to attend the upcoming conference. He told his audience that Oklahoma's governor, Henry Bellmon, would attend and present a speech. The aim of the conference was to encourage college and high schools students to embrace higher education and would be rounded off by the annual OU powwow, where he announced, with typical self-effacement, and to the amusement of others in the studio, that the head male dancer would be "some guy named Clyde Warrior, I think."[55]

Warrior noted that the event would include discussion panels on the various opportunities available to young Indians in Oklahoma, on politics, on why Indian students should obtain a higher education, and why they should pursue careers and technical training. Friday panels would discuss scholarship and assistant programs available to Oklahoma Indian college students. Saturday would be given over to discussions on technical training in the morning, and then the annual spring dance would start, hosted by the Sequoyah Club. The powwow would include war dancing and round dancing, with permission received from the university for the dancers to 49 all night after the event if they so desired.[56]

Warrior's final broadcast, on April 30, 1963 was marred by his anger at being "dragged into tribal politics by Kiowa, Comanche, Apache groups," many of whom were arguing about the tribal, and occasionally familial, origins of certain songs being played on the show.[57] These accusations of cultural theft and appropriation were an unfortunate side effect of the three tribes being forced to share the same agency since 1875. The tribes, especially the Kiowas and Comanches, had a history of shared enmity that had finally eased in 1836. Many familial disagreements and much of the distrust between members of the two had carried onto the agency, especially with individuals old enough to remember the last of their shared conflicts. This distrust had subsequently been passed down through the generations, often to the point where people of mixed heritage would acknowledge one tribal identity and disown the other. In this instance, groups from each tribe were claiming certain gourd dance songs as their own and attempting to convince Warrior not to play them unless the other groups acknowledged their claims.[58]

Warrior's intellectual growth was not confined to Indian affairs during this time, and he surrounded himself with like-minded friends who formed a lively social group. Browning Pipestem, his future wife Della (Otoe Missouria), Kathryn Red Corn (Osage), her future sister-in-law Jeri Cross (Caddo), Tony Isaacs, and Garrick Bailey (Choctaw) were the crux of this group. Bailey became friends with Warrior through their mutual friendship with the Red Corn family. While Warrior and Isaacs would talk music long into the night, Garrick Bailey remembered that Warrior "loved to talk politics or political strategy and how you motivate people." A large group of people used to meet regularly in a campus bar called Tony's, where they would meet and discuss politics, and it is here, rather than in class, according to Bailey, that Warrior developed a "very good understanding of the American political scene."[59]

Within this informal group of students and professors who would come and go was what Bailey calls an "Irish drinking society" known to each other as the Druid Society, which included Warrior. According to Bailey, Warrior referred to the group as one of "functioning alcoholics," which suggests self-awareness of his growing dependency on alcohol in the relatively short period since he had started drinking at the 1961 workshops in Boulder. He jokingly used Ernest Hemingway as an example of a successful functioning alcoholic and was already regularly drinking shots of Johnny Walker Scotch whisky alongside his beer. Membership in the society was one time that Warrior acknowledged his Irish roots, and he mixed with people of all political persuasions.[60]

Warrior's passion for politics was unusual among his peers in the Indian community at the University of Oklahoma. Bailey felt that "one of the real problems Clyde had in the Indian community was that it was not that politicized." He recalled a lot of people made fun of Clyde for his determination that core traditional cultural values were necessary to build strong foundations for the future.

Bailey remembered that many people would tell Warrior that "you can't go back in time: You can't hunt buffalo again."[61] For Warrior, however, the past contained the most pertinent tools for protecting culture, community, and tradition while building a foundation for the future. His commitment to the old ways formed the basis of his vision of Red Power as an ideology and a movement. At this time, however, as reflected in the drive for participation in the NIYC and Rosalie Wax's sociological surveys for the Boulder workshops, only a small number of the 3,141 Indian students were politically active. There seemed, to Warrior, to be even fewer who were participating in their own traditional cultures.

In addition to recalling his growing political awareness, Kathryn Red Corn remembered Warrior as a lot of fun to be around. Red Corn, who roomed with Della Hopper and quickly became one of Warrior's best friends, described that, at five eleven, handsome, and athletically built, he "kind of stood out . . . and he had a certain charisma about him."[62] Della later remembered that charisma, saying that "he was like a magnet. People were just drawn to Clyde. If you go into a room and Clyde was in there, there would be people that would just want to talk to him." It was due to this magnetism that Della was drawn to him. They became very close—"of course I fell in love with him," she admitted—although they did not begin dating until the following year.[63]

The youth councils, college classes, workshops, and informal gatherings with friends and teachers helped Warrior grow as an intellectual. He used his increased awareness to better articulate his frustration at the iniquity of the cultural and social status quo in Indian-white relations and the sense of otherness he had felt ever since attending the predominantly white high school in Ponca City. He still viewed the world through the cultural prism of his Ponca heritage, but his education at Cameron, the University of Oklahoma, and especially the Workshops on American Indian Affairs added another dimension. They gave him an intellectual framework he had previously been missing. He began to expand his cultural worldview beyond Oklahoma and beyond the United States, occasionally thinking and talking about Indigenous and Western cultures worldwide. Rather than accept the messages of assimilation that the dominant American society was pushing, Warrior became more entrenched in his determination to protect and preserve his own tribal identity and help other American Indian communities. His ideology grew through long discussions with friends and colleagues such as Mel Thom, Shirley Hill Witt, Bob Thomas, and his soon-to-be partner Della, as well as his grandparents and other elders. As he kicked down the "open door" of higher education and began contextualizing his ideas for a wider audience, his Ponca identity and cultural heritage remained his bedrock. Now he began to formulate mature concepts of self-determination and Red Power and how to go about articulating them.[64]

CHAPTER 3

THE CULTURAL FOUNDATIONS OF RED POWER

"We speak different languages, we have different social customs, we have different forms of tribal government."

If the intellectual underpinnings of Clyde Warrior's vision of Red Power were crystallized in NIYC meetings, student youth group gatherings, and the Boulder workshops, they were also a reflection of his deeply rooted cultural foundation. "Red Power" was far more than just the slogan that Warrior later claimed that he and Mel Thom had chosen because it sounded "kind of cute" in response to Stokely Carmichael's 1966 rallying call for Black Power.[1] Carmichael was national spokesman for the Student Nonviolent Coordinating Committee, and the cultural ideals and organization he sought to foster in Black Power were already present in large parts of Indian Country. The primarily reservation-based, culturally immersed National Indian Youth Council was by then already leading a campaign to protect and preserve tribal communities and cultures.

For Warrior, Red Power had existed in tribal communities long before he and Thom gave it a name. In 1953, D'Arcy McNickle, addressing an NCAI annual conference, focused exclusively on fighting unilateral termination of all tribes, had warned that "the fight for civil rights has not yet been won, but the fight for the right to be culturally different has not even started." It was this right to be culturally different that most clearly defined Warrior's vision of Red Power. It encapsulated the self in identity and self-awareness, family and tradition, and tactics of direct action. The bedrock of Red Power lay in the many complex layers of community and tradition that underscored Warrior's worldview. Although many

Indian nations had borrowed or adapted cultural traits from one another over the centuries, each still held a distinct identity and culture, based in part upon language, unique ceremonial practices, and independent tribal histories. Even in the case of songs, prayers, dances, and ceremonies shared with other nations, clear distinctions were drawn when it came to what was sacred or social. The composite American Indian of the public imagination and contemporary scholarly works was, Warrior declared, a creation of the "typical American." He noted, "To [most whites] the American Indian is dead, there is no such thing, they only appear in movies, in television . . . and sometimes it disturbs me a little bit because I am not that." Rather than being a figment of the hegemonic imagination or a relic from America's violent past of colonial settlement, Warrior was proud to be exactly himself—a "warrior, a man of the world"—saying, "I have no questions about what I am or what I will be."[2] This conviction augmented his vision for Red Power.

Too often Red Power is seen as following and even impersonating Black Power late in the civil rights movement era as American Indians finally began protesting for their rights. The role of Warrior and the NIYC in crafting Red Power ideology, long before it achieved notoriety through the actions and rhetoric of the American Indian Movement, are too often ignored. "Red Power" first appeared as a slogan in November 1966 when Warrior, Thom, Della Warrior, and two more NIYC members drove a car, against NCAI wishes, adorned with "Red Power, National Indian Youth Council" on one side and "Custer Died for Your Sins" on the other, in the NCAI annual convention parade in Oklahoma City.[3] The incident marked a dramatic shift in relations between the NIYC and NCAI. Hank Adams remembered it creating a "big scandal for the NCAI," with organizers, including Vine Deloria, Jr., demanding, "How did that 'Red Power' banner make it into the parade?"[4] As for following Black Power, it had been just four months earlier that Stokely Carmichael had announced to a civil rights rally, "We [have] been saying 'freedom' for six years and we ain't got nothin'. What we gotta start saying now is Black Power," and he was yet to formalize exactly what Black Power meant.[5] After constantly being arrested and harassed for taking part in protest marches, Carmichael

Warrior (*cowboy hat*), with Mel Thom (*left*), Della (*driving*), and others gate-crashing the 1966 NCAI parade with their Red Power banner. (Courtesy of Department of Special Collections and University Archives, Stanford University Libraries.)

increasingly called for more militant action by African Americans in the civil rights movement and eschewed the concept of nonviolent protest. In doing so he shared many of the messages of African American solidarity and economic independence previously put forth by Malcolm X and the Nation of Islam. Similarly, many of Warrior's ideas were fresh interpretations of sentiments of Tecumseh, Chief Joseph, Red Cloud, Sarah Winnemucca, Arthur C. Parker, and many others whose calls for the protection of tribal communities dated back throughout the history of European contact with Indian nations.

In 1967, Carmichael co-authored *Black Power: The Politics of Liberation* and framed Black Power as the need for African Americans to "unite, to recognize their heritage, to build a sense of community."[6]

There are many similarities here to articles by Warrior and his NIYC cohorts. Carmichael denounced well-meaning white people interfering in black communities, asserting that this exacerbated African American self-doubt, just as Warrior and the NIYC felt about social workers and religious groups helping American Indian communities. Carmichael, as Malcolm X before him, questioned the validity of "African American" as a racial signifier yet admitted to using the term due to its wide familiarity just as Warrior did with the term "American Indian." Both men called for a more equitable arrangement between coalitions rather than white oversight of projects, especially ones stemming from Lyndon Johnson's Great Society initiatives. The Red Power and Black Power movements emerged side by side, mutually exclusive yet strikingly similar in their objectives. In short, only the slogan came first and was borrowed. The cultural aspirations and political ambitions of both movements mirrored each other in their timing and urgency. The single major difference between the two was that Warrior's Red Power had a foundation in tribal traditions, communities, and identities, albeit fragmented, as Warrior's many speeches highlighted. Carmichael's Black Power was aspiring to *create* a foundation upon which it could build.[7]

At his core, Warrior was a traditionally raised, community-focused Ponca Indian, and this background shone through in his formation of Red Power. As his cousin Steve Pensoneau stated, "We have no identity crisis, because we were raised to know who we are as Ponca Indians." This security of identity, culture, tradition, and community ensured that Warrior never doubted the veracity of his words or the value of the community he was fighting for. He was raised by grandparents who taught him to never to be ashamed of his heritage.[8] His sheer conviction, and the weight of authority that this conviction added to his words, meant that by 1964 Warrior was undoubtedly the most influential young American Indian activist in the nation. His influence increased with his growing profile, as more and more young Indians took his concerns back to their tribal leaders and demanded change within their own communities. He acknowledged, though, that it would be difficult to forge a completely unified intertribal alliance in Indian Country. The issue for Warrior was not the heterogeneity of Native American cultures that many academics insist upon, but the exact opposite—that the cultural differences between nations ought to be embraced and celebrated. "There are tremendous differences in American Indians," he stated defiantly. "Not only are [we] scattered all over the country, but we [each] live in a different physical world, a different social world, a different historical environment. . . . We speak different languages, we have different social customs, we have different forms of tribal government, and this [makes it] very difficult to bring American Indians together."[9]

Warrior used the word "Indian," as it was the most commonly recognized signifier for the group of North American Native peoples with broadly shared circumstances, but he clearly signaled his belief that tribal identity superseded Indianness or alleged pan-Indian identity. He frequently referred to the innate security and self-awareness that came from total immersion in his culture, language, and tribal history, and he clearly knew the difference between Ponca identity and "Indian" identity.[10]

In January 1964, Warrior traveled to an executive meeting of the NCAI and, as Robert Burnette remembered, "laced into the older tribal leaders for having been willing through the years to let the white man rule the reservations and control the affairs of the Indian people." Burnette, the NCAI chief executive, whose removal from office Warrior would engineer later that year, noted that the conference had "begun with fireworks." In his 1971 book *The Tortured Americans,* he sympathized with Warrior's position, admitting that he had been wanting to say some of the same things for years and that he was pleased by the more militant stance that Warrior introduced. He did, however, criticize Warrior for speaking so harshly "before our guests and the Indian women."[11] While Warrior later apologized to Burnette for his intemperate words, many of the women, such as Shirley Hill Witt, were not quite as easily shocked as Burnette supposed and were enthralled by his speech. Warrior's greatest weapon beyond his love for his people and his community was, it seemed, his courage to speak out without fear of reprisal. Witt later recalled that part of what made Warrior stand out was that he would say or do "all kinds of things that maybe some of us would have been more reluctant about."[12]

It was this combination of bellicosity and a reverence for the past that drew ever-increasing numbers of young Indians within the influence of the National Indian Youth Council through a still-growing network of regional youth councils and conferences. The candidness that had shocked several of Warrior's peers at the University of Oklahoma had garnered him a growing reputation as a visionary and forthright leader. Seeking no personal gain or glory, he deemed any personal repercussions to his blunt speech irrelevant. For people like Burnette, encumbered in offices they had sought, no such freedom existed.[13]

In 1963, the concept of using direct action to protect tribal communities emerged in an article outlining concern about Public Law 280, passed in 1953. The law had given certain states primary jurisdiction over criminal and civil matters on Indian reservations. Of primary concern in the piece, written by Hank Adams (Assiniboine) and published in the NIYC's newspaper (*ABC: Americans before Columbus*), was the impact upon the tribes of Washington State. Adams, who had grown up on the Quinault Indian Reservation on the shore of the Pacific, carried his discussion over into the December issue where, after a brief summary of his disputes with the law, he specifically targeted Indian fishing rights. Adams was determined to enlist the help of Warrior and the rest of the NIYC in fighting for the tribes in Washington who were "presently engaged in a great battle to preserve their aboriginally-derived and treaty-guaranteed fishing rights." Unity was a cause for concern, as he noted that "the latest battle finds certain influential Indians allies of the opposition" and warned that "those Indians do not realize that the patting hands [of their federal overlords] move steadily closer to their own tribes' throats."[14]

In response, Warrior, Thom, Bruce Wilkie, author Eugene Burdick, and actor Marlon Brando launched the NIYC's "Campaign of Awareness" before the major news services of the world in New York, including an appearance on NBC's *Today* show. Warrior later joked that he, Wilkie, and Thom looked like "three fat chipmunks," as they informed the media that Indian people had their backs to the wall and that the present-day termination and forced-assimilation policy had to end. Brando, who would describe Warrior as "a man with a sense of dignity I'll never forget," had met members of the NIYC at the council's board meeting after an informal introduction from D'Arcy McNickle.[15] It was at the same meeting, on the Uinta and Ouray reservation at Fort Duchesne, Utah, that Adams and Warrior determined to keep their fight for Red Power separate from the wider civil rights movement.

In what was his first official NIYC meeting, Adams sided with Warrior to maintain an "independent course to guard against submersion and [avoid being] dominated by other people and other voices and other races." According to Adams, who initially found Warrior to be "overbearing almost to the point of bullying with persons who couldn't stand up to his opinion," Warrior's argument quickly convinced Brando and several NIYC members who had been in favor of reaching out to civil rights leaders to join their campaign.[16] They understood why others in the NIYC were casting envious eyes at the media attention African Americans were receiving in their struggle for civil rights and equality. Warrior and Adams were convinced, however, that joining them would result in tribal cultural and communal issues being subsumed by the other movement's goal of inclusion and equality. If that happened, then the fight to maintain the integrity of cultural distinction that was the cornerstone of Red Power would be lost.

Proving the truth in the rhetoric behind the Campaign of Awareness, unlicensed Nisqually fishers in Washington discovered the entire Nisqually River closed to them by game wardens at the behest of the powerful local Sportsmen's Club in the 1950s and 1960s. After local tribespeople defied the ban and were arrested, a state superior court issued restraining orders, in clear violation of tribal treaty fishing rights. As Adams argued in *ABC*, "For many of us fishing is still a matter of survival."[17] He was determined to get the NIYC to aid in the fight for that survival and enlisted the help of Wilkie, who had joined the council at its 1963 annual meeting, and was a fellow Washington resident. Together the two collaborated with Washington tribes to organize protests and actions against attempts to regulate and suppress Indian fishing in the state's rivers and lakes. With the help of Herb Blatchford's organizational skills, the NIYC garnered support from tribes as far away as Florida, Montana, and the Dakotas, with Seminoles, Blackfeet, Sioux, and others offering to help the tribes of Washington in staging a "fish-in."[18]

March 2, 1964, was a day Warrior described as "a landmark in American Indian history."[19] A crowd of thousands, consisting of local Indians, members of the aforementioned tribes and others in solidarity, NIYC members, and news reporters, all thronged the banks of the Puyallup River to witness game wardens' abrogation of treaty fishing rights. Marlon Brando later remembered, "I got in a boat with a Native American and a Catholic priest; someone gave us a big salmon we were supposed to have taken out of the river illegally and, sure enough, a game warden soon arrived and arrested us." The presence of Brando had the desired effect on news media, and at a subsequent protest that afternoon on the steps of the State Capitol in Olympia, reporters flocked to report on what Herb Blatchford later described as "the first full scale intertribal action since the Indians defeated General Custer on the Little Big Horn."[20]

The evening following the protest in Olympia was spent in discussion and quiet celebration of success in bringing attention to the serious issues facing the tribes in the region. The mood was light as Warrior and Brando gave short speeches to a small audience of organizers and interested parties, with Brando triumphantly holding a paddle above his head. After the speeches, Warrior, Brando, Wilkie, Thom, Reuben Wells, and Gerald Brown all relaxed by donning Beatles wigs and miming guitar playing. Brando mastered his "guitar" while clinging to a half-full shot glass. At one point he stole Warrior's glasses and placed them upside down on his own nose.[21] After the Beatles rendition and an impromptu rendition of "Ebb Tide" on a hotel lobby piano, Brando tangoed with Shirley Witt late into the night.[22]

The next day saw the number of protesters grow to somewhere between two thousand and five thousand. Warrior upped the rhetoric and proclaimed, "Today, March 3rd, 1964 marks the beginning of a new era in the history of American Indians." No longer would Indians remain in the background, he announced. They were now firmly involved in civil rights protest. Having been raised at his grandparents' feet, steeped in the traditions of his own Ponca people, and surrounded by traditional elders from neighboring tribes as a child, Warrior understood that traditions were a necessary part of a community's identity, even though he was often accused of romanticizing the past. He described these traditions as a "sacred relationship between the Indian and God." Above federal or state law, the right of tribal people to fish was a gift from the creator, he and others believed. He decried this denial to fish without license, which they had been doing "from time immemorial," as treaty abrogation and a "cancerous sore."[23]

Warrior skillfully wove the issue of American Indian treaty rights into the very fabric of American identity and demanded for tribal communities the respect, recognition, and voice that they deserved. While he never positioned Indians as being participants in the global postcolonial Cold War movement, he utilized Cold War and postcolonial rhetoric to highlight the disparity between US foreign and domestic policies. He reminded the crowd that Soviet premier Nikita Khrushchev had repeatedly denounced the United States as a dishonest nation because "it had broken so many treaties with Indian tribes." Citing President Johnson's attack on Panama for breaking the Rio Treaty of Inter-American Reciprocal Assistance as an example of American policy hypocrisy, he asked, "If this treaty is not an outmoded agreement from the past then why are Indian treaties regarded as such?" According to Warrior, in order for the United States to maintain the moral high ground in the Cold War political arena, American Indian treaties needed to be honored. This was especially necessary for the United States' conscience, he argued, because "the founders of this country . . . pledged their solemn word never to dislodge this relationship between the Indian and his God," a promise that continued treaty abrogation "made a mockery of." He demanded, "Give us Life for our tribes, Liberty for ourselves, and the Pursuit of Happiness for our children."[24] Warrior used the Declaration of Independence ironically but also because he recognized that he needed to frame the fight for treaty protection within concepts that politicians and the general public would recognize. He also clearly identified here the core triumvirate of Red Power: community, culture, and tradition.

The Washington protests and actions succeeded on several levels. Awareness of tribal treaty rights conflicts increased across the United States and globally, and in 1974, after several more protests and the continued pressure of the Survival of American Indians Association (SAIA), District Judge George Boldt in *United States vs. Washington* ruled that the Indians of Washington State had the right, under treaty, to 50 percent of the state's annual fishing haul. The ruling ensured the survival and economic regeneration of the federally recognized tribes within the state.[25]

As Warrior and the NIYC increased their visibility via protests and conferences, they were heeded by the power brokers who ran federal Indian policy in Washington, D.C. Warrior seized this opportunity to address the need to protect tribal communities, identities, and cultures. He stressed the significance of the moment, declaring this is "the beginning of the active participation of American Indians in the creation of a new society."[26] The pursuit of this new society was centered on a single complex issue: respect for American Indians' right to embrace, celebrate, and maintain their unique identities. This theme underscoring the community aspect of Red Power was one that Warrior would return to time and again. He declared that for the past hundred years Indians had been held back by being told they could not be both Indians and Americans, but he shot back, "We refuse to accept that definition. We will be Indians and we will [be] human beings. I am an American and an Indian."[27] This concept of cultural pluralism was another to which he would repeatedly return.

With the ideology of Red Power already formulated, the Washington fish-ins were, Bradley Shreve noted in *Red Power Rising*, "the true birth of the Red Power Movement."[28] Now it was up to Warrior and his cohorts to maintain the momentum. His first attempt to do so represented something of a personal mission. In early August 1964, he surprised and intrigued Shirley Witt by asking if he could borrow her beat-up Volkswagen bus. Besides being curious, she had no idea that Warrior could drive, and she was further surprised when she learned he wanted to go to Mississippi. Three young men, northern civil rights activists, had been missing there since June 21 when they had investigated the firebombing of an African American church that had been used as a freedom school. On August 4, their bodies had been found in Philadelphia, Mississippi. (It was later discovered that members of the Ku Klux Klan had murdered them.) Warrior told Witt, "The killings were on the reservation of the Choctaw in Mississippi. I would be a better warrior to go to Mississippi than to go to Vietnam." While some others from the North involved themselves in the voter registration drives taking place in Mississippi that summer, Warrior went to the Mississippi Choctaw reservation to provide whatever aid the Choctaws needed. Later, when he arrived at the annual NIYC meeting and returned the bus to Witt, he would not divulge what he had done to help in Mississippi. He did, however, have to explain a large dent in the side of her bus, sheepishly admitting, "I went off a bridge."[29] The trip reveals that despite Warrior's uncertainty about the ability to forge intertribal alliances, his view of community within Red Power extended beyond his Ponca heritage to include people from other tribes and nations, and this was a message that he constantly tried to carry forward.

As he addressed youth councils, poverty-related conferences, and academic audiences Warrior spoke of the need for community and Red Power to counter the devastating effects of federal colonialism on Indian communities. He railed against the BIA bureaucracy and the overbearing attitude of those at federal agencies who insisted upon administering Indian programs without input from the tribes. He complained about the ineffectual tribal leadership that such a policy produced; the paucity of choice available to Indians in lifestyle, occupation, and health care; the insecurity and lack of self-esteem bred by the despair of life on the reservation; and the effects that such despair had upon self-identity. Ultimately, these conditions often led to another devastating problem for American Indians—alcoholism, which was rife in many parts of Indian Country, as increasing numbers of despairing men and women drank themselves to death. The horror of Warrior's complaints lay not just in their truth but also that they reflected truths that had existed for so long. Similar indictments had been made by Society of American Indians member Arthur C. Parker in 1915, and, even further back, by Sarah Winnemucca (Paiute) in the late 1880s. Many of the conditions that Warrior described had worsened since the government's Meriam Report in 1928 had suggested sweeping reforms of federal policy regarding service to American Indian communities.[30]

Warrior had first addressed the issues facing his own community, and the complexity of what community represented to him, in his Boulder workshop essays. Here his intellectual conceptualization of community drew upon the folk-urban comparisons of his teacher Bob Thomas. Answering the question of where his community would fall on the folk-urban scale, Warrior divided the Poncas into two categories: "folk-like" and those "midway between Folk and Marginality." He proudly identified himself as belonging to the folk-like half of the community, "the ones who take an active part in all tribal organizations and functions" and never refer to themselves by saying "I" but speak of "we," meaning the tribe. He stated simply, "These are my people." Warrior revealed the fundamental distrust of white society that many American Indians wore naturally. He observed that "these people have no idea of leaving this life, they think white men are strange and have bad ways and they're out to get the Indian." In addition to his people being the traditionalists of the tribe, Warrior also marked them as the cultural core of Ponca heritage, claiming that "the majority of these people are the full-bloods, many . . . from chieftainship blood." Like his drum-making grandparents, "each one has a definite role, [and] with the role each one has a definite status and they all recognize it as being that way."[31]

In contrast, the other Poncas were "out for themselves and they don't hesitate to tell you," Warrior wrote. "They say the Indian way will not work today, that only dumb, ignorant people, and lazy people cling to a way of life that is gone." These people, he insisted, could not care less what the tribal organizations do and think tribal functions "malarkey." They were the "wealthy farmers" who have exploited their relatives' land and who "teach their children to be ashamed of being Indians." While he expressed hope that one day these two groups would come together, he was doubtful, saying that at present there was no understanding and, worse, that there was no desire for undertanding.[32] These issues had been dividing the Poncas for generations and went back to the rift that Standing Bear had discussed in his testimony after removal.

Warrior realized that the fault for this division within the Ponca community lay with external influences dating back to the pressures of assimilation, removal, and allotment. Over the next several years many of his speeches and articles would deliver an eviscerating attack on the historic and contemporary corrosive effects of US internal colonialism and the bureaucracy behind federal Indian policy. Introduced to Warrior and other NIYC members by Bob Thomas at Boulder, internal colonialism was not a new concept in the analysis of Indian-white relations. Felix S. Cohen's "Colonialism, US Style" and "Colonialism: A Realistic Approach" were required readings at the workshops, and Cohen's analysis of Indian communities as subjects of internal colonialism helped Warrior develop concepts that he would articulate in later speeches. By 1964, addressing internal colonialism was a powerful rhetorical weapon for American Indian activists such as Warrior, as it hinted at connections to postcolonial uprisings taking place across the globe in the wake of World War II.[33]

In his presentation at an Indian leadership conference in Eau Claire, Wisconsin, he discussed uprisings taking place across Africa and Latin America and described the American Indian student movement as a "quiet revolution" in comparison. This was due, he argued, to the inability to see "our young people in America as really a potent force for change." While Warrior never specifically directed Indians to join or create a global indigenous decolonization movement, he was aware of the power of such rhetoric. As the cornerstone of Red Power was retention of cultural sovereignty among American Indian communities, he hoped that by pointing to related situations in the global arena he could galvanize Indian students to take action at home. Referencing African independence campaigns, he claimed that American Indian students were sitting on the sidelines of "perhaps an even greater social movement than student protests in other parts of the world."[34] This was one of the few occasions when Warrior called for solidarity with other indigenous peoples. He would often refer to other indigenous revolutionary movements but he would never openly called for a unity of purpose across international lines the way that the NCAI and later AIM did. His focus was on more immediate matters closer to home.

Warrior argued that societal and social lack of choices available to young Indians because of the internal colonial system of federal

Indian affairs stopped them from joining social movements or expressing their unrest. Despite his own commitment to focusing on the needs of tribal communities, he also believed that there needed to be possibilities for individuals. He lamented that desperation for educated leadership within tribal communities meant that students were expected to return home and serve on their councils. He complained that this expectation robbed them of the spontaneity of choice that that other college students had, saying, "They are *in training* to be. They are not *being*. I know of no society (except Indian) that *expects* young people to be leaders."[35] The message was paradoxical considering Warrior's conviction that retention of cultural practices was crucial for Indian communities. Traditionally in such communities, the role of the individual was predestined and predefined. In this particular instance, though, it was not cultural retention but political leadership for which students were expected to return home. Also, by focusing on future political leadership, tribes were not seeing enough doctors, business leaders, or other necessary experts returning to their communities.

Even within this paradox of actively seeking change and promoting a new style of leadership while championing tradition and culture, the stifling effects of the limited choices available to Indians were manifest in the low self-esteem and insecurity of his cohorts. As Shirley Hill Witt recalled, "We mimicked the dominant society." While she was referring to gender power structures in tribal societies and the male-centric public face of the NIYC, many Indians of their generation and older had adopted personas thrust upon them by outside influences.[36] Red Power was about eschewing these personas and embracing one's own identity. The five types of Indian that Warrior described in his December 1964 article "Which One Are You?" were manifestations of the stultifying effects of federal Indian policy and societal perceptions. According to Warrior, it was as much the responsibility of individuals to shake off these unreal perceptions as it was for them to fight for the right to choose their own futures.[37]

The five types that Warrior described were as much a damning indictment of Indians themselves for adopting these personas, as they were of the institutional and societal racism that forced these perceptions upon Indians in the first place. One type reflected the worst perceptions of Indians by white society, and included "the slob, or hood," who molded himself into the white misconception of Indianness by "dropping out of school, becoming a 'wino,' and eventually becoming a court case, sent off to prison. . . . Another Indian hits the dust, through no fault of his own." The second type was the joker, the Indian man, for example, who "has defined to himself that to be an Indian is a joke. An Indian does stupid, funny things . . . and he goes through life a bungling clown." The third type was the "white noser" or sellout, who "has accepted . . . the definition that anything Indian is dumb, usually filthy, and immoral, and to avoid this is to become a 'LITTLE BROWN AMERICAN' by associating and identifying with everything that is white." Warrior called this type "the fink of finks." The fourth type was the "ultra-pseudo Indian," the man, for example, who "is proud that he is Indian but for some reason does not know how one acts. Therefore, he takes his cues from non-Indian sources, books, shows, etc. and proceeds to act 'Indian.' Hence, we have a proud, phony, Indian."[38]

The fifth and final type was the "angry nationalist," who Warrior saw as "generally closer to true 'Indianism' than the other types." The angry nationalist, with whom Warrior himself was usually associated, resented the others for being ashamed of their own kind and "tends to dislike the older generations who have been 'Uncle Tomahawks' or 'yes men' to the Bureau of Indian Affairs and whites in general." This type of American Indian, he wrote, viewed the problem of "personality disappearance" with bitterness and were labeled radicals as they tended to alienate themselves from the general masses of Indians for speaking the truth.[39]

Warrior's concern was that these personas reflected a move away from the traditional tribal values with which he had been raised and which, in his eyes, represented true, if idealized, "Indianism." He argued that "genuine contemporary creative thinking [and] democratic leadership" were needed to reject these personas. The leadership, however, needed to come from traditionalists, so that whatever processes were implemented would be "based on true Indian philosophy geared to modern times." To clarify that by "Indian" he meant individual tribes, he warned that "this will not come about without nationalistic pride in one's own self and one's own kind." Rather than commitment to the idea of pan-Indian homogeneity, Warrior subtly emphasized tribal distinction.[40]

Despite his shockingly frank words, Warrior was in many ways channeling the frustration of his grandparents' generation at the bastardization of tribal identity among younger Indians. This was evident when he declared that Indian leadership could not come "from those who have sold out, or those who do not understand true Indianism. Only from those with pride, love, and understanding of the people and the people's way from which they come can this evolve." Warrior was again using language that more traditionally raised Indians would recognize, as in most communities "the people" referred specifically to their particular tribes rather than the wider American Indian "race."[41]

Although he had been mocked by many of his peers at the University of Oklahoma for romanticizing the past, there was a deep reason for his hankering for the old ways. Rejecting traditional values and lessons was tantamount to rejecting the community in Warrior's eyes. He was aware that his generation had been raised in something of a cultural limbo, and his efforts to help his uncle revive the Hethuska Society reflected his concern about this. He had grown up listening to his grandparents and their friends discussing the old ways, but his generation could not fully experience these ways. He and his generation had often been told that the true meaning of these traditions could not be revealed to them as they had not earned the right to the knowledge. Red Power was about earning the right to learn these cultural secrets, and most of the five personas Warrior identified reflected lack of respect for elders. He complained, "I am sick and tired of seeing my elders stripped of dignity and low-rated in the eyes of their young. And I am disturbed to the point of screaming when I see American Indian youth accepting the horror of 'American conformity' as being the only way for Indian progress." Warrior's view was that young Indians should seize their cultural and communal identity, and he believed that the National Indian Youth Council was needed to "introduce to this sick room of stench and anonymity some fresh air of new Indianness." Borrowing from Mel Thom's NIYC presidential inauguration address, he insisted that what was needed was "a fresh air of new honesty and integrity, a fresh air of new Indian idealism," and he issued a simple, powerful call to arms: "How about it? Let's raise some hell."[42]

"Which One Are You?" was significant on many levels. Vine Deloria, Jr., later described Warrior as having had "a way of presenting his points crudely and effectively so that people would not forget," and his rhetoric marked an important shift in the methodology of American Indian protest.[43] While his directness was an extension of the verbal militancy first suggested by his "sewage of Europe" SRIYC election speech, it also reflected the frustration tribal elders seemed incapable of expressing to the younger generation. He placed as much responsibility upon American Indians for accepting humiliation and subjugation from white society as he did upon the system for imposing it. Gus Palmer, Jr., later remembered being shocked at how many Indians he and his friends recognized from Warrior's typology. Palmer recalled feeling awestruck and thinking, "Wow, this guy is fearsome. He's Crazy Horse. He's the real thing." Warrior was irreverent, self-assured, and unafraid.[44]

At the core of the article was the issue of respect. Warrior had witnessed many within his own community falling victim to the stereotypes and demands he described. He had seen this on reservations and college campuses across the country. It was respect that was lacking, respect that had been denied him by schoolteachers, church leaders, and the people of Ponca City as he had grown up. Most importantly it was a lack of respect from Indians within their own communities that needed to be rectified. Rather than submit to people who "tried to make us be like them," as Palmer later put it, Warrior wanted Indians to be respected for who they were.[45] For every Gus Palmer, Jr., who was galvanized by Warrior's rhetoric, Browning Pipestem surmised that many Indians hated Warrior "because he was right."[46] Palmer recalled that the article hit a nerve with many people who read it and felt exposed: "[Warrior was] looking at you, and you were one of these guys and you knew it."[47]

Warrior reiterated his commitment to community, family, and tradition in a follow-up article, "How Should an Indian Act?" He told his readers that the answer was simple: "Indians should act appropriate[ly] to their circumstances."[48] By this he meant that Indians should look for self-respect and be confident enough as an Indian to act like one, no matter what tribal or cultural manifestation that might entail. The article clearly deferred to the concepts of folkways and urbanity that had been so prevalent in his workshops education. Warrior was convinced that Indians who took behavioral and attitudinal prompts from outsiders, as he described in "Which One Are You," were not acting appropriately according to their circumstances.

Warrior insisted that to be truly successful, all Indian students needed to embrace their families and communities and traditional institutions such as the Hethuska Society for inspiration and guidance, as tribal people had always done, rather than seek help from outsiders.[49] This was not merely rhetoric or a romantic embellishment of lost traditions on Warrior's part. For a Ponca man such as he, the Hethuska was a way of life. Contemporary member Jimmy Duncan proudly proclaimed, "You join Hethuska, you think Hethuska, you act Hethuska, you live Hethuska." This ethos also applies to the Gives Water Service Club, of which Warrior was also a member.[50] In addition to the service role adopted by his grandmother, Gives Water clan members (or *Wanidhe*—life-givers) had long held a special role within Ponca society. In pre-reservation days, when captives were brought into the tribe, "If the Wanidhe gave you a drink of water, you were adopted into the tribe. If not . . ."[51] Similar water-carrying functions were carried out by young Gives Water boys at the Hethuska ceremonials, a tradition continued when the society was revived and also at the Ponca powwow. At the annual powwow, water carriers take a bucket of water and ladle to each of the attending straight dancers to refresh them and honor the dance's connections to the Hethuska. Warrior's role in both organizations was clearly defined and based upon the traditional rules of care, respect, and honor, with which his grandparents had inculcated him from birth. Reflecting this debt, he acknowledged family as probably the factor that gave him the most important cultural and societal cues.[52]

Warrior knew that in many tribal communities this focus on tradition was not as strong. The modern urban world had changed

Warrior (*fifth in procession*), during the entrance of the service flag at the Gives Water Service Club dance on Memorial Day 1964; his grandmother Metha Collins (front) carries the flag, upon which forty-two stars on the flag denoted Gives Water family members and other Poncas who had served in the US armed forces, with one gold star denoting the single fatality. Warrior's grandfather Bill Collins is next to her. (Courtesy of Western History Collections, University of Oklahoma Library.)

much of that dynamic within tribal life, according to Warrior. "Most tribal institutions have been smashed and replaced," he mourned. The issue was not merely changing times, evolving concepts, or "foreign" interlopers, however. Much of Warrior's rhetoric focused on the conflicting worldviews that had dominated Indian-white relations since first European contact. He argued that the reason Indian students acted so inappropriately to their circumstances was because, still having a "tribal outlook," they were attempting to make their way in "alien institutions, alien because they are out of context." He did add a caveat again about individual responsibility, saying that Indian students needed to "'WAKE UP' and decide if he is going to accept these definitions that are being cued to him by this alien society and institutions."[53]

Warrior concluded "How Should an Indian Act?" with a few pointers as to how Indian students could avoid being dragged down into a state of bland cultural anonymity. He suggested that his readers "decide where your loyalty and reference group lies in today's world and decide what you are, what you want, and set a goal." Get your mind out of the status quo, he urged. Most important: when the chips are down, it's family that counts—in any society.[54]

Somewhat ironically, Warrior's unrelenting campaigning for the protection and preservation of cultural and community identity and tradition almost cost him his place as a Hethuska tail dancer. In the summer of 1965, at the same time "How Should an Indian Act?" was published, Hethuska Society leaders held a committee meeting. They discussed Warrior's increasing activism and its potentially detrimental effect upon the society. Sylvester Warrior, as Nuda'ho"ga, shared his concern that Clyde was neglecting the office of tail dancer—conference commitments had kept him from the April ceremonial. The attendance of the tail dancers is essential to the integrity of the ceremony. Clyde, after a long and fraught meeting, finally convinced Sylvester and the other society members who had approved the organization's revitalization that his April absence had been unfortunate and misguided and would be the only one. He counted his reprieve as a blessing. The April absence aside, he took the role so seriously, that "when he tail danced he wore the small [crow or eagle feather] bustle on his back."[55] This was part of the original Hethuska regalia that was eventually replaced by the otter-skin sash after the tribe relocated to Indian Territory. He did own a sash as well but maintained that for Straight Dance purposes rather than Hethuska ceremonials.

For Warrior, there needed to be a way for the two worlds of youth and traditionalism to coexist and for young Indians to be able to communicate with their people, especially the "old traditionalists who are still very nationalistic in their own thinking."[56] Warrior himself already personified this, with one Cherokee tribal elder describing him as someone who "may not have the power of the medicine way, but he knows how to talk to those who do have the power and can't express it in a modern way. Some of the young Indians don't know how the old Indians *feel*. He knows. . . . He understands the tribal ways. I mean he really feels it."[57]

Understanding of the old ways and ability to vocalize this understanding for a modern audience marked Warrior as a cultural carrier to tribal elders of all nations. Seeing his ability to mix with the dominant society without his vision or worldview being tainted, they viewed him as a bridge between their world and modern America. Warrior, in turn, empathized with the frustration of his elders. He was haunted by the continued breakdown of tribal communities, the cycle of perpetuating misery fostered by paternalistic federal oversight. He discussed the situation at length before an audience at Wayne State University's Montieth College in February 1966. He observed, "It is getting worse, the social breakdown . . . you have situations where sons will come in drunk and slap their mothers—unheard of in tribal societies." He lamented the lack of opportunities for tribal communities, which meant diminishing self-worth within individuals. People were turning to "unconscious suicide," he observed, thinking, "Man, life ain't worth it. Best we should stay drunk and die or best we should kill each other than . . . live the life we have to live today."[58]

Acknowledging his own increasing struggle with alcohol and his growing despair at the lack of opportunity within Indian Country, he confessed, "I am one of them but I am not at [the] suicide point."[59] His drinking, which had grown from social late-night drinking sessions with Bob Thomas in Boulder and the Druid Society in Norman, Oklahoma, to full-blown alcoholism, appeared to have been weighing on his mind since the birth of his first daughter. He admitted that it was also something for which he was becoming known in Indian Country besides his activism, despite the fact that he was not alone in his drinking. He later told Murray Wax, his mentor from the Boulder workshops, that many of the students at Sequoyah (the high school in Tahlequah where he would serve an internship) "have heard [of] my tremendous drinking capacity somehow or another."[60]

Regarding social breakdown and devastating poverty on reservations, Warrior was certain that death was preferable: "The best American Indians should have to die rather than live in the environment and social structure that they are presently in." He tended to drink while he was away from his home and family, but he had seen the effects of alcoholism on reservations and Indian communities, first as a dancer and later as an activist. In his darker moments he saw that unless change was swift and drastic, many Indians faced death by alcohol and their communities faced further cultural fragmentation. "This may sound extreme," he warned, "but I am sure many of you here if . . . you have come from ethnic minorities . . . [know] that this is true."[61] High levels of alcoholism among American Indians had been a problem for generations. Linked now to loss of culture and low self-esteem, it had begun after the deliberate introduction of alcohol to Indian communities by whites with genocidal intent. The loss of land and tribal sovereignty were also seen as highly contributing factors to the epidemic. Warrior was not alone in recognizing the need for change, drastic change, although he was among the best at articulating this: it was devastatingly apparent and deeply personal with every word he uttered.[62]

Warrior had highlighted the disconnection between his Ponca community and the outside world in an article published in *New University Thought* in the summer of 1965. In "Poverty, Community, and Power," Warrior wrote, "[The] Ponca tribe of which I am a member lives in Kay County, Oklahoma. You could call Kay County a community, it is a legally designated unit, but if it is a community my relatives are not part of it." The Poncas were acknowledged by local whites only when necessary, Warrior argued. "Our Indian community, as far as being part of Kay County, might as well be on Mars."[63] Although the Poncas of White Eagle were (and are) only nine miles from Ponca City, the two were polar opposites in many ways. Community for the traditionalist Poncas was sacred, as it ensured continuity of identity and culture. They were surrounded, however, by political entities and societies that had no desire to help them economically, politically, or socially, in any way, and saw little value in helping or even allowing the tribe to prosper. For Warrior, community meant equality and respect and participation and inclusion in social and political life, such as he had seen in his upbringing in Bois D'Arc and in the Hethuska Society and Gives Water Service Club. The politicians of Ponca City only saw poverty and statistics.

These problems were typical for other Indian communities too, and Warrior envisaged three possible outcomes unless the status quo changed dramatically and soon. The first was Indians getting completely assimilated and intermarried: "bred out, our blood diluted, . . . there wouldn't be any American Indian problem." Blood quantum was a contentious issue for Warrior, who resented federal ownership of Indian identity as a colonial imposition on sovereignty and freedom. The second possibility entailed the formation of "Mau Mau societies among the tribes, very radical, violent." He was astonished that "the government knows of [Indian nationalist movements], and how they don't do anything about them is beyond me!"[64] He was unaware at this time that his friend Bob Thomas had labeled him a leader of the "Red Mau-Mau."[65] A third possibility was one he suggested would be the most economically devastating for the tribes, while probably the most culturally beneficial. He foresaw tribes further withdrawing from "the American scene" as he had seen with many of the traditional Cherokee communities surrounding Tahlequah. He predicted that in this case "a tribe will become more cohesive and the relationship with the outside world will be less and less," writing that this had happened before.[66]

As an avid reader of *Newsweek, Time,* and the *New Republic,* which was then a left-of-center political magazine, Warrior was well aware of the political rhetoric and opinions being voiced around the country that time. He was convinced that if the whole of American society was erupting in protest and clamor for change, then sooner or later those in power would have to acquiesce or face revolution. This conviction was bolstered by the increasing militancy of antiwar and free speech protesters among the general US student population as well as the increasing militancy of the civil rights movement. In 1965, however, he had little faith that he would ever see dramatic change for American Indian communities, whether via revolution or governmental acquiescence. His rhetoric was now often more militant than during the fish-ins of 1964, and

Warrior with fellow Hethuska Society members; *left to right*: Abe Conklin, Richard Poweshak, Alfred Waters, unidentified, unidentified, Sylvester Warrior, John Steel, unidentified, Norm Heights, Del Ray Scott, Clyde Warrior, and Roscoe Conklin at Osage Inloshka event, Gray Horse, Oklahoma, mid-1960s. (Courtesy of Frank Turley.)

Warrior was quite comfortable too with direct action. His greatest frustration was his sense of his inability to foster changes immediately. Not for the first or last time he admitted, "How this is done, I haven't figured . . . out yet and I doubt if I ever will."[67]

Warrior was determined to keep fighting for change, however, and was quick to defend any perceived threat to community integrity. In June 1967, he was involved again in militant protest, this time on behalf of traditional Cherokee communities. That month, the Cherokee government announced the grand opening of the Cherokee Village and Heritage Center. Located in countryside south of Tahlequah, the center was designed as a tourist attraction where Cherokee history and culture were taught through a performative "living history" program. Traditional members of the Cherokee community were horrified, and they accused the village organizers of misrepresenting Cherokee culture and creating a "monkey house." Many of them had earlier formed the Original Cherokee Community Organization (OCCO) as a method of collective cultural preservation against federal interference, which they perceived to include the federally appointed Cherokee tribal government. The OCCO called on Warrior and the NIYC to support a planned protest, and on the opening weekend Warrior and Della joined a picket line of protesters that included traditional Cherokees from all generations.[68]

Protesters carried slogans in Cherokee and English from the OCCO, and the NIYC paid for flyers highlighting their concerns about the Cherokee Heritage Center. Rather than simply handing out flyers to visitors, however, Warrior and Al Wahrhaftig hit upon the idea of distributing them all over the surrounding area by dropping them from an airplane. Wahrhaftig had returned from Colombia to resume working as an instructor at the Boulder workshops and was also a researcher for Sol Tax's Carnegie Project on Cherokee literacy among traditional communities. He had been taking flying lessons in his spare time and had passed his pilot's exam the previous October. For a single day the Cherokee National Air Force, with Wahrhaftig as its commanding officer and first pilot, was born. Wahrhaftig rented a small Cessna plane at the Tulsa airport to avoid getting the Tahlequah airport operator into trouble, but as he reached the protest site with his Cherokee copilot they faced a brewing thunderstorm. Wahrhaftig and his friend hurriedly dropped stacks of handbills from the plane, but the winds shifted strongly and carried them who knows where. "Suffice it to say," Wahrhaftig later recalled, "we threw all the folders, all the leaflets, out of the plane, handful by handful, and not a goddamned one of them landed on a demonstrator." After racing the storm back to Tulsa and landing safely seconds before the storm struck, the pair returned to Tahlequah. Still exhilarated from racing and beating the storm, the two were greeted by Warrior's laughing retort: "Every goddamn boll weevil in Texas knows about this demonstration but nobody here does." Despite the mishap with the leaflets, those involved, including Warrior, saw the protest as successful in raising awareness of their concerns about cultural exploitation, especially from within, and the need to maintain cultural integrity.[69] The demonstration was also Warrior's distinction between political and cultural leadership writ large.

Warrior knew that Red Power would evolve as a more militant ideology if the NIYC's proposed changes of greater autonomy and cultural control within tribal communities were not successful, and he powerfully articulated this vision in a conversation with Stan Steiner in September 1966. Steiner was interviewing Warrior, who was now president of the NIYC, for his weekly radio show and for his forthcoming book on Indian activism, *The New Indians*. By now, Warrior was married to Della, with two small children, and he was working as a researcher on Cherokee education for Murray Wax. He was also president of the NIYC. The interview took place at Warrior's home in Tahlequah, with an Oklahoma thunderstorm raging outside, and his daughter Mary Martha Warrior playing nearby. Warrior described his vision of Red Power, despite not yet calling it that, seeing it as being "community driven." He discussed joblessness, poor education, societal "peonage," and political and economic exploitation of the local traditional Cherokees as a microcosm representing similar situations within Indian communities elsewhere. "If the country doesn't want to listen to logic," Warrior warned, then violence appeared to be the logical outcome. Having seen the way the civil rights movement had progressed, with

Warrior relaxing with a Navajo elder at the Boulder Workshops. (Courtesy of Newberry Library.)

nonviolent protests increasingly replaced with violent clashes be-tween protesters and authorities, so he saw Red Power evolving. Perhaps referencing the 1965 riots in Watts, Los Angeles, he told Steiner to "look at the Negroes. Nothing was done in their favor until they got violent, and I guess if this country really understands violence then this is the only way to do that." Of eastern Oklahoma, he snorted, "Southern rednecks in this area only understand vio-lence. Slap them in the mouth or shoot them, then they'll pay at-tention to you."[70] Such rhetoric reflected the lingering bitterness toward his own experiences at the hands of whites in and around Ponca City.

Steiner challenged Warrior's view of the future, suggesting that an alternative to violence lay, for example, in "community actions among Cherokee villages and Creek villages around here." Warrior

acknowledged that local groups were forming to address the poverty they were surrounded by, and that communities were discussing some kind of policy or plan of action. While these projects
epitomized his vision of Red Power, he argued that such efforts
would flounder, saying that they would be manipulated by "the
powers that be." His experience with the OCCO protest was an example of local action, and with the Cherokee Village opening as
scheduled he knew that many people did not see raised awareness
as a victory. He insisted that change was needed now before a more
violent form of Red Power was expressed by the generation to come.
Repeating a theme that would dominated his rhetoric against Johnson's Community Action Programs, which allowed local bureaucrats to control the funding, programming, and decision-making
process, he feared that the next generation of activists would decide
that the only way to change the bureaucratic structure would be to
smash it, to "turn it over sideways and stomp on it."[71]

When Steiner asked if this tendency to violence was exclusively
youth-driven, Warrior argued that it was not. He described tribal
communities in Oklahoma as a "happy medium of elders with their
power in the community working with these younger ones who
have some idea of how urban America works." These two groups,
Warrior claimed, "know that they're getting the short end of the
deal and that it must be stopped."[72] In his book *The New Indians*
Steiner called elders and youth working together "new Indian nationalism coupled with traditional tribalism."[73] This was in direct
contrast to the image within academia that activists like Warrior
and other NIYC members were rebelling against their elders. As he
had made clear numerous times, culturally immersed traditional
elders and federally appointed political leaders were entirely different. To Warrior and others, traditional elders, with their knowledge and experience, were the true cultural power of the tribes, to
be protected and honored at all costs.

As catchy as it was, Steiner's observation was hardly a new one. In
1893, when battling in vain to convince the Poncas to sell their "surplus" land to the government, the Jerome Commission had made
the same observation about the Ponca people collectively.[74] Warrior
elaborated on this issue when Steiner asked him the whereabouts

of the Martin Luther Kings or the Tecumsehs or the Pontiacs, of the Indian movement. Robert Burnette would later admit that he and fellow tribal leaders described Warrior as being the "Stokely Carmichael of the Indians," but Warrior did not see himself that way. Rather than compare himself to contemporary leaders or traditional Indian leaders such as Crazy Horse, as a young Gus Palmer, Jr., had done, Warrior reiterated his commitment to the old ways, saying, "Leaders come about at the will of the people. A true leader is representative of the people. They make him a leader."[75] Again expressing his vision of Red Power, he told Steiner, "Communities decide a plan of action, then an articulate spokesman voices for them, but he is not really the leader. It is the community that is the leader." This unwillingness to be called a leader, despite that title often being bestowed upon him, spoke clearly to the Cherokee elder's insistence that Warrior knew the old medicine ways. This was true for Warrior in Tahlequah among the traditional Cherokees, at home in Bois D'Arc and White Eagle with the Poncas, among his cohorts at the NIYC, and all across Indian Country. These communities included women and children who voiced opinions on what directions to take, while he and others were merely "articulate spokesmen."[76] This concept of communal leadership emanating from within reached back to Warrior's Ponca upbringing, where, although fragile, a clan system still existed within the tribal communal structure. This viewpoint not only epitomized Red Power, it also underlined Warrior's distrust of tribal political leaders who sought office rather than follow traditional protocol.[77]

As far back as the inaugural meeting of the NIYC, Warrior had argued against people using the organization to appoint themselves leaders, and he lamented to Steiner that "today it's become a political springboard where they were bought off with government jobs." He called for NIYC members to appoint new speakers, saying that "the ones who started the movement are now considered Uncle Tomahawks because there is a more and more angrier bunch coming up—which I like." This was the group that he foresaw becoming violent: "They'll be . . . angrier and also have more awareness about how to work the [system]."[78] Although his view of Red Power was based upon culture, community, and tradition, he was comfortable with the idea that if violence was necessary to protect these, then violence would be used.

Warrior knew that the country's problems were not isolated to American Indians and African Americans, and he saw a wider malaise throughout the United States: "bureaucracy out of control, over-institutionalizing, the alienation of individuals, and the exploitation of people." Warrior drew Red Power parallels to the free speech movement and anti–Vietnam War protests, saying, "This is what the students in Berkeley are mad about. There's not that much difference in their thinking or anger. This is what people are screaming about Vietnam." It was not just students and Indians who felt this way, and Warrior referred to US senators Wayne Morse and J. William Fulbright, who were among Lyndon Johnson's most outspoken critics over the Vietnam War. Warrior told Steiner he agreed with "what Fulbright says, and Morse, that maybe we should stop and re-evaluate ourselves as . . . a group of people, as a community, as a nation, and see what we are doing not only to each other but also to ourselves."[79] He asked, "Is this the American Way, a process of hollowing out the insides of themselves?" If this was the price of assimilation into American society, all the more reason to defend tribal cultures and communities, he believed. Individualism and alienation were anathema to Warrior's worldview.[80]

Warrior was ahead of his time. His rhetoric for Red Power echoed many of the theories of cultural pluralism that had been propagated during the immigration explosion at the end of the nineteenth century. The concept, however, would not become intellectually acceptable in the United States until the late 1970s. His ideology also went several steps further than the cultural pluralists. While they called for the right to commingle as dual identities within mass American culture, Warrior demanded the recognition of the rights of the tribal communities to maintain "distinct cultural allegiances." He envisioned a broader version of democracy that would protect these rights of cultural diversity in the United States. He reasoned, "The problem of what we want as individuals, as Indians, and as Americans are inseparable. We cannot talk about one without talking about the other because we are individuals, we are Indians, and we are American." He urged people to "think about how we as Indians can help our communities break out of the trap we find ourselves in . . . think about what kind of community we want to live in—then think about how we are going to bring that about."[81] This assessment of community contrasted starkly with the one that emerged to form the bedrock of Johnson's "War on Poverty."

Warrior chose to anchor his vision for the future in the past, saying that "in the old days . . . it was young people who became the hunters and the warriors and led our people out onto the plains." It was the young, he asserted, who had "created the golden age of the Indian" by serving their communities. He was convinced that young Indians could do that again but that great "courage, imagination, and dedication" were required.[82] Warrior's confidence had been bolstered by the success of the fish-ins of 1964, when young Indians, led by Hank Adams, had brought national and international media attention to Washington State's abrogation of Indian fishing rights. For Warrior, Red Power was a complex web of interacting themes and issues that drew inspiration from all aspects of his life, with culture, community, and tradition in combination the driving force. It was born of a worldview fostered by his culturally immersed upbringing and bolstered by his acceptance within the traditional communities of Cherokees with whom he had helped protest a contentious new cultural center. It was based in his absolute conviction in the crucial role of the community in maintaining tribal culture and identity.

CHAPTER 4

MAKING THE CASE
FOR SELF-DETERMINATION

"We must make decisions about our own destinies."

As much as Red Power focused on a return to, or a retrenchment of, traditional values and principles in order to retain tribal culture and identity, Warrior's call for tribal self-determination focused on the contemporary social, economic and political means with which to do so. As Warrior and the NIYC increased their profile and influence nationally, his calls for "real, not fictional self-government, true self-determination" became more strident.[1] Warrior's vision differed from the NCAI's proposed Point IX Program of 1954 (presented to Congress as an alternative to federal termination legislation and based on assistance programs designed for underdeveloped countries), which had promised ultimate tribal acculturation into mass American society. While the NCAI defended tribal treaty rights and fought vociferously against termination policy, many saw its Point IX program as a compromise with the federal government.[2] The self-determination demanded by Warrior and the NIYC entailed sustained tribal political and economic independence, retention of federal treaty obligations, community leadership, and cultural freedom, without assurances of acculturation.

Warrior saw the biggest challenge to self-determination as being the government apparatus currently serving American Indians, writing that "this bureaucracy [the BIA] is actively using all its resources and manipulating powerless tribal governments against their own communities." He complained that Indian-related programs implemented by Congress "only serve to divide and conquer a helpless people," saying that "even the people of Angola, under the Portuguese, or Zulus of South Africa or the Negroes of Mississippi do not have to suffer this type of discrimination."[3] In many ways his complaint was pertinent to programs implemented prior to Johnson's War on Poverty, but it ignored the strides that many communities had made by taking advantage of Office of Economic Opportunity (OEO) programs.

Warrior exposed the burden of dependency within tribes that had been created by federal oversight of American Indian programs, highlighting a "horrendous combination of colonialism, segregation, and discrimination has been going on for over 100 years." Reflecting examples made by Felix S. Cohen is his critique of US federal colonialism, he noted that his own community had been left "uneducated, and poverty stricken, helpless and without hope and divided among themselves" and "confused and threatened beyond belief."[4] The system of federally induced peonage that Warrior described to Stan Steiner was reflected in the manner in which the Poncas and other smaller tribes of Oklahoma, such as the neighboring Otoe, Kaw, and Tonkawa peoples, were indeed having trouble sustaining themselves economically compared to the much larger Cherokee and Creek nations. President Johnson's War on Poverty program did offer OEO programs aimed at alleviating poverty and hopelessness in tribal communities, but the system was organized in such a manner that even among communities that were improving, these improvements were occurring too slowly to be truly effective.

The steadily growing membership of the NIYC and subsequent increase in readers of *ABC* meant that Warrior's concerns were being heard all over Indian Country. Along with his overall criticisms of the failures of the War on Poverty, Warrior and the NIYC urged a change in federal attitudes toward treaties and called for serious economic and educational reform. Warrior believed that decision-making power over Indian communities needed to be put in the hands of the people and the communities themselves, and that this might be done without eliminating the BIA.[5] As it stood, political leaders of the vast majority of tribes were appointed by the BIA, and new tribal laws required the approval of the secretary of the interior. To Warrior and many others, the ultimate veto power of the United States rendered tribal government ineffective and true leadership unattainable.

As he had in Olympia, Warrior referred to the Soviet Union, this time likening federal oversight of American Indians to Communist repression of indigenous peoples. Writing in "On Current Indian Affairs" in *ABC*, he said that Indians should be granted "at least the self-determination that other American communities have" instead of a having to suffer under a system "of repressive internal colonialism which parodies the Soviet treatment of its national minorities." An essential element of real self-government was the protection of treaty rights, as had been highlighted in Washington State. Warrior acknowledged that the majority of treaties had been made by the . United States when it was "a small emerging nation [struggling] to survive," but twentieth-century US size and power did not justify their blatant violation. "If the United States is to be the moral force in the world which she has aspired to be, morality must begin at home," he wrote. "We only ask the American people to honor their word."[6]

Warrior was adamant that Indian communities were prepared to bear the consequences of making policy decisions for themselves. Echoing Shirley Witt's withering assessment of the behavior of tribal leaders at the Chicago conference in 1961, he asserted, "The indignity of Indians with hats in their hands pleading to powerful administrations for a few crumbs must be removed from the American scene." Warrior also tied self-determination to Red Power, seeing that in order to move forward, tribal nations required the solid foundations of the past. But he acknowledged, "Members of NIYC have to ask ourselves constantly and very clearly, which are the things in the past . . . we mean to carry forward . . . and which are those we shall leave behind."[7]

Warrior was convinced that self-determination would ensure the retention of ideals and traditions that had previously identified communities that were culturally, socially, and politically distinct as self-governing, mutually independent nations. Self-determination would enable tribal communities to continue in the modern world without compromising their cultural integrity, a situation which would ideally ensure that traditional elders, rather than politicians, occupied the areas of power, in a manner specific to each tribe's particular cultural heritage. He argued that the NIYC was leading the way by being "the first to hold our annual meeting in the tradition of our forefathers, the open council." Warrior also pointed out that the NIYC had been the first group to successfully protest against abrogation of treaties. Protest and direct action would later be regarded as the signature of Red Power, but for Warrior it was important to assert that it was but a means to an end: "We believe that everything is still ahead for us. The history of our people is not over."[8] So Warrior and the NIYC bridged the past with the future. As Shirley Hill Witt later testified, "We Native peoples, we walk with a beautiful shawl around us, and that shawl is our history, and we live with it every day. It's on our shoulders and around us and protects us."[9]

In 1964, Warrior used the histories of other minorities in the United States as examples of how to retain cultural integrity and resist complete assimilation into mass American culture. In the same month that "How Should An Indian Act?' was published, Warrior spoke before the Vermillion Conference, an annual anthropological gathering at the University of South Dakota, which that year was cosponsored by the NIYC. Here he compared Indians, and their role in American society and culture, to the Irish and Jewish American peoples. He argued that these two groups had thrived in America, surviving "as whole communities." In contrast to Indian people, "they did not separate themselves off from [each other], they did not try to please powerful people by trying to change their community to fit some image handed them on a platter as is done in American Indian communities." Jewish Americans, he argued, had seen education as the way for people to contribute to the Jewish community, "not necessarily to leave it or coerce it," and education policy would later become a cornerstone of Warrior's interpretation of tribal self-determination.[10]

Warrior had a bleak view of the conversations taking place between Indian communities and those purporting to help them. Bemoaning the lack of consultation with Indian communities, he argued, "The first thing that happens is that everyone wants to talk about the Indian problem . . . and it always turns out that the Indian problem is defined implicitly as those ways in which Indians are a problem to powerful whites."[11] His message was clear. Not only was it time for Indians to act for themselves, it was also time for Indians to begin thinking for themselves and putting themselves and their communities first. Rather than Indians being a problem to powerful whites, it was the opposite: powerful whites stood in the way of Indians defining progress for themselves.

This was the crux of Warrior's view of self-determination, as much as it was with Red Power. While the ultimate aim was empowerment of the community, the cause began with individuals within those communities. In making the case for self-determination, he argued that the problems of poverty, alcoholism, and unemployment "are only symptoms of the total situation in which Indians find themselves." He asked, "Do we really want to help our people or just please the powerful?" and asserted, "We have to throw away these old categories and talk about the situation as a whole and how we as a people can use our talents to make a place for ourselves on the American scene, just as the Irish and Jewish people have done."[12] The challenge, however, was to do so as Americans and as Indians, in a framework of pluralism that acknowledged the right of tribal communities to maintain their cultural identities.

Warrior challenged Indians to think beyond their own communities, about how they could shape not only their immediate surroundings but also the political, social, and cultural landscape of the United States. He argued that as Indians were already Americans, they had no need to cast off their cultural identity to become more American. They did, however, need to "think as Americans about what kind of country we want to live in so that we as Indian people can find and make our place in it."[13] This talk of dual identity was not something people expected to hear from Warrior, whose first known commentary on Indian-white relations, after all, had been that the sewage of Europe did not run through his veins.[14] Yet this idea of being Indian and American was one of the foundations of the NIYC, which carried the ambition of forging a "greater Indian America."[15] To Warrior, leader of an organization that included such identities as Ponca, Paiute, Mohawk, Navajo, and Shoshone-Bannock under the banner of Indianness, adding "American" into the equation required no great leap of faith.

In the Cold War United States, the concept of cultural plural-ism—in this case, the idea of American and "other" existing simul-taneously in the same people—was as alien as it had been when proposed in the late nineteenth century. Assimilation of "others" and conversion to Christianity had been the primary social motif since Europeans first landed on the continent. During the colonial period before the United States, there had been countless attempts at forced Europeanization of Indian nations. After this, the process of Americanization—largely through forced language and educa-tion programs—was extended beyond Indians, and immigrants of all nations, including African Americans, were pushed to as-similate. This process underpinned the "melting pot theory" that the United States was a single homogenous culture that absorbed and assimilated all others. When immigrants in the late nineteenth century began to question this theory and pushed for pluralism, a movement began for the recognition and retention of their origi-nal cultures in coexistence with "American" culture. The most vocal proponents of this were German-Jewish immigrants, and the movement peaked during the early years of the twentieth century. For Warrior the issue was not simply about his own cultural integ-rity but also one of redemption for the United States. He observed that the United States had taken the "moral high ground" in the Cold War but had not done enough to protect Indian sovereignty or identity "within her own borders."[16]

Warrior originally thought that the best way to change the fed-eral approach to Indian sovereignty would be a joint campaign for tribal self-determination in partnership with the NCAI, but by 1966 the relationship between the NIYC and the NCAI was strained. This was primarily due to the breakdown in relations between their respective leaders, especially between Warrior and Vine Deloria, Jr. Neither saw value in the other's singular approach to Indian af-fairs. Warrior and the NIYC viewed the NCAI's methodical lobby-ing process as too slow and ineffective, while Deloria and the NCAI felt that Warrior and the NIYC were too brash and abrasive.

The division went back to 1964 events, and those actually started with a friendship forged in 1963. Warrior and Deloria (Standing Rock Sioux) met at the 1963 Boulder workshops and became fast friends for a short, fortuitous time. Deloria had been interviewing for a position with United Scholarship Services, a fledgling organization that would play an important role in the life of Warrior and many other American Indian students, when he was invited to visit the workshops. As with recollections by many other friends and acquaintances over the years, one of Deloria's earliest memories of Warrior was of Clyde dancing "while Bob (Thomas) and I just stood measuring each other" at one of the after-hours 49s, which Deloria later dismissively claimed were "the real activity of the workshop."[17] He remembered Warrior and Bob Thomas as intellectual cohorts who were determined to test him. Warrior was impressed enough with Deloria to invite him to join the NIYC but quickly developed other ideas about how the young Sioux could be a useful ally. Although their friendship eventually settled into acquaintanceship, there was mutual respect between the two from this meeting.

Deloria later credited Warrior with winning him the position of executive director of the NCAI. In a testimony to Bob Thomas, he recalled that "Clyde had set various political traps for Robert Burnette and triggered a general rebellion against him which then rebounded to my benefit."[18] The general rebellion resulted in Burnette resigning as executive director several months before the election was due to be held, so Deloria was contesting for a vacant position. Hank Adams reiterated this point, recalling that "it was Clyde's determination that Vine should be the executive director of NCAI and he did the political work to make it happen." Warrior's intent was to take "the NCAI away from the older generation" but the ultimate goal was a closer working relationship with the NIYC than had previously existed.[19] His successful maneuvering showed that the many hours he had spent in Tony's Bar at the University of Oklahoma, where he "loved to talk politics or political strategy and how you motivate people," now had a practical outlet.[20]

Maneuvering Deloria into office in the fall of 1964 did not, however, yield the results Warrior had hoped it would. Deloria claimed that his refusal to use the position to sponsor another Chicago conference under the guidance of Dr. Tax, as he claimed that Warrior and Bob Thomas intended, resulted in Warrior vowing to remove him from office at the following year's NCAI convention. There is, however, no record of such a request or of such an attempted coup being made. Wary of the political opposition his appointment had generated, Deloria was not prepared to risk his newly gained position by steering the NCAI away from a campaign path with which its members were comfortable. Many of those members were the same leaders who had called Warrior and his cohorts communists in Chicago three years earlier and were now comparing Warrior to Stokely Carmichael. The NCAI was confident that its approach had won several successes, while they viewed the NIYC and its youthful cohort with disdain.[21]

After a short settling-in period, during which Warrior was formally acknowledged as a close advisor, Deloria was quick to publically distance himself from Warrior, despite the debt he owed him in gaining his position. At this point Deloria also appeared to inherit the disdain toward the NIYC felt by other NCAI leaders. Although the two remained on cordial terms with each other professionally, they were often on opposing sides politically and ideologically for the remainder of Warrior's life, as highlighted by the Red Power parade incident. Although Deloria eventually acknowledged Warrior's significance in Indian affairs, at that time he was more likely to occasionally make personal attacks on Warrior's intellect and eloquence, such as dismissing his rhetoric as "brash and abrasive."[22] He also damned Warrior with faint praise, referring to him in his 1969 book *Custer Died for Your Sins* as "perhaps the greatest wit in Indian Country." Despite Warrior being one of the most influential figures in Indian affairs at the time of the book's writing, the only reference Deloria made to Warrior's activism was to retell one of his jokes. "Do you realize," Deloria quoted Warrior as saying, "that when the United States was founded, it was only 5 percent urban and 95 percent rural and now it is 70 percent urban and 30 percent rural . . . Don't you realize what this means? It means we're pushing them into the cities. Soon we will have our country back again."[23] While Warrior's humor was famous among his friends and colleagues, such selective remembrance did him a disservice.

Hank Adams later accused Deloria of "undergoing some revision" in his memories of Warrior.[24] Warrior, who died long before

Deloria forged a career as one of the most formidable American Indian intellectuals and critics of federal Indian policy in the twentieth century, preferred to simply include Deloria as one of the many Indians he saw as failing to fight enough for Indians, as he railed against the "finks" in the NCAI. In later years, Deloria grudgingly conceded that Warrior "had a way of presenting his points crudely and effectively so that people would not forget," although Warrior's influence in Deloria's own rhetoric is plain in *Custer Died for Your Sins*. Deloria's apparent animosity extended beyond Warrior, though, and included much of the NIYC leadership, suggesting that scars from the rift between the two organizations had never healed. He remembered listening to Mel Thom and Herb Blatchford testifying before the secretary of the interior in 1963 and recalled feeling "a bit betrayed that Thom and Blatchford did not have ideas of their own—but merely recycled the concepts they had learned from Bob Thomas at the Workshop."[25] This was actually quite a feat for two of the driving forces behind the NIYC, as neither had at that point attended the workshops as students (Thom did several months later), and Deloria himself had yet to meet Thomas either.

By 1966, Warrior was in a position to more closely influence the direction of the NIYC board's activism when he won the presidency of the organization. In a repeat of their 1961 contest for the presidency of the Southwest Regional Indian Youth Council, the election pitted Warrior against his friend, colleague, and incumbent president Gerald Brown. This time, rather than decry the "sewage of Europe," Warrior campaigned with the slogan, "Up, Up with Persons." Warrior won the election, and in his victory address he told assembled council members, "This is my country and I want to see which way Indian America is going to go."[26] He would remain president of the NIYC for the rest of his life.

In a September 21, 1966, press conference in Washington, D.C., Warrior was forthright in his condemnation of federal Indian policy. He declared that the organization's policy was to "seek radical and drastic changes in Indian affairs in order that the nature of our situation be recognized and made the basis of policy and action." In a short but damning statement, Warrior condemned the federal government's policies, actions, and attitudes toward American

Indians, calling the policies ineffective, inoperable, and ill conceived. He argued, "Nothing meaningful for tribal people has ever been accomplished in the world unless it has been with a drastic change, and American Indian Affairs is no exception." In a clear call for tribal self-determination, he asserted that "the government, through its agencies such as the Bureau of Indian Affairs and the Office of Economic Opportunity, [is] not structurally or functionally designed to work out solutions for tribal people." The primary reason for this was because "most administrators, including some Indians, know nothing or care nothing of how the average Indian operates or what the Indian wants."[27]

This was a message that Warrior returned to in various conference appearances as NIYC president. At Wayne State University he issued a vitriolic attack on Indian affairs insiders, calling them "white colonialist fascists, uncle tomahawks, and bureaucrats who are concerned only with procedures, progress reports, and regulations, and who could care less about the average Indian." Warrior was doing his best to prove right Gerald Brown's fears that he would take the organization in a radical new direction and demanded to know "How long will Indians tolerate this?" He pointed to the other minorities in the United States, who had been much more vocal in the civil rights movement, and reminded people that "Negroes, Mexican-Americans, and Puerto Ricans could only take colonialism, exploitation, and abuse for so long; then they did something about it." Reminding his audience of the combined threat of the government's termination and relocation programs, he asked, "Will American Indians wait until their reservations and lands are eroded away and they are forced into urban gettos [sic] before they start raising hell with their oppressors?"[28] The talk was the springboard for a more militantly vocal Warrior raising issue with government policies and their effects upon America's tribal peoples.

Warrior felt that the degraded situation of Indian communities across the United States demanded an urgency that he perceived the NCAI as ignoring. He also felt that without sovereignty, these communities would never revive economically, socially, or politically. Under the status quo, he reasoned, "Many times our tribal governments, which have very little legal power, have been forced into the position of going along with programs they did not like and which in the long run were harmful. They were powerless to do otherwise." Further, such an environment fostered greater inequality and inefficiency for Indian people. "Of this I am certain, when a people are powerless and their destiny is controlled by the powerful, whether they be rich or poor, they live in ignorance and frustration because they have been deprived of experience and responsibility as individuals and as communities."[29] Such comments were a common refrain of the times, from the anti-imperialist rhetoric of Vietnam War protesters to the Port Huron Statement of Students for a Democratic Society. What made Warrior's lament unique was that, for Indians, this was a generational inheritance that had created despair of epidemic proportions.

Another unique aspect of American Indian sovereignty that Warrior often referred to is the issue of American Indian identities and communities being tied to the land of their ancestors. He emphasized the religious and spiritual connection to the land in contrast to the economic framework with which most Americans viewed it. Warrior argued, "Many American Indians . . . are living in the Holy Land, land that has belonged to them for generations. This is similar to the relationship that Jews have to Israel."[30] Here Warrior was referring to the continental land mass rather than traditional tribal homelands, as the vast majority of Indian nations had been forcibly relocated during the brief history of the United States, although there were a few who considered themselves lucky enough to have resettled in landscapes that closely resembled their traditional homelands. The similarity of landscape in their new surroundings allowed some communities to preserve their belief systems. This, in turn, allowed tribal members to grow securely self-assured in the bosom of their community.

To Warrior, this spiritual connection to the land was fundamental to cultural survival and identity. Framing the imagery within terms of masculinity that were pertinent of the era, he revealed that this connection ensured that from the time one is born, an Indian "knows what he is and he knows his position in life; therefore he is not bugged about this verb 'to be,' what he is or hopes to be, because he 'is.' He is already a complete man, he knows his place in the world." In contrast, he argued that when Indians move outside the boundaries of their communities, whether through forced or voluntary relocation, quite often, they are completely ignored.[31] The effect of such a jarring conflict of worldviews has often caused Indians to doubt themselves when left in the unfamiliar surroundings of Western society without the protection of the community to fall back on. For Warrior, maintaining a land base was not simply politically and economically vital but absolutely essential for the preservation of these distinct tribal worldviews.

Warrior was determined that a bridge needed to be found that enabled Indians to move comfortably within both worlds. He saw greater Western awareness of Indian cultures and communities and worldviews as foundations of that bridge. But he revealed the fundamental obstacle in reaching this awareness, arguing, "People begin to become concerned about how come American Indians don't want to compete or better themselves, . . . [but] how can they better themselves when they already are what they are?" Noting that there were still Indians around "who were involved in the last rebellions to stop this and to maintain our own personal good life," he added that this sentiment of resistance was alive and well. "Many [of these] still consider the United States as invaders and also liars and not holding up their word." Others, he admitted, were "completely frustrated by the results they have received by the American way," such as removal, allotment, relocation, and termination.[32]

Of the requirement that the secretary of the interior approve new tribal laws, Warrior wrote, "This happens no place but America and it happens with American Indian communities."[33] But BIA control over many Indian communities was more than this. Warrior complained that even something as simple as owning a car was deemed too complex for individual Indians to handle alone. He insisted that many local dealings of American Indians were handled by the bureau "with something like Power of Attorney" and accused the BIA of "treat[ing] us like babies. We are a group of people regarded by the Bureau of Indian Affairs as incompetent."[33] His words evoked the ghosts of the allotment era's "competency hearings" (in which

competency was decided through tests based purely on assimilationist policies), which were the nadir of tribal sovereignty. The
NIYC campaign for self-determination was grounded in eradicat-
ing this soul-destroying micro-management.

The pinnacle of Warrior's role in the campaign for self-
determination was his impassioned and powerful testimony in
1967 on the connection between the material and spiritual paucity of American Indians and their lack of self-determination. Appearing before the President's National Advisory Commission on
Poverty in Memphis, Tennessee, on February 2, 1967, four months
before Stokely Carmichael and Charles V. Hamilton published
their Black Power text, Warrior addressed Indian education and
self-determination. The hearings were one of three organized by
the commission to canvas firsthand accounts of poverty, unemployment, and potential solutions, the others taking place in Tucson,
Arizona, and Washington, D.C. Warrior's role as NIYC president
and his work with the OEO and Upward Bound (described in chapter 5) meant that he was approached to testify as one of 105 selected
"representatives" of the rural poor, for whom he saw causal links
between poverty, ethnicity, and lack of adequate education.[34]

He had long spoken out against Johnson's War on Poverty, developing a blind spot to instances where the program benefited Indian communities. In his interview with Stan Steiner, Warrior had
gone so far as to assert that the president was merely "paying lip
service to a group of people that are finally . . . becoming more and
more aggressive in trying to do something about their conditions
and situation in which they live."[35] Warrior's dismissal of LBJ's approach to Indian affairs was prompted by the selection of Robert
Bennett as commissioner of Indian affairs and signified the level
of cynicism with which he viewed politicians. The NIYC opposed
the appointment on the grounds that Bennett was a BIA careerist,
and they did not see an appointment from "within the ranks" as
an approach that promised the radical change to the system they
demanded.

In the swearing in of Bennett, Johnson claimed that he would
"put the first Americans first on our agenda" to work out "the most
comprehensive program for the advancement of the Indians that the

Government of the United States has ever considered," and many in his administration felt that he was acquiescing too much to the Indians.[36] Recalling the speech and the reception it was receiving from the numerous Indian leaders in the room, speechwriter Robert Hardesty remembered later, "Will Sparks and I were standing at the back of the room, wondering how it was going to end, when Jim Duesenberry, of the Council of Economic Advisors, rushed over to us and said in a stage whisper, "Holy God, someone run over to the Budget Bureau and get Charlie Schultze [its director]. He's giving the country back to the Indians!"[37]

Johnson had referred to Thomas Jefferson's observation that colonial European settlers had found Indians "occupying a country which left them no desire but to be undisturbed." He told the assembled aides and media, "We cannot turn back the hands of time today, but we can, after 161 years of neglect, honor Jefferson's plea." It was this comment that set pulses racing. He continued by saying that, despite "some success" by previous administrations, "far too many of our Indians live under conditions which [have] made a mockery of our claims to social justice."[38] While some in the White House feared that Johnson was promising too much, logistically and financially, in his support for Bennett and Indians, Warrior was cynical. The government's top-down approach to fixing the "Indian problem" was anathema to his campaign for tribal self-determination.[39]

By the time of his appearance at the poverty hearings, Warrior had identified clear ideas about how change should come about. His solutions did not entail violence as he had advocated in his interview with Stan Steiner, although he did still warn that this was a viable option. Foremost they entailed trusting tribal communities to take back control of their lives. Warrior was determined that the government ask Indians how they envisaged rectifying the problems their communities faced. He advocated tribal self-determination through the recognition of cultural and political sovereignty in the true sense of the word, with the community, and not the BIA, determining what was best for them.[40]

In Memphis, Warrior emphasized to the commission the difference between the tribal worldview of community and the Western one, highlighting the spiritual and intellectual bond between his generation and their elders. He reminisced that "most members of the National Indian Youth Council can remember when we . . . spent many hours at the feet of our grandfathers listening to stories of the time when the Indians were a great people, when we were rich, when we lived the good life."[41] Warrior was referring to pre-reservation times, which were now just a distant memory for the oldest surviving elders in tribes across the nation. For his own grandparents and other Poncas, those were times when member-ship in the Hethuska Society was earned through endeavor rather than offered through invitation, when traditions such as the winter camps were still strong, when the people were still in Nebraska and wealth was measured in cultural rather than monetary terms. Those stories he had listened to as a child, from his grandparents and their many visitors to the Collins family farm, formed the tem-plate for his vision for self-determination. Warrior acknowledged, "It was only recently that we realized that there was surely great material depravation in those days, but that our old people felt rich because they were free." Warrior's ancestors had been "rich in things of the spirit," but "if there is one thing that characterizes Indian life today it is poverty of the spirit." What was needed was freedom from stifling federal oversight and bureaucracy that pre-vented "basic human choices about our personal lives and about the destinies of our communities."[42]

He called the freedom to make these choices "the mark of a free mature people." Without self-determination and the freedom it of-fered, he contended, "We sit on our front porches or in our yards and the world and our lives in it pass us by without our desires or aspirations having any effect." He reiterated that "we are not free. We do not make choices. Our choices are made for us. We are the poor."[43] In an earlier article he had used the bison hunt to symbol-ize freedom, lamenting that "in the old days . . . no one went out and found the buffalo for us and no one organized our hunts for us . . . we did that ourselves." He emphasized in that article that "there can not be responsibility unless people can make decisions and stand by them or fall by them" and added, "It is only when a community has real freedom that outside help can be effective."[44]

What made Warrior's lament so powerful was his connection to Indians' freedom of the past. Rather than view the past as something from which communities should veer, he saw it as foundation upon which modern, sustainable nations could build. For Warrior, the only real solution remained to appeal directly to the federal government for support in the push for self-determination. While OEO programs were supposed to have entailed self-management, administrators had often intervened. In essence what Warrior was calling for would mean a return to the nation-to-nation relationship between tribes and the federal government, although he did not go as far as the American Indian Movement would several years later. AIM would demand the revival of the treaty-making process itself.

Seeing the BIA as paternalistic in the worst way, Warrior berated administrators and social workers who classified Indian children as "deprived," saying that "exactly what they are deprived of seems to be unstated. We give our children love, warmth, and respect in our homes and the qualities necessary to be a warm human being." He countered, "Perhaps they get into trouble as teenagers because we give them too much warmth, love, passion, and respect. Perhaps they have trouble reconciling themselves to being a number on a IBM card." He reiterated that self-determination was about more than the freedom to choose: "We must make decisions about our own destinies. We must be able to learn and profit by our own mistakes. Only then can we become competent and prosperous communities."[45] Free from the careful planning and statistical evidence that D'Arcy McNickle and the NCAI had produced in their 1955 Point IX plan for self-determination and ultimate acculturation, Warrior's address to the poverty hearings in Memphis recalled Arthur C. Parker's 1915 essay indicting the government for its actions. Parker, editor of the journal of the Society of American Indians, published critiques of federal policies in the first two decades of the twentieth century, accusing the government of stealing rights of "intellectual life, social organization, freedom, economic independence, moral standards and racial ideals, [an Indian's] good name, and a definite civic status." He saw each of these rights as fundamental to freedom, without taking into account loss of territory and of resources.[46]

Warrior (*far right*) with (*left to right*) Robert Reitz, Galen Weaver, Dave Warren (Ojibwe-Tewa), and D'Arcy McNickle (Flathead) at the Boulder Workshops. (Courtesy of Newberry Library.)

Warrior was adamant that freedom was not merely a rhetorical weapon upon which to pin his vision for self-determination. He told the commission in Memphis, "We must be free in the most literal sense of the word—not sold or coerced into accepting programs for our own good [that are] not of our own making or choice." This meant that even if tribes were successful in dealing directly with the federal government and bypassing local agencies, there still needed to be a major shift in the dynamics of the relationship. Assigned to run community programs that are not of their own design, Indians "cannot but ultimately fail and contribute to already strong feelings of inadequacy," he asserted. These feelings of inadequacy then became generational, pervading the self-worth of the enter tribe and its worldview, keeping them from even attempting to rectify their problems.[47]

Warrior declared, "Programs must be Indian creations, Indian choices, Indian experiences because only then will Indians understand why a program failed and not blame themselves for some personal inadequacy." To him it was clear: "a better program built upon the failure of an old program is the path of progress." But to achieve experience, competence, worthiness, a sense of achievement, and resultant material prosperity, Indians must have "responsibility in the ultimate sense of the word." In this Indians were the same as any humans: "freedom and responsibility are different sides of the same coin and there can be no freedom without complete responsibility." Not the secretary of the interior, not Congress and its whims, but the people themselves needed to make policy decisions. He was convinced that "the real solution to poverty is encouraging the competence of the community as a whole."[48] With self-governance and therefore people with vested interest in the success of tribal programs, some of the best of the Indians' past might be recovered.

Again in Memphis, Warrior made international references for rhetorical effect. When it came to Indian affairs, he argued that the global reputation of the United States was at stake, especially given its vaunted ethic of freedom. Here Warrior echoed Society of American Indians leaders, who spoke up after World War I as America helped fund postcolonial rebuilding in Africa and the Middle East, and NCAI leaders after World War II as the United States sent reconstruction aid to foreign nations. Rather than her being the land of the free, he declared to the commission, "America has not . . . been diligent enough in promulgating this philosophy within her own borders."[49]

Warrior closed his presentation with a dash of cold water in the face. Saying that members of the National Indian Youth Council realized that complete freedom and self-governance "within the present structure [are] not possible," they further recommended "that another avenue of thought be tried, such as junking the present structure and creating another." Continuing with existing federal Indian policy would be simply reinforcing and worsening "existing ills."[50]

Warrior's ideas were ahead of his time, and ultimately President Johnson and his successor, Richard Nixon, adopted many of his suggestions as they sought alternatives to the status quo that was slowly strangling the life out of America's Indian communities. The speech was one of the most eloquent and dramatic calls yet for tribal self-determination, resonating with the anger and frustration of a people used to having their demands for freedom ignored. This was far from the conservative route that Warrior felt the NCAI had traveled under Vine Deloria, Jr. Warrior's speech carried the NIYC to the forefront of the campaign for self-determination and ensured that it was an organization to be taken seriously.

On the same day that Warrior spoke in Memphis to the poverty commission, his words were bolstered by tribal leaders in Washington, D.C., who offered a reproof, albeit mild, of the government's proposed omnibus bill of new economic legislation related to American Indians. The bill fell far short of the demanded repudiation of termination and did not guarantee Indians title to their own lands. The proposed Indian Resources Development Act, approved by Commissioner Bennett, never made it to Congress after the dissent of the tribal leader. Although a small victory, this was a significant step in the direction of tribal self-control that Warrior and the NIYC demanded. It was clear what direction Warrior and the NIYC considered the way forward in Indian affairs. Warrior's words reverberated around Indian Country, and it seemed that Commissioner Bennett had been paying attention. Just a few days after the Memphis hearings, February 6–7, 1967, Commissioner Bennett met with Warrior and other NIYC officers at a conference in Denver to discuss Indian poverty, education, and reservation resources.[51]

Warrior's rhetoric in the mid-sixties often upset tribal leaders and disturbed more conservative Indian organizations such as the NCAI, but his rhetoric was effective and inspired many Indians across the United States. His campaign for self-determination drove home exactly what was needed for communities to protect and preserve their identities, cultures, and traditions, and even maintain their hold on their land. He identified a need to end the colonial politics that had dominated the relationship between the United States and Indian nations for far too long. He envisioned actual Indian oversight, tribal and individual, tied to traditional community action and worldviews, as the only way to achieve this end.[52]

CHAPTER 5

RISING TENSIONS
IN CHEROKEE COUNTRY

"We need to make the shit we all waded through
a little shallower for those who follow."

Warrior's determination to reduce colonial oversight of Indian nations by the United States went beyond the political and cultural arenas. Educational issues were a common theme in many of his speeches as he sought answers to how better to educate and retain Indian students in schools, including colleges, across the country. In 1963 Warrior added lecturing to his résumé as he attended the inaugural Alumni Weekend of the Boulder workshops to give a presentation there. While Alumni Weekend was afterward deemed disruptive in the organizers' yearly report, the return of alumni as guest instructors and role models would continue in future workshops.[1] Warrior's relative celebrity on the Indian youth council circuit that year reflected his growing reputation among the younger, more politically aware Indian student community. Della, whose relationship with Warrior was still in the formative stages then, recalled that prior to his arrival, "Everybody was [saying], 'Clyde Warrior is coming; Clyde Warrior is coming.'"[2]

Two years later, as a college graduate, Warrior observed students and educational standards professionally, as part of Murray and Rosalie Wax's Cherokee education research project based at the University of Kansas Sociology Department. Participating in the project affected him more profoundly than lecturing at the workshops did, as he connected the experiences of the children he observed with those of his own childhood. As a result of his experiences, he proposed changes to the local Tahlequah public school system in relation to how American Indian children were taught. Later, he attempted to change the curriculum at the Boulder workshops to ensure greater cultural connectivity with the students rather than continue the focus on anthropological theory. In both cases, cultural relevancy and lesson plans that fit students' cultural worldview were his primary objectives. Although both attempts—on the local level and at the workshops—were rebuffed, the rejection simply made Warrior more determined to effect change. By the end of the decade, the influence of students attending the workshops was so great that the NIYC now acted as the event's main sponsor and organizer, even renaming it in Warrior's honor after his death in 1968. And in the case of the school-level education project, Warrior and the NIYC would eventually embark on a national, rather than Cherokee-focused, initiative designed to connect curricula more closely to the particular worldviews of tribal schoolchildren.[3]

Before Warrior began researching for Murray Wax's project, he worked unofficially for the Carnegie Project in 1964, an opportunity made possible after he transferred from the University of Oklahoma to Northeastern State University in Tahlequah. He traveled back to Norman fairly regularly, though, as his relationship with Della Hopper blossomed. The Carnegie Cross-Cultural Education Project had begun in 1963 under the direction of the University of Chicago's Anthropology Department, with funding from the Carnegie Foundation. Robert Thomas directed the project under the guidance of Sol Tax. The project was an experiment to assess the effects of encouraging literacy in English among the full-blood Cherokees in Tahlequah and surrounding areas. Guided by Tax's commitment to action anthropology, the project studied how long it would take traditional Cherokees, those who were the poorest and most illiterate of the Cherokee Nation but fluent speakers of their own language, to become literate in English after they learned to read the Cherokee syllabary devised by Sequoyah in 1821. Tax's idea was to collate the Cherokee results and formulate a plan to roll the project out to groups working with indigenous peoples around the world in order to facilitate their own literacy projects. Thomas, however, had an entirely political motive for improving literacy in the full-blood communities, in that he intended to "catalyze a grassroots movement to heal the traditional community and prepare the way for [a Cherokee] renaissance."[4] Thomas had complained years earlier—in a refrain similar to Warrior's about the iniquity of the federal trust relationship—that many full-bloods were withdrawing as far as possible from the "white world," and he saw the literacy project as a way for traditional Cherokees to reassert themselves "as modern, 'for real,' worthy people."[5]

Cherokee Chief Counsel Earl Boyd Pierce, who was generally viewed as pessimistic and paranoid, quickly seized upon Thomas's ulterior motives, and warned Cherokee Principal Chief W. W. Keeler in a letter, "I do not think there is any doubt that the main effort to drive a wedge between the Executive Committee and the full bloods has been launched."[6] Pierce's skepticism was well-founded on this occasion, even though he was prone to embellishment. In 1963, Pierce wrote to the NCAI chief executive, Robert Burnette, claiming, "Thomas is a plant by Sol Tax . . . to get even with Keeler and me, and you and all of us, for what we did to them at Chicago."[7] Pierce and his colleagues' achievement at Chicago was the insertion of a pledge of allegiance to the United States in the Declaration of Indian Purpose; this Pierce interpreted as "having frustrated an un-American conspiracy."[8] In an effort to subvert what he saw as potential factionalism among his Cherokee people, Pierce planned an extensive and exhaustive counter-intelligence program against the Carnegie Project. As a result, in 1966, Warrior and several other researchers were arrested, detained, and questioned by the FBI as "subversives." Pierce also spread rumors against the project through different Cherokee communities to the point that many members of the Cherokee Nation refused to take part in it and openly distrusted the "outsiders."[9]

It was in this context of educational debate, political intrigue, and community sabotage that Warrior spent his final semester at NSU and as a Carnegie Project volunteer in the fall of 1965. At the same time, the NIYC was moving closer to becoming an advocate for educational reform, as it agreed to become the third major sponsor of the United Scholarship Service (USS). The USS had, since 1960, provided scholarship funding for American Indian and Mexican American secondary and college-level students. The NIYC's sponsorship was the first major commitment of its leaders to engage directly with education policies rather than to merely discuss them at conferences or in workshops. Its role included "board membership . . . the planning of program and budget, decision making and organizational development, and the staffing of the USS office itself."[10] Warrior became involved in USS matters, alongside his continuing Carnegie Project research.

In addition to his volunteer work with the Carnegie Project and the NIYC sponsorship contract, Warrior had also taken personal steps toward a more involved role in education by changing his undergraduate major from anthropology to education when he transferred to NSU. Part of the degree program included a semester-long internship, and Warrior volunteered to undertake his at Sequoyah High, which had originally operated as the Cherokee Orphan Asylum. In 1914 the BIA had purchased the building as a boarding school for children of all the area tribes. In the mid-1960s, the building, located in downtown Tahlequah, hosted mostly Cherokee schoolchildren, with a smattering of Creek and other students. Given his disdain for "Indian leaders, teachers, [and] adults interested in Indian affairs who . . . (are) keeping Indian students from being students," Warrior found the prospect of teaching there daunting.[11] He confessed to Murray Wax, "I would have had a difficult enough time in a public school, much less in a BIA school."[12] However, it was the students at Sequoyah High—not any paternalistic attitude of his BIA paymasters—who offered Warrior his greatest challenge. One of the first things he noticed was that student perception and responsiveness to classroom material was largely dependent upon upbringing and level of traditional tribal cultural immersion. This became the foundation of his push to provide a culturally relevant educational system for American Indian schoolchildren.

Warrior was also forced to reevaluate his own teaching practices as he struggled to connect with many of the students. He despaired that with the students dismissed as "slow kids," he had "tried every educational method which I had been taught and a few I created on my own to absolutely no avail." He ultimately concluded that this was a cultural issue, saying that he couldn't explain in English anything that they could understand about American history: "There is a tremendous language difficulty with the ones I couldn't [reach]." Many of the students spoke English as a second language, as Warrior had as a child, and this made teaching what was essentially an alien history to these children extremely difficult. The experience taught him valuable lessons that he used later in his teaching projects, and he began to attempt to "draw whatever subject matter at hand into their perspective, somehow hoping they could identify with something or another." In doing this he noticed responses that displayed a distinct difference in the worldviews of the students, again dependent upon their level of cultural immersion. Whereas some would catch on and understand "the middle class perspective" quickly, he found that the "tribal types" would "pick up on the 'tromped on' powerless group of people," displaying, he believed, empathy that reflected their own experiences.[13] That such a response reflected his own tribal worldview was not lost on Warrior.

He found the psychologically detrimental effect of the educational system upon the students to be extremely problematic and would raise this issue in several speeches. He also talked about it with Murray and Rosalie Wax. Warrior surmised that in most cases, by the eleventh grade they had erected "a block against Indianness somehow or another and it is very difficult for them to talk about anything like that." He was adamant that racism, in historical portrayal of Indians as savages and other classroom remnants, caused the most damage to these children's self-identity. Warrior knew from personal experience the steadily deteriorating effect that such a portrayal had upon a young Indian's psyche. He was horrified that students shrank from their past, using their reaction to President Jackson's Indian removal policies as an example, saying, "They want to get away from anything that tends to identify them with those people." Conversely, he told the Waxes, in the contemporary Indian world students suffered from a lack of role models: "They absolutely know nothing of anything or anyone outstandingly successful and could care less." He complained, "All they know is that they are alone in this world and that is what they have been taught and they have to get out and get an education."[14] Whether or not the education was culturally, psychologically, or intellectually uplifting for the children appeared to be irrelevant to most educators. Even more damning was that under the current system, as throughout the past, parents and communities felt powerless to change things.

Many of Warrior's observations reflected his views about the effects of federal Indian policy on tribal communities. He noticed that as the system turned these children away from Indianness, they fell into three groups. The first, he told the Waxes, "want to get an education so they can get out of that situation and somehow or other accomplish [something]." The second and larger group, he noted, was made up of young Indians who "tune out the system and also tune out Indian-ness," while those of the third group "tune out the system of education but do not tune out their identity because they are [the] very solid and very stable ones in their class." While this last group reflected his own background, he found no programs in place to encourage a more holistic experience for any of the children. What he discovered instead was an almost institutionalized racism among the teachers. He despaired that "they always blame the kids, the family or outside activities but . . . never . . . look at the God damn system [which] all it does is alienate and cull the optimism of life and youth." Such was the lack of support for these students that "by the time they get to be 15, 16 they have absolutely no optimism about Indians," viewing them—and thus themselves— as "toothless and useless." Despite his misgivings and calling it a "horrifying semester," Warrior managed to successfully complete his internship and graduated from NSU in the spring of 1966.[15] The experience made a lasting impression of the deep-rooted problems that the American education system created for Indian schoolchildren, but it also fostered several ideas for positive changes that could be made.

Moved by his experience with the Sequoyah schoolchildren, Warrior accepted an educational research position with Murray and Rosalie Wax rather than head to graduate school as he had planned. Both scholars had worked with Warrior at the Boulder workshops, and they contracted with other workshop alumni too, including Kathryn Red Corn and Della Warrior. Clyde and Della were officially a couple now, having married in the summer of

1965. (Much to Della's mother's chagrin, the impromptu wedding had taken place in Montana where the couple had gone on NIYC business—"it was the only free time we had to do it," Della later noted.)[16]

Funded by the federal Office of Education, the project studied the relationship between Cherokee schoolchildren and their families and the public school system in and around Tahlequah, Oklahoma. The Waxes had worked with Bob Dumont on a previous study of Oglala Sioux schoolchildren at the Pine Ridge Reservation in South Dakota, which had resulted in a 1964 report for the Society of the Study of Social Problems. Unlike the civil rights movement, where desegregation for African American schoolchildren was still an emotional and combustible issue, American Indian educational integration was not considered to be a problem. Assimilation policies and the Johnson-O'Malley funding program from the New Deal era had already integrated American Indian students with whites, with many educators and policy makers hoping that such immersion would educate the Indian out of the students. The Waxes' new study was designed to compare the educational experiences of rural Cherokee schoolchildren in Tahlequah with those of urban Cherokee children living in Tulsa. While the two were less than eighty miles apart, the gulf in experience and educational attainment was expected to be huge. Intellectual gains and cultural losses of assimilation in contrast to those of cultural retention were two issues the Waxes planned to study.[17]

Warrior signed a twelve-month contract to observe the classroom behavior and environments of schoolchildren in the Tahlequah area, encompassing Sequoyah High School, Tahlequah Junior High, and Tahlequah High. His research field notes, which included his observations on the students and their abilities, offer an intriguing perspective considering that Warrior had recently been on the other side of the teacher's desk. In contrast to the general behavior and attitudes of the student body, which seemed to Warrior fairly consistent across all three schools—a gamut from disruptive antics, lack of interest, and flirting, to hard study—he noticed how markedly different the attitudes and approaches of teachers were in each of the schools.[18]

These attitudes ranged from the positive attitude of the US history teacher at Sequoyah, who "did something there that I had never seen any other teacher in any other school do," to that of the Tahlequah High history teacher, who relied on authoritarianism to cow the students into learning. In an effort to help the students overcome their resistance to the curriculum, the Sequoyah teacher "would go through a chapter and pick out words he knew for sure they couldn't understand," and he would get this out of the way, teaching them the words, before he started the chapter. In contrast, the Tahlequah teacher, rather than make the material less intimidating, issued threats such as assigning thousand-word theme for talking out of order. Warrior called this particular class "a horror story or a travesty on the American education system," saying that it was the students and not the teacher who had control of the class.[19]

The discordant worldviews of Native and non-Native cultures was a prominent theme in Warrior's early field notes for the project. He despaired of a system whose administrators and teachers failed to make any effort to connect materials being taught to individual students' personal experiences or environment, as he had during his semester-long internship. His frustration at this neglect was exacerbated by what he perceived to be the ill intentions of Tahlequah High administrators. He noted that the school principal and counselor, and the majority of the teaching staff, had repeatedly assured him that "we don't care what they are, and we aren't concerned with [who] they are. We treat them all the same." For Warrior, this was a mistake of huge proportions, as he saw that efforts to ignore students' ethnicity actually exacerbated the problem by helping students become invisible and slip unnoticed through the system. The approach also smacked of an unwillingness to create a greater workload for themselves. He surmised that the attitude of many teachers toward failing grades was, "I guess the only reason they can't learn is because they are just Indians."[20] Warrior argued that "the duty of the education system is to take what they are into context, to take the various differences into context and thereby adjust the . . . system whereby they might learn something." Whether or not the attitude behind "we don't care what they are" was well intended, he felt that it was very important to take into consideration what students are and who they are.[21] Warrior was convinced that Indian students would only benefit from the education system when cultural identity was accepted, recognized, and incorporated into the curriculum.

Warrior cited two examples that perfectly exemplified why the system and its alleged colorblindness was wrong, and he used these examples to question the veracity of the principal's claims. The first was the Tahlequah High School principal's admission that he could not figure out why Indian students did not place much value on speaking, reading, or writing English. As Warrior noted, "It obviously hadn't occurred to him that English . . . isn't their language and they see no need to learn English in the world they live in." The second entailed a boy Warrior discovered in a ninth-grade vocational mechanics class. "[Here] we have an Indian student who has gone through nine years of public school education and now he's a Sophomore and he can't read," Warrior reported, though he also noted that the boy could speak English fluently. Warrior saw this illiteracy as proof of underlying racism in the school's "colorblind" system. He perceptively questioned in his field notes whether or not "overcompensation or overstating that there is no discrimination" actually represented fear or guilt because there is an "understood policy of discrimination," adding, "Thus far all my dealings tend to make me believe that this is so."[22]

The same ninth-grader led Warrior to notice a correlation between the culturally and linguistically immersed children and those attending manual or vocational classes. While the principal and his counselor merely noted that students in these vocational classes tended to be Indians, "usually 50% or better" (by which they meant blood quantum ratios), Warrior noted that the Indian students fared better in classes that correlated with their worldview somehow. He noted that no one enjoyed history, and so therefore there was no learning in those classes. Whereas, "in regard to the carpentry and mechanics class, the students were interested and therefore they were learning." The majority of students understood spoken English even if they were illiterate. In vocational classes, once a teacher had taken the time to explain each tool, "what its use is and . . . how it is employed," they flourished.[23] In academic settings, they messed about, talked, or daydreamed, either through frustration, lack of interest, or, as Warrior had noted in his own teaching semester, an utter lack of context. But tools, building, mechanics, and cars were all within the worldviews of even the most rural culturally and traditionally immersed Indians in the Tahlequah area.

In early 1966, Warrior was given the opportunity to apply a practical solution to the problems he had identified as key in the failure of Indian children to complete or even attend school. He and Robert Dumont, who shared his beliefs, together pushed the NIYC to build upon the sponsorship of the USS by involving members in the OEO's Upward Bound courses, albeit with specific cultural caveats. Upward Bound was part of the same OEO philosophy that had led to the creation of Head Start but targeted students farther along the educational age spectrum. The plan was to help prepare high school students for college life. In the summer of 1965, a year after Head Start was introduced, eighteen pilot Upward Bound programs were rolled out across the country. These were so successful that the following year there would be 220.[24] Dumont and other NIYC members had joined the Indian Advisory Committee of Upward Bound and hoped to convince Warrior to follow suit. As he had noted in his Tahlequah field notes, however, Warrior was convinced that high school was far too late in a life to begin offering students tangible cultural support. Thus he was reluctant to join a project he felt was targeting students too late in their development to make a meaningful impact.

After cajoling from his cohorts, Warrior agreed to attend an April 1966 Upward Bound conference in Washington, D.C., and there he wasted no time in making his opinion known to the Upward Bound directors present. He contended that if Upward Bound was simply an extension of standard educational practices then it was just another attempt "to wash students in white paint."[25] His words were far more visceral and harsh before an audience than in his Tahlequah field notes. He argued that Indian children became "warped and twisted" by their experiences in the classroom, and, for Upward Bound to help, the organization needed to "make the shit we all waded through a little shallower for those who follow." Cultural relevancy was the key to a more successful educational experience. There needed to be lessons and programs that "fit into the context of the world of the kids—so they won't be scared."[26]

Fellow attendees Tillie Walker (Mandan) and Browning Pipestem added a note of compromise to Warrior's words by insisting that these measures needed to take place without a complete rejection of Western culture. They acknowledged that there needed to be a balance between competent Indian educators and teaching "white culture" so that "Indians can take advantage of it." Warrior was not prepared to back down, however, and suggested that more meetings were needed in order for their ideas, with Indians involved centrally in the planning, to become actual programs.[27] Despite arriving at an initial working consensus with the Upward Bound directors, Warrior still mistrusted the OEO and other government agencies and continued to push his own solutions.

Despite his mistrust, Warrior agreed to conduct a review of two Upward Bound projects in New Mexico and Oklahoma designed to help Indian students attend college. While the review was at the behest of the OEO and Upward Bound, Warrior was suspicious of the methods and motives of the organizations' directors and had his own reasons for studying the projects. He and fellow NIYC member Browning Pipestem were applying for funding for an NIYC-sponsored Institute of American Indian Affairs as an alternative to the Boulder workshops. They felt that the lessons learned at Boulder were no longer sufficient for the more culturally and politically aware generation coming through the educational system. Neither condemned the workshops and both agreed that they served a valuable purpose, but they felt that the workshops had not kept up with changes in Indian affairs since their inception in 1956. The research and funding applications offered a brief respite from campaigning and publicity work, and later that year Karen Rickard teased Warrior. "We'll have to start an impeachment movement!!!" she threatened him, if he didn't "get on the stick" with "all the NOISE & ACTION."[28] It was an apt expression of how Warrior was viewed by friends and opponents alike: someone to be counted on for "noise and action." For the moment, however, he focused on appraising the summer programs.

The first consisted of five Mescalero Apache students attending Eastern New Mexico University at Portales, New Mexico, while the second was based at Southwestern State Teachers College in Weatherford, Oklahoma. Writing the project reviews, Warrior told similar stories of bored, disaffected students comparable to those he had witnessed during his spring semester of research in Tahlequah. His analysis was that all Upward Bound classes were designed to create "sophistication in the American culture." Such an education consisted of field trips to such places as the Santa Fe Opera, Albuquerque's historic Old Town, and Oklahoma's National Cowboy Hall of Fame (known locally to Indians as the "Hall of Shame"). Each of these locations was deemed an example of true American culture.[29]

Warrior's primary critique of the projects was that they were merely summer extensions of the same educational structure and material that students struggled with during the regular school year. His dissatisfaction was obvious in the report, where he wrote, "Upward Bound is a good program and instructed by well-intentioned people, [but] it will not work because it does not reach the people . . . intended." The students themselves declared that they would have graduated anyway and all knew of other students from their communities who would have benefited more. According to Warrior, the schools were sending students who were poorer and therefore "qualified economically for Upward Bound" rather than sending the students who needed the program academically. As always, he argued for cultural relevancy to be the cornerstone of any educational projects involving Indian students, instead of what had been typical: "teachers . . . pressuring them to participate without any knowledge or idea of cultural differences." The Upward Bound directors thanked Warrior for his "eloquent" report but deemed that "the evidence was inadequate for the total picture."[30] As a government agency, the OEO would not approve any changes without statistical analysis to support Warrior's findings and requested that he conduct further research.

Warrior's Cherokee research took precedence over the Upward Bound project, however, and he returned to Tahlequah to a hornet's nest of political intrigue created by the growing tension between

Cherokee leaders and the Carnegie Project. Matters reached such a straining point in the summer of 1966 that Murray Wax began making clear territorial distinctions between his research project and Sol Tax's Carnegie Project, led by Robert Thomas. His first step was to try to reassure Commissioner of Indian Affairs Bennett that "while Rosalie and I have been critical of some of the operations and programs of the BIA, we are by no means its opponents." He also requested access to agency information on Indian education in the area, admitting that the "presence in this area of the Carnegie Cross-Cultural Educational Project of the University of Chicago does add an interesting complexity to our research effort."[31]

The intensity of the political hostility in the air when Warrior returned to Tahlequah was made obvious when he revisited the Tahlequah high and junior high schools in which he had conducted his previous semester's research. Tribal leaders and local educators were growing increasingly hostile toward the Carnegie Project, and, despite Wax's attempts to distinguish his own researchers from Tax's, the ill feelings spilled over. When Warrior informed the high school principal that he wanted to resume his observation and interview project, the principal angrily told Warrior that he did not "care to be associated with, or for his school, or any of his students, in the controversy that was going on in the area." Warrior noted that the administrator "didn't want to be caught in the middle between [the Tax project] and us."[32] Wax had already warned Bob Dumont, when he recruited him, that "everyone buzzes like a hornet . . . having been thoroughly upset and frightened by the Carnegie . . . Project."[33] Locally powerful Cherokee families were also unhappy with the growing discontent displayed by the usually reticent traditional tribal members. With the help of Bob Thomas, as opponents of the project alleged, traditional families had organized the Original Cherokee Community Organization, (OCCO), with whom Warrior later protested the opening of the Cherokee Village and Heritage Center, and they had begun to demand a greater voice in community affairs.

For the second part of their project, the Waxes wanted Warrior to interview the students, and parents of students, who had dropped out of school. Warrior was pleasantly surprised by the response of the county superintendent, who "made no mention . . . of the turmoil that is going on. He seemed to be completely unaware of it." The superintendent's views on education were, however, totally at odds with Warrior's and those involved in both research projects. While Wax, Warrior, and his fellow researchers all identified racial and cultural differences as the reason why so many Indian students were failing, the superintendent deemed the problem one of geography and setting. His opinion fit far more closely with President Johnson's idea of poverty being the cause of poor educational standards, and he declared the problem as one of all the area's rural schools. He saw "economic retardation and social maladjustment" irrespective of race, as did Johnson's War on Poverty.[34]

For Warrior, this opinion was problematic. Poverty and class were obviously issues that needed to be addressed urgently, but without an acknowledgement of racial and cultural differences there would be no viable solution to these educational failings in the case of American Indians. Warrior was still convinced that the problem was caused by a lack of understanding or appreciation about contextual differences in worldview. He and others in the NIYC and Indian Affairs saw this as a major and unacknowledged flaw of the War on Poverty. He and his cohorts were determined that without cultural relevancy the education system would continue to fail Indian students. Lifting Indians out of poverty would help, but, as he had stated on many previous occasions, without educational reference points to which Indian students could connect, they would remain confused or bored and adrift in the classroom. It was an argument and a campaign that Warrior would continue until his death. Regardless of their different viewpoints, the superintendent and Warrior shared frustration at the lack of progress in rural education. The superintendent despaired of a workable solution so much that he lamented to Warrior that, "outside of a gallon of gas and a match and burning down the country schools," he had no idea what could solve the problem.[35] In other words, in an ideal world he would be able to start from scratch.

The turmoil in and around Tahlequah reached a new level. On September 21, 1966, in the same month that Della gave birth to their second child, Andrea Imogen Warrior, he learned that he and other researchers were to be investigated by law enforcement agencies.[36] Kathryn Red Corn later remembered, "We all ended up down in Tahlequah being interviewed by the government, and we were supposed to be involved in something, or they thought we were communist or something. It was kind of crazy."[37] The OCCO was campaigning more openly against the Cherokee National Council and projects they deemed at odds with traditional Cherokee values, and Chief Counsel Earl Boyd Pierce was increasingly agitated by their complaints. Al Wahrhaftig, although not arrested or detained, later discovered personal correspondence between Pierce and the local FBI agent accusing members of both research projects of instigating civil unrest in the area. The correspondence showed that Wahrhaftig too was under FBI surveillance.[38]

The unrest in Tahlequah reached neighboring counties and towns, and educators there too became reticent about allowing Warrior back into their classrooms. One superintendent, Mr. Thompson of the Hulbert School District, told Warrior and Dumont that he had heard the rumor that there were several factions among the Cherokees in the county and announced that he didn't want them around or associated with his school. At the same time, Warrior noted, Thompson revealed that "he had heard a lot about me and my activities," in a tone that was "rather slanderous." Warrior did not know if this referred to his activism or his drinking problem, which was becoming steadily worse, and he began to "feel guilty of being a hindrance to the project."[39]

At this point, Murray Wax was compelled to write to his local congressman in Kansas, denouncing the "hostile political pressure" his project was under and decrying the "congressional investigation" underway due to the Waxes' supposed ties to Tax's research. He acknowledged that in helping to "bring to light the discontent and unrest that had been fermenting among the traditional Cherokee," the Carnegie Project had been accused by Earl Boyd Pierce of actually "fomenting unrest among the traditional Cherokee." Pierce had a history with Tax that went back to Pierce's initial disapproval of the 1961 Chicago conference. Although he had eventually participated in the Chicago conference, Pierce had subsequently held reservations about Tax's motivations, seeing them as a potential threat to his own power. Such were the personal and professional connections between the members of both projects, with Warrior, Thomas, Wahrhaftig, Red Corn, and Dumont all friends, and the Waxes and Tax having studied together at Chicago, and all being involved at one point or other with the Boulder workshops, that Wax admitted that it might lead to the assumption that he and Rosalie were "in league with Tax and his researchers." He denounced this assumption, however, and told Congressman Robert Ellsworth, "We resent the effort to brand our project with any political label or to terminate it before it has accomplished its goals."[40] The project eventually resulted in a paper by Bob Dumont, "The Quality of Indian Education and the Search for Tradition," which was first presented at the NIYC's 1967 annual meeting, held at the Ponca Powwow.[41]

In October, the Waxes were sufficiently impressed with Warrior's work to consider him a useful member of the team, as his October 19 memo of feedback from Rosalie Wax showed. While she noted some areas for improvement, she generally encouraged Warrior to "continue, continue, continue, continue," as "your accounts of conversations with educational administrators could not be improved upon." Her advice for the remainder of the year was for Warrior to work closely with the other researchers on the project, declaring, "God save the Plains Indian peer group. Don't ask me how it happens, but no sooner do you, Mr. Dumont, and Miss Redcorn [Kathryn Red Corn] reside in the same town than your work improves by leaps and bounds."[42] Dumont himself appears to have had an ambivalent working relationship with Warrior, praising him in some field notes but at the same time telling Murray Wax in exasperation that "they're [your] research assistants. I assume no responsibility."[43] In January 1967, Wax recognized their strained relationship, asking Dumont if they could continue working "amicably together without either feeling exploited."[44]

Earlier Wax had written to NCAI Chief Executive Vine Deloria, Jr., to further clarify the position of his project and his researchers. He insisted that Warrior had no connections at all with either the Carnegie Project or Thomas's *Indian Voices*, but was instead "a full-time employee of the Indian Research Project of KU [the University of Kansas]." As with his letters to the BIA and his congressman,

Wax reiterated that the two projects were "dissociated in fact" but complained that "certain parties," which in essence meant Earl Boyd Pierce, "have found it convenient to insist that they are a joint conspiracy." Wax was finding the strain of defending his project quite telling and ended his letter to Deloria by pleading that "we would like to be allowed to go about doing our research."[45]

In one respect Deloria was more aware of Warrior's commitments than Wax was. He knew that Warrior had been coediting Thomas's monthly *Indian Voices* newsletter since April 1965. Warrior's involvement in *Indian Voices* is somewhat ironic considering his earlier warning to his NIYC cohorts that the newsletter stood in direct competition with *ABC*. Once involved, though, he had an immediate effect on the newsletter, as the content shifted from a purely political outlook to one that encompassed Indian cultures as well. Warrior's Plains Indian influence shone through as, in a reprise of efforts he made as Sequoyah Indian Club president at OU, the pages included updates on the powwow circuit and news of ceremonials and social dances, alongside news of rallies, conferences, and scholarships. Even Thomas himself left the safety of his Stomp Dance heritage to accompany Warrior on the powwow circuit around Oklahoma. It was not until 1966 that the Cherokee people held their first powwow, so Thomas was in unchartered cultural waters. Warrior's involvement with Thomas and *Indian Voices* meant that while he was no longer involved in the Carnegie Project, he was often seen in the company of Thomas in and around Tahlequah. In addition to this added complication for Wax, Warrior's involvement with *Indian Voices* increased his exposure across Indian Country and especially in traditional communities, while Thomas constantly praised him inside the newsletter for his intellect and commitment to Indian causes.[46]

Slowly, however, just as Warrior was receiving praise for his work on the Cherokee project, personal issues began to interfere with his productivity. In the midst of his unstinting work as an advocate for cultural relevancy in education and tribal political and cultural self-determination, his growing alcoholism was becoming an issue for those around him. By September 1966, just two months before he and Mel Thom adopted "Red Power" as a slogan, he was signing off his field notes as "Agent 49" in a clear reference to the more social, after-hours events of the powwow circuit. In November, Murray Wax chastised him for his lack of productivity as a researcher, and Wax later confided to Mildred Dickeman, Warrior's research supervisor, that he was worried about Warrior's long-term health. In truth, Warrior's increasing activism, public speaking, and greater responsibilities were affecting his health and work for Wax as much as his drinking was.[47]

Adding to Wax's frustration, the work Warrior did produce for the project was of very high quality. A week after the OEO recruited Warrior to serve as a VISTA conference consultant, Wax wrote to him to "confront the issue of Spring Semester" and whether or not Warrior would be retained beyond his initial twelve-month contract. Wax complained that during his employment as a researcher, Warrior had submitted a "very small quantity of work." This, however, had been of a "tantalizingly" high quality: "you demonstrate that you understand the dynamics of Indian education and of Indian affairs as well as anyone I know." Wax declared himself at an impasse. "I like having [you and Della] about," he wrote to Warrior, and "if I were to replace you with a conventional graduate student, it would take him years to understand as much about Indian education and Indian affairs." Conversely though, he reasoned, such a student would be providing the volume of material that Warrior had not—to produce a "presentation, perhaps building it into articles, or a thesis, or even a book." Warrior's lack of "formal background in social science," given his major in education, was also a problem for Wax. Wax ultimately suggested that Warrior should "make other plans for spring" but offered the possibility of a consultancy role.[48]

Whether the intention of the letter was to relieve Warrior of his duties or shock him into being more productive, Wax eventually decided to retain him. Wax wrote to Dumont in early 1967 that Warrior had "begged me to let him continue: and, after reflecting on the matter, I agreed to continue [employing] Della [too], providing he went for treatment."[49] Warrior agreed to the conditions and left for Denver in early December after having a talk with Bob Dumont. He also allowed Dumont to help him by arranging for a friend's father to visit, since the man was "one of those upper class reformed alcoholics [with] a pretty sharp brain [and] Clyde might enjoy him."[50] The following month Warrior was back in Tahlequah and abstaining, which was quite usual according to Della. She remembered that in the periods after rehab, he would not drink while he was at home, but "if he got asked to be someplace, then that's when it started again."[51] Wax assured himself that "Clyde and Della . . . can keep usefully busy until the end of the month when Millie [supervisor Mildred Dickeman] arrives and can provide local guidance."[52]

The following year brought fresh problems, however, after Warrior left to testify before the President's National Advisory Commission on Poverty in Memphis, Tennessee, on February 2. Five days after his testimony at the poverty hearing, and on the same day that Warrior was discussing policy initiatives with the commissioner of Indian affairs, Millie Dickeman wrote to Wax to inform him that during a recent check up, "Clyde's liver showed no cirrhosis, but promised to do so soon if [he] had a couple more binges like his last. They told him it was severely damaged . . . but could recuperate if he treated it properly for six months." Warrior's solution, Dickeman wrote to Wax, was to forgo hard liquor "except for an occasional breakdown," as at government hearings. Significantly, though, Warrior continued to drink beer, Dickeman told Wax, even though he did not know whether he would be able heal his liver by doing this. Like many alcoholics, Warrior was convinced that he could control the problem. Dickeman wrote, "He doesn't really want to give up liquor in toto, but wants to cure his liver and then drink sensibly." Having already tried rehab, he also eschewed the idea of seeking further help, for despite being aware that alcoholism is hard to cure, he did not want to "go for any AA type approaches," Dickeman told Wax. Despite it all, she concluded, "This is very premature at this point . . . Clyde does seem eager and active, so let us enjoy some guarded optimism."[53]

That optimism appears to have been misguided, however, and while his national reputation as a speaker and activist was gaining strength, Warrior's personal demons were slowly eating away at his daily working relationships. Wax was becoming increasingly disappointed, having retained Warrior only on the condition that

Clyde sought help. From his point of view, Warrior's drinking, as at the poverty hearing, reflected badly upon his research project and undermined its seriousness. Dickeman wrote to Wax that "Della [is] the more sensitive and reliable worker, [while] Clyde is full of ideas . . . but is impervious to any kind of coordination with the outside world via reading or discussion with other project leaders." By April, she reported, "Clyde is really in a bad bind now, and hasn't really worked in the last two weeks." He was "restricting his psychological support to beer," she wrote, while Della mailed all his applications to graduate school, including Harvard, Kansas, and Haverford College.[54] Wax replied, "I'm not surprised that he gave out: all one could ever do is hope that he might take fire." He also seemed to wash his hands of Warrior, declaring, "It seems to me that every project has its share of people who don't belong, for whom it is the wrong project at the wrong time of their life." He bemoaned, "You tried, Dumont tried, I tried, and perhaps so too did RKT (Thomas)."[55] Citing Thomas here was ironic, given that several sources cite him as a major facilitator of Warrior's drinking problem.

The correspondence between Wax and Dickeman is not the only testimony to Warrior's alcoholism, although many of the stories can best be described as hearsay and exaggeration. Wax's wife Rosalie also gave several accounts of his drinking in her text *Doing Fieldwork: Warnings and Advice*, in which she recounted the research projects she and Murray had directed between 1943 and 1967. As is standard practice in a work such as this, Wax changed the names of all her subjects except for herself and Murray. Warrior was given the code name Arthur Braveheart. In the text, Wax describes how in his youth "Braveheart" had been "one of the finest Indian dancers in the United States," and that he was "passionately devoted to improving the situation of the Indians," having written some "brilliant essays on the situation and plight of American Indian youth." By April 1967, she and Murray "were obliged to face the fact that Arthur was an alcoholic" and "had been for many years." Complaining that she and Murray had been the last to know among "everyone in Indian affairs," she also admitted that they had initially ignored the evidence of his drinking because "he never appeared intoxicated or stupid, and his work, for a beginner, was of reasonably high quality." The event that brought the matter to a head was a spectacular Easter party hosted by "Braveheart" that she reported as lasting an entire four-day weekend. The day after the party "Braveheart" became so ill that he could not keep food down for several days until he found a doctor "who gave him a powerful sedative." By this time, Rosalie noted, "He looked like a walking dead man."[56]

One factor in Warrior's continued drinking was his concern over graduate school. The more immersed in the research project he became, the more convinced he was that it was crucial to transform American Indian education. In order to help make this happen, he needed more experience and a better education—graduate school—but he was torn because of his increasing sense of the lack of cultural relevancy in his own schooling, and he was nervous about spending more time in a Western educational setting. D'Arcy McNickle, who urged him to apply to Harvard, recommended him for a John Hay Whitney Foundation grant, describing him to the foundation as "one of the outstanding young Indians in the country."[57] Confirmation that he had received the grant created agitation that Warrior tried to calm with beer, according to Dickeman. While McNickle described Warrior in complementary terms, Dickeman was unsure how to proceed with her own requested letter of recommendation. She confided to Wax that she felt Warrior "has no business in graduate school. His Indian anti-intellectualism is so incredibly strong."[58]

Wax responded. "My policy is to be diplomatically honest: he is bright and insightful; his educational background and training are abominable, he is active and successful in national Indian affairs; etc." He proceeded to dismiss Warrior's credentials in the same vein as he had washed his hands of his role in the research project. He told Dickeman, "My guess is Stu Levine at KU will think Clyde wonderful as a resource in American Studies, and that Clyde may be nursed along as the pet Indian of the program." Based on Wax's unmet demands for completed project work, he told Dickeman that he believed Warrior would "surely fail quickly out of a decent graduate program, or even a partially competent program such as

Sociology or Anthropology at KU," adding that "it might be good for him if he did."[59]

Besides the rather arrogant manner in which he dismissed both Warrior and the KU American Studies program as inferior to his own, Wax also showed a deep misunderstanding of the man he had mentored and worked with since 1961. He wrote of Warrior, "It seems quite clear that what he wants is a safe job that will not pinch his conscience too hard, but his opportunities are limited as long as he is branded both as red and lacking in academic credentials."[60] Perhaps Wax had spent too much time dismissing Warrior's activism as reflecting poorly on his project, and perhaps he never read Warrior's application to Kansas, where Warrior described his purpose in seeking a master's degree: to enable him to "assist the various ethnic groups and types of people that are trying to survive in America today."[61] This ambition is certainly not reflective of someone seeking a "safe job."

While some were already urging Warrior to ultimately pursue a doctorate (such as Dr. Joseph Feathers of Western Montana College, who had worked with Warrior in the previous summer's workshop), Wax attempted to find him work away from academia entirely. He wrote to the Industrial Areas Foundation of Chicago seeking employment for a "person of insight, ability and tenacity." He confided that while Warrior had a "bright and perceptive mind, his interests are not academic but political." In contrast to what he told Dickeman, Wax revealed that he was worried that Warrior would be "battered about [by] the aridities of academic life, when his motivation is much more to assist his people . . . in lifting the yoke that oppresses them."[62]

In April 1967, Wax wrote to Warrior informing him that he had written him a glowing reference for the Department of Political Science at Kansas, then cautioned him that his choice of major needed careful consideration depending upon his desires for the future. Political science would work if he wanted to be a teacher, while he would need law if he desired to be a politician. He ended the letter by suggesting American Studies, as he had done to Dickeman, because "you have shown little aptitude or interest that anthropologists or sociologists do. You will need much less of that for American Studies and KU will be easier by far than Chicago or Harvard." He assured Warrior, "You do have a gift for writing and speaking when you are affected by events and it is likely that you will be able to work and swindle your way through American Studies at KU in the pattern of most graduate students."[63] On May 15, 1967, Warrior received a letter accepting him into the American Studies Program at Kansas on a probationary basis.[64] Ironically, this offer came with the opportunity to continue working with Murray and Rosalie Wax.

By 1967, with the research project ending and Warrior preparing to attend graduate school, it appeared to some as though his plans for crafting more culturally relevant education for young Indians were on the wane. They were wrong. He continued to formulate ideas to address the educational needs of American Indians and intended to use graduate school to professionalize his concepts. In the meantime, the forthcoming Ponca Powwow was the perfect forum to put forth those ideas.[65]

CHAPTER 6

CREATING A CULTURALLY RELEVANT CURRICULUM

"Our Indian community . . . might as well be on Mars."

Although Murray and Rosalie Wax expressed concern over Warrior's workload in the research project and the effects of his alcoholism upon his research, Warrior was firmly committed to overcoming
this obstacle and crafting a culturally relevant curriculum for Indian
schoolchildren. Hank Adams later recalled, "Clyde had so much
more to offer to educational concerns of Indian communities."[1] For
Warrior, the concept of a curriculum that spoke directly to tribal
worldviews was linked to his own childhood resistance to learning
English. Now, after his research in Tahlequah, he was convinced that
cultural relevance in education was an urgent necessity. It could, he
believed, create a space where Indian children could grow as Indians and Americans, secure in the worth of their tribal identities.[2]

Warrior believed schooling grounded in tribal knowledge and
culture would reverse the trend of the school system creating Indian children desperate to conform to dominant cultural norms.
He hoped for young Indians to see the value of their parents and
grandparents through a traditional lens rather than the Western
prism with which they currently judged their elders worthless. The
1967 Ponca Powwow and annual NIYC conference would allow
him to showcase his ideas before his own people, especially those
who were skeptical about the relevancy of his activism to their
community.[3]

Warrior had continued dancing despite his increasing commitments as NIYC president, conference speaker, and researcher, and

the Ponca Powwow was a return home in more than a literal sense. Increasing weight gain had necessitated a shift from Fancy Dancing to Straight Dancing, but he was as graceful in this new category as he had been in the former, as it was a secular derivative of the Hethuska Society ceremony, and he continued to win titles despite the change. His role as a Hethuska tail dancer meant that he was already equipped with the necessary regalia. At the Ponca Powwow in the fall 1967, he divided his time between NIYC duties, dancing, and spending with his family at their encampment just west of the dance grounds. For Warrior, family time at such events was a vital component of immersing his daughters into the Ponca culture, having previously paid them both into the arena at Gives Water Service Club Memorial Day dances in Bois D'Arc. Mary had been paid into the arena in 1966, while Andrea was paid a year later in 1967.[4]

Leading up to the powwow, in the summer of 1967, Warrior focused more closely on affairs at home, but national politics were still a concern. He sought to involve the NIYC with the Southern Christian Leadership Conference's (SCLC) planned Poor People's March on Washington for the following year. Of continued concern, however, was Warrior's commitment to creating a curriculum that could be amended to fit the worldview of any Indian community. The creation of the White Eagle Community Project gave Warrior the opportunity to introduce the concept of culturally relevant education to his own community.

On July 26, 1967, Warrior and the NIYC applied to the Ford Foundation for a grant of $27,500 to develop programs within their newly created educational branch, the Educational Services to American Indian Communities (ESAIC). The NIYC hoped to use the ESAIC to expand its involvement in Indian education beyond summer workshops and college students. The idea was to reach out to the grass roots of community development, as described in Warrior's and others' speeches attacking the War on Poverty. In the NIYC grant proposal Warrior stated that "the tribal kin group or extended family within the larger tribe is the locus of control and power, yet these groups are systematically excluded in current community development."[5] Community control of all aspects of tribal life was the cornerstone of his vision of Red Power and self-determination, and, as Warrior had put it in "We Are Not Free," the "ability and competence of [grassroots] groups is rarely utilized in the development and working out of programs for their communities."[6]

Warrior wanted the NIYC to create programs that enabled tribal communities to embrace the modern world while retaining their cultural identity and integrity. In the proposal to the Ford Foundation he stated that the role of the NIYC was to "provide a bridge between the tribal community and the urban technological worlds." Within this role was the responsibility of "defining and altering the forces of change, so that the tribal community is allowed at least an equal decision in the direction and method of change." Warrior argued that, "to the extended family, NIYC has a policy of interpretation, protection and development of their desires, obligations, and rights of decision." Conversely, to the "urban technological worlds," the NIYC was "an agency of communication and articulation for tribal communities, in order to implement and insure the right of continued growth and development."[7]

NIYC leaders refused to continue to allow government agencies to dictate policy to Indian communities. They refused to sit back while the NCAI offered support to tribal governments, such as that of the Cherokee Nation, when faced by protest from tribal members. Warrior's upbringing had instilled in him a conviction that in such instances, the will of the people should outweigh the desires of the political elites. Warrior's philosophy of both sides talking and listening to the other, and contributing dialogue on an equal footing, exemplified Hank Adams's description of Warrior as a "cultural carrier."[8] It was as much an intra-tribal vision as it was intertribal and cross-cultural, and it was also a fundamental base of Red Power and the fight for tribal self-determination.

There were three divisions—research, training, and development—under which ESAIC was developed to facilitate the cultural conversations that Warrior envisaged, and in October 1967 the research side was contracted out to the Far West Laboratory for Educational Research and Development, based in Berkeley, California. The partnership would facilitate the NIYC temporarily relocating its headquarters to the Hotel Claremont in Berkeley after receiving Ford Foundation grant funding. The Far West Laboratory was one of twenty regional laboratories appointed by Congress to "find practical ways to improve the education of our nation's children by 'bridging the gap between research and practice.'" The research project consisted of a ten-school study that would collate data to be used in developing "model schools" in specific American Indian communities. Warrior used his influence as NIYC president to ensure that the White Eagle School in the Ponca community was one of the community schools included. These ten schools would serve as the basis for the ESAIC development division, under which formal summer-school programs for sixth, seventh and eighth graders "would be structured around the basic notions of Upward Bound but whose primary base of operation [would] be within the community and secondarily in the school and college."[9] In a reflection of his idealized style of community action, Warrior heeded his own concerns about the weaknesses of Upward Bound programs and demanded that he retained the control to implement alternatives if he desired. In the NIYC proposal to the Ford Foundation he had made it clear: "Planning and development of the program will be done in the community in order to avoid the current pre-packaged plans of OEO, BIA, and HEW that have local tribal community involvement on a secondary level rather than a primary [one]." In addition, plans were set in motion for an "Intercultural Planning Exchange" program, which, he argued, would bring other "relevant projects and programs in minority and tribal education on the administrative and community level of planning and development."[10] Rather than wait for Johnson's Community Action or Upward Bound programs to change, the NIYC set about creating new community opportunities themselves.

In August 1967, the NIYC reelected Warrior as president at its annual conference, held in White Eagle to coincide with the annual Ponca Powwow. The event dated back to 1878, making it the oldest continually running intertribal powwow in the southern plains. Besides his NIYC conference responsibilities, Warrior placed first in the Straight Dance category, no mean feat given the attendance of many exceptional Ponca, Osage, Quapaw, Tonkawa, and other dance contestants.[11] Commissioner of Indian Affairs Robert Bennett, having accepted Warrior's invitation to attend the conference and powwow, addressed the crowd on the "racial and economic conditions surrounding Indians in Northern Oklahoma."[12] As befitting Ponca hospitality, Bennett was guest of honor at a family dinner hosted by Warrior's grandparents. The dinner was held at the family encampment "under pecan trees on the banks of the Salt Fork River."[13] The meal included "Wah-bthoo-gah, Indian hominy cooked with beef; Wahshing-ah Shza-zee, fried chicken, pumpkin and corn cooked together; Wahshungeh, corn and bread dumplings"; and fry bread. Warrior's grandmother, Metha Collins, who at the time was representing the Ponca Nation before the Indian Claims Commission, showed that Warrior's candidness was a family trait, when she gave Bennett a stern lecture on the unfairness of BIA policy to "lease Indians' land and mineral rights without consulting [them]."[14]

Bennett's address reflected NIYC concerns about Indian peoples' abilities to connect with the contemporary world, and he told his audience that American Indians "need to educate ourselves for the world of today. There are few survivors of the modern day environment who are not equipped with the modern day tools of learning." He admonished young movement members, though, for their militant attitude toward federal Indian affairs, telling them that while they had the right to criticize, they should be responsible for "constructive criticism," and he warned them that they needed to distance themselves from the burden of traditionalism. Referring to Red Power, he scolded his audience, "Before slogans swallow us up . . . let us face life in our time. Let us draw on the past but not rest on it."[15]

This advice was at odds with the ethos of Warrior's Red Power. He had previously responded to criticism that he and the NIYC spent too much time talking of the "old days," by asserting, "We feel that talking about the past means talking about the future."[16] For Warrior, embracing the past and bringing it forward with them was the only way for tribal communities to achieve a sustainable future. Shedding the past would mean shedding their culture, heritage, and ultimately their identity. The concerns of the conference's other main speaker, Robert Dumont, the chosen NIYC representative to address the conference and powwow attendees, also reflected this ideology. In a speech titled "The Quality of Indian

Education and the Search for Tradition," Dumont argued that there ought to be *more* traditional knowledge and learning in the Indian classroom, not *less*. Dumont's argument drew from areas that Warrior and other NIYC members had previously discussed, and it explained much of the thinking behind the NIYC's forthcoming educational projects with the Far West Labs. It was also a pertinent speech, given that White Eagle was the location for one of the NIYC's model school projects.[17]

Dumont highlighted the lack of community involvement in American Indian education that the NIYC had exposed in its arguments against the War on Poverty. The differing worldviews of Indian students and Western educators, as discussed by Warrior in his Tahlequah field notes, was another issue that Dumont addressed. He argued that the current state of Indian education was the "unification of two different cultural traditions." What was needed, and what he, Warrior, and the NIYC hoped to achieve with their model schools, was cultural relevancy. Dumont insisted, "What is needed is to involve on an equal or a shared basis the traditions of Indian communities." Traditionally, Indigenous peoples taught and learned using methods vastly different from those used by Western nations, and the absence of any of these methods in the classroom was hindering American Indian students from learning. This is not to say that all Indigenous teaching methods were the same. Rather than take a one-size-fits-all approach to educating Indian students, as in white society, Dumont insisted that each school needed "to recognize, incorporate, and work with value tenets of the particular Indian community, utilizing how they define goals of learning and how one is to be taught and how one is to learn."[18]

Dumont committed the NIYC and other participants in the new project to ensuring that these goals were met. He explained that the process would involve "recognizing and validating the different intellectual traditions of Indian communities." This would require getting involved with the communities in a fully cooperative way, "redefining, reordering, and restructuring from practical to ideological and philosophical levels."[19] If the NIYC, Far West Labs, and chosen Indian communities could achieve this, they would remove some of the fear and alienation that Indian children felt in the classroom. From Warrior's perspective, achieving such a goal would enable readjustment of the children's sense of what constituted worthiness, and they would look at their communities from a new, more appreciative viewpoint. It would also increase the probability of student retention in high school and eventually facilitate growth in college enrollment numbers.

Dumont drew from the observations that he and his colleagues, namely the Warriors and Kathryn Red Corn, had made in Tahlequah. He asserted that Indian children were overwhelmed when they first entered the public school classroom. This was a disconcerting message to the Ponca parents listening, as their seventh and eighth graders were scheduled to switch from White Eagle to Ponca City schools the following academic year. Dumont told them that when the students first entered the classroom they were "met by an overwhelming and sometimes frightening pervasiveness of the American society with its power of socialization." Alluding to the earliest tenets of education as a tool of assimilation, he argued that "the cultural uniqueness, in fact, the whole life of the Indian child seems to be kept at a distance, to be kept out of the classroom and to be taught out of the child." Again echoing Warrior's comments about conflicting worldviews undermining the education process, he asserted, "The cultural distance between what the teacher wants and what the child will and can do seems too great for positive and effective education."[20]

Arguing against the policy of "we treat them all the same" that Warrior had complained about so much in his Tahlequah field notes, Dumont insisted that sustained academic learning for an American Indian student would only occur if there was a blending that included "social and cultural learning." This would only work, however, when a teacher "recognizes and implements the cultural differences of students." As vaunted as the Western education system was, and particularly the American one in the wake of educational reforms made by presidents from Truman to Johnson, the issue of cultural bias was an accusation that had lingered. Dumont insisted that these "crucial issues in Indian education" were important "not only to Indian people but to a good many others in this country and throughout the world."[21]

The issues raised by Dumont's talk and the plans laid out in the Ford Proposal were well received. Dumont, Warrior, and the NIYC pressed on with their educational reform projects and pursued grants totaling $122,000. In October, Dumont, Mel Thom, and Browning Pipestem met with Glenn Nimnicht and Jack Forbes of the Far West Labs in Berkeley to hammer out the finer points of the joint project and formally sign the contract that would allow work to begin.[22]

As these education plans progressed, the President's National Advisory Committee on Rural Poverty published its findings from the poverty hearings earlier that year. Titled *The People Left Behind*, the report, published in September 1967, made a series of recommendations for "major change" in the government's antipoverty programs. American Indian reservations were acknowledged as one area of concern, as were poverty clusters across the country, including parts of New England, Appalachia, and the Southwest. The report made no exception for reservations, however, when it declared that "the community in rural poverty areas has all but disappeared as an effective institution." This was exactly the problem that Warrior and the NIYC had campaigned against, saying the War on Poverty did not recognize the existence, or value, of tribal structures. Indeed the report validated Warrior's complaint about the difference between how Indians and non-Indians viewed community. In the section titled "Community Organization," the commission argues that "community must now be defined in terms of an area that encompasses several counties grouped about a town, city or metropolis."[23]

Warrior and the NIYC had vehemently argued that if the government and antipoverty campaigners continued to view Indian communities in such a manner, they would continue to create programs destined to fail those communities on even the most basic support level. The report also confirmed Warrior's accusation that Community Action Program (CAP) projects worked in conjunction with local "power agencies" and county or state governments.[24] Since CAP's creation in 1965, it had funded one thousand and forty Community Action Agencies (CAAs). Of these CAAs, 620 operated in rural areas and "most are organized along conventional political

lines . . . half are based in single counties, and half in multicoun-
ties [*sic*]."[25] As Warrior had written, such was the level of racism
toward the Poncas in the surrounding area that they were part of
Kay County, Oklahoma, in name only: "Our Indian community
. . . might as well be on Mars."[26] The Poncas were undoubtedly not
alone in having their needs catered for by political entities that had
no desire to understand their cultural dynamics or help them economically, politically, or socially, in any way whatsoever.

The report did state, however, that opportunities were available for communities to circumvent these political bodies, and that
"CAA's may be formed to represent any urban or rural area . . .
or any sufficiently homogenous area . . . without regard to political boundaries or subdivisions." In a series of recommendations
to ensure that people were made aware of these possibilities, the
report demanded that "activities and projects undertaken must cor-
respond to the basic needs of the community and to the expressed
needs of the people." This suggested to Warrior that the government was finally beginning to listen to the issues he, his cohorts,
and other poor people were raising. The issue of tribal responsibility also appeared to be addressed in the call for community devel-
opers to "aim for increased participation of people in community
affairs and revitalization of the existing forms of local government."
While the statement undoubtedly referred to city, county, and state
governments, Warrior was convinced that there was enough lee-
way to include tribal governments in this category, especially as the
report states that "the identification, encouragement, and training
of local leadership should be a basic objective of any program."[27]
The People Left Behind appeared to offer the chance of greater tribal
ownership of CAP projects for the future, and Warrior sought the
advice of his grandmother as to potential for the Ponca community.
He felt that if proposals were applied correctly, Red Power and self-
determination could be achieved through community action.

In the meantime, Warrior continued with the education projects already set in motion by the NIYC. The encouraging reception at the Ponca Powwow suggested that there was potential for
real educational reform if the projects succeeded, especially in his
home community. At the same time, Warrior's drinking problem

progressively worsened as he spent greater amounts of time away from home, testifying before congressional committees, meeting with youth councils, discussing policy initiatives with the commissioner of Indian affairs, and coordinating efforts for national education reform. He was not alone in his drinking but did consume more than most. The 1960s were a time when business and political meetings were commonly conducted in bars or conference halls where beer and liquor flowed freely, making it much harder for him to resist than when he was home with his family.[28]

What was most remarkable about Warrior and his cohorts, including Mel Thom, Shirley Witt, Bob Dumont, and others, was that none of them were formally trained for what they were doing. Workshops and regional youth councils had given them insights into the world of national tribal politics, but this was not enough to prepare them for the scrutiny they were now under as leading tribal rights advocates. As comfortable as Warrior felt in these circles, he was going back and forth between two worlds—as his cousin Steve Pensoneau described him, "an extremely traditional person speaking confidently before congressional hearings the day after a ceremonial in White Eagle"—and the pressure from this began to tell.[29] His drinking had evolved from a fun and social activity at the Boulder workshops to an almost necessary salve to ease the pressure and loneliness of the intense workload and responsibility that he and the NIYC had shouldered, especially when he was away from Della and his daughters.

With Warrior now based in Lawrence, Kansas, as a graduate student in KU's American Studies Program, his alcoholism reached the point where Della contacted his friend (and "almost an adoptive father") Bill Center for intervention. Center sent him to a rehab center in Los Angeles that Della remembered was "some new kind of a treatment that the movie stars went to."[30] Murray Wax commented to Millie Dickeman, "I think it's too late and that he has given up, and is ready, both psychologically and physiologically, to die."[31] The treatment procedure that the clinic used, Della recalled, was a very aggressive technique where "they said very derogatory stuff about his mother and his Indian people." He called Della from California and asked her to come and collect him, telling her that "you just have to sit there and take it, and I guess not even show any facial expression."[32] Knowing how jarring such treatment was to Warrior's worldview and pride in his community, Della arranged for him to return home.

The treatment did appear to work, however, and he returned to Lawrence "looking chipper and healthy . . . and making a genuine try at graduate studies," according to Murray Wax.[33] It may have been the racist slurs against his mother and Indians in general that galvanized him, slurs that he had fought his entire adult life to disparage and counteract, but, regardless, he threw himself back into his role as NIYC president. The following month he accepted a two-day consulting commission in Washington, D.C., from the Far West Laboratory. In keeping with the idea of encouraging the community to become involved with the project, he decided to seek help from within White Eagle. He also recognized that he had not lived in the community for almost a decade and wanted somebody "living here, being from the grassroots and knowing what we needed."[34]

There were people within the tribe who saw Warrior as a troublemaker and agitator who brought unnecessary attention to White Eagle, which meant that although he needed support, he could not get it easily.[35] This attitude ironically stemmed from those with the traditional worldview, with whom he identified. As far as many Poncas were concerned, the real world ended at White Eagle's borders. To circumvent this community reticence to get involved, he sought advice from his grandmother, Metha Collins, as to whom he should approach. Of those she suggested, he chose Martha Grass because of the respect she, as a woman and an elder, had within the community. Despite the fears he expressed in his speech before the poverty commission about the way Ponca women were now being treated, elders like Grass still commanded huge respect within the community.

Martha's daughter, Thomasine, remembered that Warrior, complete with a cast-covered broken nose, "came to our home and asked our mother if she would join him and help him to go to a meeting in Washington, D.C., to speak on behalf of the Ponca people." Warrior, who had broken his nose in an accident prior to going into rehab, talked with Martha Grass for a "very long time" about "tribal rights and activism," trying to convince her to travel with him. Thomasine, who would be left behind to babysit her younger siblings, recalled being very surprised that Martha said yes. "A little grandmother that stayed home all the time and got involved in small community activities down here in White Eagle" agreed to accompany Warrior to the capital.[36] Warrior's invitation led to Grass becoming a pivotal figure in American Indian activism in the following few years.

In the same month, Warrior and Browning Pipestem pushed forward with NIYC plans for introducing their own summer workshops to supplant the Boulder workshops. They acknowledged that the Boulder workshops addressed the cultural differences inherent in the American learning environment and bridged the gap between the standard "technical" American curriculum with an increased focus on social sciences that Indian students generally lacked. They also admitted that the Boulder workshops helped students address their feelings of marginality and helped them realize that what may have seemed to be individual problems were not unique and personal. This marginality was "in the total context of Indian-White relations" and part of a historical process.[37] In a November 1967 letter to Warrior, Bob Dumont agreed with him that the one thing the Boulder workshops lacked was emphasis on "self-determination, responsibility and free choice for Indian students."[38]

For a program designed to "create new Indian leaders" to be categorized this way by two such leading alumni was damning. Dumont encouraged Warrior that NIYC workshops could offer "this kind of experience" for students who had not "gotten this needed development . . . in their home communities *or* in their education." He also reminded Warrior, "You can make this point as well as I can."[39] This assertion marked a major shift in the direction of the NIYC and Warrior. The decision signaled a break in relations with American Indian Development (AID) and D'Arcy McNickle, who sponsored the Boulder workshops. The council was already at odds with the NCAI, which NIYC leaders saw as standing with tribal governments rather than tribal people. They viewed this as an attitude and approach diametrically opposed to theirs, as it was the people who continued and defined tribal identity rather than their governments.

On December 11, 1967, Warrior sent a formal proposal for the NIYC workshops to the OEO, the Department of Health, Education and Welfare, Dr. Tom Billings at Upward Bound, and Commissioner Bennett. The proposal laid out a three-phase program for Indian college students: four regional conferences to be held in the spring of 1968, followed by a six-to-eight-week summer course, the same size and format as the Boulder workshops, and finally the development of a coordination and resource center for American Indian students. The resource center would focus on "socio-cultural change in a historical and contemporary perspective, concentrating on issues and problems of American Indian community development." The ultimate goals of the workshops represented the concerns of the NIYC in general and Warrior, Pipestem, and Dumont in particular. They were designed to "provide Indian students means toward developing tools and skills, both practical and abstract, to work effectively in their tribal-urban-technological society."[40]

The four regional conferences were to be organized under the direction of local Indian groups in Colorado, Wisconsin, Oklahoma, and somewhere in the Northwest. These conferences would serve as recruiting posts for the summer workshops and as introductions to them, while utilizing summer lecturers and curricula to initiate a "framework for a continuing dialogue in issues of American Indian affairs."[41] Unlike the Boulder workshops, where students were recruited but offered no preparatory instruction, students in the NIYC workshops would already be contributing to, and learning from, the programs before they arrived.

Warrior and Pipestem identified the Haskell Institute in Lawrence, Kansas, as the ideal location for the summer workshop, both because of its longstanding history in Indian education and its potential as a home for the resource center envisioned in the proposal. Warrior admitted that the model for most of the "academic orientation" was the Boulder format, with many of the same instructors recruited as guest speakers. There would be "major revisions and innovations in [the] total program," however. Undergraduates would receive six credit hours for participation, and graduate students were eligible to participate. "Indian ethnohistory and sociopolitical issues of contemporary Indian and general US history" constituted the majority of the coursework.[42] This was a departure from the focus upon folk and urban societal contradictions that Bob Thomas favored in Boulder.

The final phase of the proposal, the coordinating center and resource center, was one under which the NIYC wished to add continuing involvement for alumni beyond reunion conferences and occasional guest lecturing. Ultimately, the successful implantation of phase three would result in a "year round center and institute . . . that is devoted to the training of American Indian college students and others who will be working with American Indian communities."[43] In short, this "Center of Indian Studies run by Indian people" was the prototype for the American Indian studies departments that later opened on college campuses across the United States. The scale of influence that Warrior and the NIYC now had on American Indian students meant that their ideas were broadcast widely, and local, unofficial NIYC branches began opening on college campuses to coordinate the campaign for such departments.

With regard to the model school project, Bob Dumont informed Iola Hayden (Comanche) of the Oklahomans for Indian Opportunity (OIO) on January 26, 1968, that the White Eagle situation was far more complex than had first been thought. Especially challenging was the attempt to create a parental educational organization other than the PTA. In a testimony before the OIO at a conference in Norman, Oklahoma, the previous month, Martha Grass had exposed a culture of teacher delinquency that was little short of abuse of Ponca schoolchildren. On a single visit to the White Eagle School, she discovered that the children, from six to fifteen years old, had been locked outside on a frosty morning while their teachers "sat in the cafeteria, drinking their morning coffee, catching up on their newspapers." Once they were allowed inside the building, first graders were instructed to "sit and color" while the teacher sat at the front reading her newspaper. This sort of neglect had led to a situation where most of the "second and third and fourth graders didn't know how to read," Grass reported incredulously. The tragedy for her, Warrior, and others was that this neglect undermined the work that she and other parents were doing at home in preparing their children. Parents would say, "You are going to school to learn to read. You are going to learn to spell. You are going to learn to count." But the parents were wrong.[44]

Grass complained that the academic inadequacy of the children was endemic to every grade. "Fifth and sixth graders were studying from their fourth grade book and yet, they couldn't do the work."[45] In Tahlequah, Warrior had felt insulted and angry when teachers blamed families for the poor academic development of Indian children, and he had focused his anger on the education system. In his home community of White Eagle there was not even a system being used. The model school program would change this and also have a far-reaching influence beyond the ten projects that the NIYC initially planned, with later organizations following similar methods of educational cultural immersion.

In the seventh and eighth grade classroom the situation crossed from negligence to outright abuse. While many of the children slept the day away, there was an overpowering odor that "smelled like fingernail polish" in the room, Grass reported. Several of the children exhibited signs of substance abuse, as "their eyelids were puffed up until they were almost closed," the result of sniffing glue and spray paint. The advice Grass had received from officials and doctors was to "watch the children and if they cramp up and start to vomit and can't, rush them to the hospital."[46]

After these conditions were exposed, Warrior dropped out of graduate school in Kansas and returned home. He realized that he would be far more help there than he would be in preparing for a future career of fieldwork at graduate school. The NIYC funded Warrior for the following month to "see what he can dig out in terms of possible candidates, voters and program direction," according to a letter from Bob Dumont to Iola Hayden, and to help install a program at the school to reverse the neglect. Warrior was scheduled to meet Ponca parents immediately after Senate subcommittee meetings on Indian education convened in Oklahoma to create "real programs and projects—educational in nature but not necessarily oriented to the school—that will take shape." The projects, it seemed, were the rhetoric of Warrior's speeches made real, community action driven by the community to create its own programs and stand by their success or failure. To Dumont, Warrior's success in this project was an absolute necessity: "From what little I know of Oklahoma and Indian education, the White Eagle case is one of those situations fundamentally important to further development of education in Oklahoma."[47]

Warrior's research into the situation resulted in a brief résumé of the White Eagle School, in which he also made several suggestions for necessary change. Warrior's report was every bit as damning as Martha Grass's testimony had been harrowing. Many of his findings substantiated observations he had made about his community as a callow twenty-one-year-old student at the Boulder workshops and examples he had used about Indian Country in subsequent speeches and articles about the effects of schooling on Indian children. The dropout rate from White Eagle School for Ponca children was an astounding 87.8 percent, which he blamed on the school not being viewed as part of the community. The teachers deliberately positioned themselves as outsiders, he declared, and were essentially excluded from any role except to educate. This led parents to avoid involvement, to the detriment of their children. According to Warrior, they would say, "I don't know what goes on over there or what they do; I don't want to interfere and get into it with the teachers." When parents did attempt to get involved, they discovered outright violence. "One [teacher] in particular, the sixth grade teacher," Warrior wrote, "delights in kicking, pulling hair and calling the children names, such as jackass and other comparable names."[48]

Alarmingly, teachers and administrators alike encouraged the parental distance. Warrior discovered that parents were very much "out of it" as to how a school was run and was shocked to see that "measures are subtly or openly taken to keep the parents naïve." The clerk of the school board exacerbated this situation, Warrior wrote. "[She] considers the school her domain and intimidates parents, fires teachers she dislikes and openly runs the school according to her own judgment." As Martha Grass attested, the majority of parents had never visited the school or the teachers, and, as the teachers did not visit parents, "no interaction takes place between parents and teachers." The parents viewed the school as a place they sent their children to be educated, but, Warrior lamented that, the "idea that a parent can influence a school is inconceivable to them."[49]

Despite White Eagle School having no white students and Poncas far outnumbering whites as eligible school board voters (158 to 12 according to Warrior), the school board was entirely white-controlled, because "these whites are property owners and pay taxes (and) they feel they should have the right to run the school and the Indians should have no part in running the school as they do not pay taxes." The majority Indian population of White Eagle was "uninformed of the functions of a school board," Warrior wrote, and clueless about eligibility for running for school board, their potential power as parents in relation to their children's progress in school, and "many other facts." For Warrior, this situation was symptomatic of the colonial attitude that exemplified all that was wrong with the power dynamics of Indian-White relations and perfectly represented the fallacy that tribal sovereignty was honored.[50]

As part of Warrior's month-long project to decolonize the White Eagle School, he and the NIYC registered Ponca parents as voters, got them into the PTA, and "succeeded in getting the first Indian in over twenty years on the school board." He noted that when he and the NIYC had informed them of how easy the voting process was, "several Indians were astonished at the simplicity of it all and at the same time resentful toward school officials and the local registrar for failing to inform them of their rights." The victory was savored by a community that had for so long been surrounded by racism, and it "encouraged the Indian citizens of White Eagle district to work toward getting an all-Indian school board, and if possible, some Indian teachers."[51] Unfortunately, as the Poncas began to assert their communal voice in the school board, the Ponca City school district undertook a feasibility study investigating the benefits of closing the school and incorporating the students into the Ponca City schools. This was yet another example of white power elites ignoring the needs of an American Indian community and assuming control and ownership of programs directly involving that community.

Warrior saw that high school for Ponca students was similar to how it had been for him and for many of the Cherokee and Creek children he had observed in Tahlequah. He noted that many children "gave up on school" because they were made to feel like second-class citizens. He also noted the degree to which tribal immersion (in northeastern Oklahoma the Poncas were considered to be the most "tribal" people) was considered to be directly correlated with high school dropout rates. Those Indians immersed in traditional culture were often viewed by whites, Warrior noted, in terms of "rowdiness, stupidity and being dirty," and therefore the Poncas were considered the rowdiest, most stupid and dirtiest of all the tribes. "After a while they accept this definition of themselves," Warrior wrote, and they "eventually drop out and go home to act out of this definition."[52]

Warrior's list of solutions to these issues was typically bellicose. No small reforms would do. Seeking to completely transform the educational experiences of Ponca children, his first idea was to sack the entire teaching and administrative staff and replace them with teachers "who have a genuine interest in teaching the Indian children." He also encouraged the implementation of programs to inform Indian adults of their "power and role in the education of their children," while also finding ways to bring the school into the community. He wanted to create a situation where the parents would feel comfortable visiting the school and having their expectations acknowledged and met. More idealistically, given the long history of racism in Ponca City, he also wished to find a way for the Poncas to stop accepting racial insults. He recalled, "Our two children were recently called 'nigger babies' by two three-year-old white children," and he called this "an everyday episode . . . in this town." His final recommendations were to create a tutorial program for sixth, seventh, and eighth graders to prepare them academically for the public school system and to bolster their confidence so that it "would not be eroded by the white students and teachers in Ponca City," and to create a teen center for children already enrolled there.[53]

Warrior felt that these recommendations would be "advantageous to Ponca Indian education," and on May 1 Della sent a "Proposed Tutorial Program" to Glenn Nimnicht, the program director of the Far West Laboratory, for his consideration. The idea was for the program to be jointly funded by Far West and the NIYC. A second copy was sent to Bob Dumont and the NIYC to "formalize it and put it in proper form."[54] Della had taken temporary responsibility for continuation of the project while Clyde recovered from the sudden death of his mother, Gloria Collins, on April 13, 1968. Despite having been raised by his grandparents, Warrior had maintained a close relationship with his mother throughout his life. Her death was exceptionally painful for him, and he began drinking heavily again to ease his pain, leaving Della in control of the White Eagle Project and Browning Pipestem in charge of the summer workshops. Unfortunately for the Warriors, this latest lapse into drinking spurred the serious health repercussions that doctors had warned him about.

As optimistic as Warrior was about the future of the model schools, he was less sanguine regarding changes in the paternalistic bureaucratic system for which he had been campaigning. In an interview with the *Kansas City Star* a month before the death of his mother, he reprised much of the rhetoric he had used in his earlier campaigns, blaming "bootlickers" and "Indian finks" who were happy to "be Indian leaders for the BIA" rather than for their people.[55] None of his anger, impatience, or disdain for appointed tribal leaders had dissipated. At times, though, such rhetoric simply offended those it was aimed at, rather than inspire them to change, just as Robert Bennett had cautioned at the Ponca powwow.

It was around this time that Clyde and Della introduced Martha Grass to Tillie Walker and Mel Thom as they organized an Indian delegation to take part in Martin Luther King's Poor People's Campaign. Due to Warrior's failing health, Thom had taken over from him in organizing Indian involvement in the campaign, and Thom also was increasingly involved in resolving the White Eagle School issues. Grass quickly became an important and forthright member of the Indian delegation of the Committee of 100, a group of people chosen by the president as representatives of the poor. She was as blunt and direct as Warrior had ever been, scolding Secretary of State Dean Rusk over the Vietnam War, for example, saying, "We have no business in other countries' affairs, when we have enough trouble of our own." She also upset the Ponca tribal government by her words to the Senate Subcommittee on Employment, Manpower, and Poverty: "We were very lenient with all the foreign people when they came to our country. We shared with you all. Now you took all of it and we are back there just starving and hungry and suffering." She added, "I'm not only talking of food in their stomachs, but of the hunger for housing, clothing, and employment that has robbed the people of self-respect and confidence."[56]

Grass's concerns were not unique to the Ponca community. In March 1968 President Johnson had addressed on "the problems of the American Indian." The speech, subtitled "The Forgotten American," addressed problems created by generations of "defeat and exploitation, neglect and inadequate effort." Johnson's words echoed Warrior's most recent rhetoric and addressed issues Warrior had raised before the poverty commission in Memphis. As president of the NIYC, which had grown in strength and stature since its inception in 1961, Warrior's words clearly now carried far more import than they had before. His conversations with Commissioner Bennett seem to have ensured that his message and agenda were finally heard in the White House. Johnson proposed a "new goal for our Indian programs," one that "stresses self-determination . . . and erases old attitudes of paternalism and promotes partnership self-help."[57] This was a welcome message from the White House, if belated by several generations.

Johnson's message covered a wide range of subjects, from education of Indian children to tribal and community leadership and economic self-help and self-determination. Many of his objectives could have been taken directly from Warrior's speeches and vindicated the time and effort that he and the NIYC had spent over the past decade fighting on behalf of Indian communities. Johnson called for "greater freedom of choice," as had Warrior in Memphis. He called for "full participation in the life of modern America, with a full share of economic opportunity and social justice," as had Warrior, and a "policy of maximum choice for the American Indian," as had Warrior. He demanded, "Indians must have a voice in melding the plans and decisions in programs which are important in their daily life," just as Warrior had insisted since his emergence on the national stage.[58]

With regard to education, Johnson followed the precedents set by the NIYC and NCAI: "I am asking the Secretary of the Interior to establish a model community school system for Indians." This proposition mirrored the program implemented across numerous reservations, including the White Eagle Community Project. As innovative as Johnson's proposals appeared to some, they were simply catching up with existing locally oriented tribal initiatives. As Warrior had urged, Johnson requested "an enriched curriculum, special guidance and counseling programs, modern instruction materials and a second program to teach English as a second language." Warrior viewed this acceptance of English as a "second language" as a monumental breakthrough in the attitude of the federal government toward Indians. Previously, his ancestors had been conditioned to speak only English. Now, children would learn English in addition to their native tongues rather than instead of them. In regard to community control of children's education, the NIYC received a major fillip in the form of Johnson's avowed determination to "establish Indian school boards for Federal Indian schools." This was supplemented with a promise that newly elected Indian school board members "will receive whatever training is necessary to enable them to carry out their responsibilities." This was exactly the type of educational reform and community-enabling policy that Warrior, the NIYC, and the White Eagle Community Association had longed for.[59]

In the White Eagle School project, Della was still confident of Clyde's ability to recover from his mother's death and told Dumont that he would be the social studies instructor in the tutorial program. In a letter to Glen Nimnicht she informed him that a new second-grade teacher would have to be found to replace one who had been fired, and she revealed that the tutorial program would focus on English, mathematics, and social studies, the three areas in which the Ponca students were weakest. The idea was to keep costs down by using local VISTA volunteers as well as qualified Indian parents as tutors. Clyde's role as social studies instructor, Della wrote, would be to teach "Ponca tribal history, cultural differences, self-pride, evaluation of white citizens' attitudes and definitions of Ponca Indians, and topics of this sort."[60] With increased self-awareness and appreciation of tribal culture gained during the summer, the Warriors believed that the nineteen proposed students would find transition into public school a little easier to negotiate.

The program proposal offered a more detailed breakdown of the lesson plans. The English classes would cover the basics of vocabulary, grammar, and literature, and the math classes would entail basic arithmetic, fractions, and problem solving. Social studies would discuss the folk and urban world dynamics that Warrior had been schooled in at the Boulder workshops and include a class intriguingly titled "The Art of Being Ponca in Ponca City."[61] This class would teach the students skills needed to withstand the daily reminders that they were social and racial outcasts to the white community that surrounded their own. Besides preparing students academically, boosting their confidence, and teaching them how to deal with racism, the Warriors hoped to get students to "realize the superficiality of Middle class values."[62] From this basis they were confident that they could "enable these students to . . . reach some type of adjustment in today's world."[63]

The Warriors estimated the cost of the project to be as little as $490, using VISTA and college students as lecturers, especially if they used the White Eagle School as the meeting place. Within two weeks Far West had approved funding of the program and on May 16 Nimnicht offered Della a contract running until August 31, as a consultant on Indian education. Two weeks later he made the same offer to Clyde, specifically for the White Eagle Project, at a rate of twenty-six dollars per day. The pair immediately set the program in motion and within two weeks teachers and cooks had been employed and field trips planned. The cost of the program rose from $490 to $2,870 once salaries and transportation costs were included, and once calculated properly, Clyde's salary alone was $2,392.[64]

The program, which was housed in the Indian Baptist Church, rather than the school building, in White Eagle, was ultimately considered a great success by the organizers and Ponca community, despite the summer weather contributing to several dropouts: the number of students fell from twenty to twelve. In a *Ponca City News* article, Della celebrated the students who persevered, saying, "After all it is vacation time, and like other kids they want to stay

Warrior (*front*) at Osage Inloshka ceremonial event, Gray Horse, Oklahoma, mid-1960s. (Courtesy of Frank Turley.)

outside and play too." A 60 percent completion rate, compared to national dropout rates for Indian students of 87 percent (as at Ponca City High School), was something to savor, and suggested the project could be replicated in other communities. Francis McKinley (Ute), associate director of the Far West Labs, a longtime BIA employee who had previously chaired the 1964 and 1965 Task Force on Indian Poverty, lauded the program and proclaimed that it was "something to start with and build on."[65]

At the end of June, Warrior attended the Osage Inloshka ceremonial in his role as Hethuska tail dancer, celebrating the event with his uncle Sylvester and whip man Abe Conklin. In pre-reservation days, society "dignitaries" deemed attendance of such ceremonies as an essential diplomatic duty. In the modern era it was a matter of recognizing traditional rituals, maintaining cultural relevance, and ensuring that the cultural respect between the Osage and Ponca nations continued unabated. Shortly after the Inloshka celebration, the Warriors left for the Navajo Nation in Arizona, where Della was employed from July 1 to August 10 as a program specialist in the jointly sponsored BIA–National Association on Early Childhood Education Kindergarten Project. (Della's Far West contract allowed her this break in her schedule.) The project focused on the expansion of the Dilcon Community School, named after a mountain, "Tsejin Dilcon" (meaning Smooth Mountain).[66] The project had begun in 1967 and entailed addition of twenty-six classrooms and nursery facilities to the school, and Della was employed to oversee the summer training program for kindergarten teachers and assistants. The couple left the White Eagle tutoring program in the capable hands of instructors Paul and Mary Jane Meier.

The Dilcon Project was expected to be another block in the culturally relevant, community-based education that the Warriors and the NIYC were building, and it allowed Clyde Warrior to put his ideology into practice. For the first time, and in a complete reversal of the educational policies that Warrior and several generations before him had endured, children at the Dilcon School would be actively encouraged to embrace their culture, history, and identity. Together with the summer workshop programs being run by Browning Pipestem, in which college students were experiencing the same cultural and intellectual affirmation, the template for Clyde Warrior's vision of Red Power appeared to be building upon solid foundations that would allow a greater and more robust expression of traditional culture and identity. Ultimately Warrior's vision was for Red Power and self-determination to become one ideology, with self-sufficient Indian communities funding Red

Power efforts rather than relying on federal sponsorship . For Warrior, self-perpetuating cycles could be positive as well as negative. Culturally immersed, intellectually invested tribal leaders, he envisioned, would foster programs to ensure the continuation of culturally relevant education programs he and the NIYC had started. These programs would also help create new tribal leaders who were sufficiently knowledgeable of the modern world to manipulate it in such a way as to preserve and protect the future of their communities. Self-determination would then be in the hands of leaders who held the community dear, rather than ones who looked to the federal government for the protection of their individual power.[67]

CHAPTER 7

LEGACY

"Clyde leaves us with our struggle just beginning. . . .
He opened the doors of self-realization for us."

In the summer of 1968, Warrior and the NIYC planned to forge ahead with their campaign for greater cultural, social, intellectual, and political sovereignty through tribal self-determination. They were pursuing culturally relevant education programs through model schools and revised summer workshops, and they were preparing to push the project further in the fall. Due to Warrior's health, however, as the doctors' warnings about his continued drinking were proven right, the issue of his legacy came to the fore far sooner than anybody expected. Warrior became seriously ill almost as soon as he and Della settled in Arizona for Della's summer project. Fearing that this was more serious than previous times he had fallen ill, he told Della that he wanted to go home rather than to a hospital, saying, "If I go to a hospital I am going to die."[1] As he was in no pain at that time, Della agreed, and the family began the twenty-hour-hour drive back to Bois D'Arc. His condition worsened en route, however, and they were just three hours from home when Della made the decision to take him to the hospital in Enid, Oklahoma. There, a doctor "gave him some medication and he said he will be all right," and then left the room, Della sadly remembered.[2] Moments later, on July 7, 1968, Warrior, twenty-eight years old, died from cirrhosis of the liver. The condition, which he had been warned about in early 1967, had worsened quickly over seventeen months. Warrior's increased drinking after the death of his mother had proven fatal.

Warrior's death, as sudden and unexpected as it was to most, despite his ailing health and repeated warnings about it, threw the NIYC leadership into turmoil and had a profound effect upon the NIYC and around Indian Country. Mel Thom's lament, "We have lost our leader," was more than mere rhetoric. "Clyde leaves us with our struggle just beginning," he declared while thanking Warrior for opening "the doors of self-realization" for young Indians.[3] Shirley Hill Witt and Della Warrior both remember a sense of hopelessness, as people wondered what the movement would do now without him. "He was the type of person that, if he was there, everybody wanted to be around him," Witt boasted. "[His death] was such a great loss."[4]

His death devastated Della, especially as she thought about the abruptness of his hospital care. She felt the doctor there should have stayed with him longer, and she remains convinced that Warrior suffered undiagnosed conditions that exacerbated his liver condition. She thinks of the poisonous sludge proven to have been pumped into the Salt Fork and Arkansas Rivers from the Marland Oil Refinery in Ponca City, which had caused the Poncas to abandon their winter camps in the vicinity in the decade before Warrior's birth. The watershed of one of these rivers supplied the Collins family well from which Warrior drank as a child. Della firmly believes that polluted water gave Clyde a delicate immune system, which made it difficult for him to digest certain foods and also caused him to be extremely susceptible to alcohol when he began drinking as an adult.[5]

Warrior's funeral was held at his grandparents' farm two miles due west of White Eagle, where between three hundred and four hundred mourners visited to pay their last respects. For his grandparents the tragedy was twofold, having lost their daughter and grandson in just four months. In keeping with Ponca tradition the funeral was a four-day event, with Ponca religious songs, lots of cooking, and praying every night. All of the guests were fed four meals a day for four days, as was Ponca tradition, with family friends Joe and Marcella Herribeck volunteering to supervise the culinary assignment. Also in keeping with tradition, a small dish of whatever the family was eating, and a small drink of water, were placed by the side of the casket by a family member. Warrior's sister Betty Pensoneau described including him in the meals in such a manner as a traditional symbolic gesture to Warrior of feeding him first, with the food prayed over—and no-one else eating—"until that little bit of food is placed there."[6] Della remembered many mourners sitting under the old cottonwood trees that stood next to the farmhouse, with others sitting in an adjacent plowed field because there was "not enough room for them under the trees." The Hethuska Society provided benches from the ceremonial grounds, while others brought their own powwow chairs, and they sat eating "corn soup, pork and hominy and chicken, fry bread, and coffee and Kool-Aid, cakes and pies, fresh fruit, apples and oranges."[7] This was a very similar meal to that which the Collinses had prepared in Commissioner Bennett's honor several months earlier.

Warrior's body was laid out for viewing in the farm's living room. He was dressed in his Hethuska regalia, holding an eagle feather as was the Ponca tradition. His face was covered with a scarf and the man responsible for lifting the scarf during the viewing was Warrior's childhood friend, Garland Kent (Otoe, Ponca).[8] The service was overseen by a nondenominational "Indian minister," and the pallbearers were Kent, Browning Pipestem, Bob Thomas, Mel Thom, Tony Isaacs, and Frank Turley.[9] A grief-stricken Pipestem challenged the two non-Indian pallbearers, Isaacs and Turley, as the latter recalled, as to "whether we should be allowed to carry the casket." Turley gratefully remembered that the family stood up for the two.[10] At the burial site, at two o'clock in the afternoon on Wednesday, July 10, Warrior's two daughters were helped as they walked over the suspended coffin in the old Ponca way, which served as a symbol of letting Warrior "move on with his life and not look back."[11] As the girls were aided along the length of the coffin, Ponca singers drummed and sang a warrior song that was usually reserved for the closing of Hethuska Society gatherings. Despite its being the closing song, it was not funereal. It was "a goodbye song," according to Frank Turley. "It says stand up—'Hethuska no jinga' means 'stand up'—and then it says 'God gave us the war dance,' loosely translated. It's a good song."[12] It was a fitting tribute to one of the men who had helped revive the ceremony just ten years earlier.

The gate to the Ponca Tribal Cemetery, where Warrior's remains rest; situated on a high point according to Ponca belief systems, the cemetery overlooks the tribal complex of White Eagle.

After the burial, the family conducted a giveaway, as was the custom among the Poncas, and, indeed, among most Plains tribes. The practice, which had been described a "wanton disregard for property" by Secretary of the Interior Henry Teller in 1883, was the way in which the family of the deceased repaid those who attended the funeral to pay their respects.[13] Della, who wore a blue suit and white blouse to the service, recalled that the family gave away "a lot." "A lot of people had given me, they sent money and wired money," Della remembered gratefully, "and people brought things: just baskets and baskets of blankets and shawls and groceries."[14] The blankets represented shelter, the groceries represented feeding and sustenance, and the money, to be used for gasoline or bus tickets, represented a safe journey home. Each of these were contemporary versions of a tradition that, in the pre-reservation days, would see horses given away, a feast laid down, or a place to sleep offered for as long as a person needed it. For someone as immersed in his culture as Warrior had been, a giveaway of this scale was an appropriate farewell.

The eulogies for Warrior spoke of his strength, honor, courage, conviction, and vision. Those who honored him remembered his capacity for truth, belligerence, hope, and despair. They acknowledged his flaws and celebrated his brilliance, mourned his departure, and thanked him for his legacy. This was a legacy of trying, despite seemingly insurmountable odds, to change a system that had been ingrained in Indian-White relations over generations, and a legacy of almost succeeding, and at least of planting the seeds of success. At a Washington, D.C., memorial two days after Warrior's death, Upward Bound director Tom Billings described him as "a troubled, heartbroken, but determined man, listening for a response from the world which would be equal to the warmth and strength of his own good spirit." When that response was not forthcoming, when "the great emotional silence which surrounded him, the cold emotional emptiness which confronted him, hurt his heart and tormented his spirit," he recalled, "Clyde Warrior became thunder and lightning and tears." Billings concluded that Warrior had "wanted, like few persons I have known, to believe in the integrity of this nation."[15] Commissioner Bennett was later quoted as saying of Warrior, "I bridled at his criticism, and questioned his tactics, but of his basic philosophy I could find no argument."[16]

His long-time friend and colleague Mel Thom mourned simply, "Our leader is gone." Thom remembered Warrior "teasing, laughing, cussing, singing, and talking as few men would." He spoke of the "new hope" that Warrior had brought to Indian people, and he talked of how Warrior had frightened some "with his fight against oppression of Indian people." Describing Warrior as a "great American," Thom added that "Clyde was a great Indian patriot . . . He was a free man in bondage." It was the "white man's alcohol" that had struck Warrior down, as "surely as the assassin's bullet has struck down so many great men," Thom argued, before concluding, "Clyde is gone but never forgotten."[17]

Warrior's grave was initially marked simply with flowers. To commemorate his friend's life and legacy, Thom sent out a request to "friends of the late Clyde Warrior" for help to purchase a

Warrior's headstone inscription: "A Fresh Air of New Indian Idealism."

headstone. He reminded people that Warrior had died poor, and he proclaimed that Warrior "never would have been independently wealthy as long as his Indian people remained poor." He asked, "As a fitting tribute to our fallen leader, to dig into your pockets and contribute for a monument fitting of the man Clyde Warrior was, and fittingly, to have the monument in place by the time of the forthcoming Ponca Powwow." That monument was placed and bears the legend "A Fresh Air of New Indian Idealism."[18]

Warrior's work did not end with his death. The community action projects that he had set in motion at White Eagle continued unabated. On July 20, 1968, the Far West Laboratory presented an interim report on its eighteen-month study of Indian education. Della Warrior was employed part-time at the White Eagle School as a temporary field assistant to gather notes and interview students and parents to "ascertain attitudes to Indian education." In addition, she recalled "family participation programs" being introduced to involve the parents in "some meaningful educational activity."[19] Aided by these programs, parents were expected to help prepare students socially and culturally and academically for the adjustment in moving to the public schools in Ponca City.

A September NIYC proposal to the Carnegie Foundation for further funding of its Indian education program presented progress reports of the demonstration schools. The White Eagle report, incorporating much of the Far West Lab observations, noted that the Ponca community "was known as one of the most difficult ones with which to work in the state of Oklahoma." In keeping with this, proposal authors claimed that at first they had no success establishing rapport with residents "without antagonizing others." It had only been after they began working with Warrior that "they took advantage of the strong sense of pride that the Ponca Indians have when operating in their own surroundings and within their own culture." The report noted, "This pride is seldom shown outside the context of their own culture and it is particularly absent in the dealings in Ponca City, where they show themselves as weak and submissive and assume a defeatist attitude."[20] Warrior had done much to try to change this attitude, and he had been angry with the system that had precipitated such an attitude. He had been determined that not just Poncas but all Indians should be as outwardly proud of their culture as they were inwardly proud. It was this determination that had driven his continued calls for tribal self-determination.

The report also noted that this defeatism among the Poncas was "reinforced by the way that most Ponca Indians are looked down upon by those few who are educated, and by the way members of other Indian tribes and white people in the larger community look down on Poncas."[21] This had not been the case with Warrior, however. Revered for his candid attacks on the federal Indian affairs bureaucracy, sometimes feared because of his caustic wit, Warrior was someone few people looked down upon. While he may not have been welcome at most dinner tables in conservative and racist Ponca City, he was very well respected by most educated people, white, Indian, or otherwise, who encountered him. And he was not alone. The NIYC proposal credited Della with organization of a voter registration drive to elect a Ponca Indian to the White Eagle school board, acknowledging the couple as powerful allies in driving the early success of the White Eagle School.[22]

This success was in stark contrast to many of the other schools in the project, and the number of participating schools had dwindled from the original ten to just four: White Eagle, Pine Ridge, the Crow Agency, and the Mescalero Apache Reservation. Ultimately the NIYC abandoned the project, citing epistemological differences with Far West. For Mel Thom and Bob Dumont, the much-vaunted attempts to integrate each Native community's learning strategies into the model school system, a ground-breaking strategy had it been faithfully applied, was ignored, as Far West focused on primarily Western ideas. The White Eagle Community Project continued until the school was closed in 1969. Building upon their early successes, Martha Grass and her cohorts were able to force the Ponca City school system to adopt Johnson-O'Malley funding to employ Indian tutors to help their children. Previously the children had been expected to assimilate without such support.[23]

The White Eagle Community Association, now led by Warrior's widow, Della, also decided to commemorate Warrior's life. To reflect his pride in being Ponca and his desire to carry his people's history forward with future generations, they obtained a grant from the National Council of Arts and Humanities to pursue the Clyde Warrior Ponca History Project. Under the auspices of the project they recorded the memories and stories of Warrior's grandparents, his uncle, and other tribal members. The project recorded and preserved Ponca children's stories, much of the tribe's history since relocation from Nebraska, and more ancient tribal history, as well as the origins of tribal ceremonies, dances, games, and prayers, many of which Warrior himself had heard and seen as a boy. Despite his national prominence in Indian affairs, Warrior had always been happiest when "he was at home talking to his grandparents [and] participating in the ceremonial dances that they have in May," Della remembered fondly. The history project in his name thus reflected his cultural immersion and lifelong dedication to the Ponca ways.[24]

Further afield, Stan Steiner wrote to Della in October 1969, describing the "incredible talk of Clyde by people, young people, who never knew him." He told her that Warrior was "becoming a legend, larger than life: but then he always was."[25] The first attempt at ensuring that Warrior's legacy continued was a bloodless coup of the NIYC leadership led by his close friend Browning Pipestem. Believing that incumbent board members of the NIYC had led the organization into financial disarray, Pipestem orchestrated the removal of those board members at the 1968 annual conference in Gallup, refusing them the opportunity to sit at the council, never mind speak to defend themselves.[26] The annual election resulted in all board members losing their positions to Pipestem's cohort. Perhaps fittingly, the coup was achieved with a group of student graduates from the NIYC's Clyde Warrior Institute of American Indian Studies, which the summer workshops had been renamed in his honor and over which Pipestem had assumed total control.

The NIYC quarterly report for July 1–September 30, 1968 states that "the Clyde Warrior Institute in American Indian Affairs [has] had the most influence on the present status of NIYC," although this was more conjecture than fact. Pipestem wanted to give his friend the credit for the coup that he had led in Warrior's absence. The report was accurate in calling the institute "an experiment in self-determination and the operating of a modern institution responsive to Indian direction and aspiration." It ignored the foundations upon which the Clyde Warrior Institute had been built, however, saying that, "for the first time, Indian students were able to learn how to order, control, restructure, and balance the cross-cultural experience." From this experience, they had been "able and willing to assume the responsibilities of the National Indian Youth Council."[27] There was symmetry here with how the NIYC had been created, which Warrior would have appreciated even if he would not have agreed to ignore or disavow the influence of such early workshops stalwarts as D'Arcy McNickle.

The new NIYC leaders focused their attention on expanding the movement's activities beyond education, sovereignty, and self-determination. In 1969, aside from Executive Director Gerald Wilkinson and five other members, the new board included Warrior's cousin Bill Pensoneau as president, his best friend Browning Pipestem, his widow—Della, and Stanley Snake, Warrior's younger half brother. Under their guidance the NIYC organized five Clyde

Warrior Institutes: one each at the University of Colorado in Boulder, the University of California at Los Angeles, Stout State University in Wisconsin, the University of New Mexico in Albuquerque, and in Kansas, at the Haskell Institute. The intent was to reach as many Indian students as possible and cement Warrior's legacy in the process. In another move of which Warrior would have been proud, the organization held the first "protest powwow"—in objection to conditions on the Fort Totten Sioux Reservation in North Dakota. Six hundred Indians turned up there to combine "traditional Indian culture" with "modern day methods of protest" to drive home their dissatisfaction at the abject poverty and poor living conditions on the reservation.[28]

Warrior himself had advocated such protest for much of the 1960s, watching as other minorities' and antiwar protests gained attention for their causes. He wanted to build on the success of the fish-ins and push a much more aggressive agenda for Indian rights than organizations such as the NCAI were advocating. Gate-crashing the 1966 NCAI parade in Oklahoma City with a car proclaiming "Red Power" and organizing a plane to fly over the Cherokee Village in Tahlequah in 1967 had been two such actions. Red Power—the retention of culture, community, and tradition—was a fight that began at home. While Warrior had acknowledged and often referenced the global push for freedom and independence, his primary concern had been domestic and community-driven.[29]

Warrior was as quick to castigate tribal leaders, Bureau of Indian Affairs personnel, and leaders of other Indian organizations for their complicity in the subjugation of their people as he was to denounce the system of paternalism and colonialism that had led to this subjugation. The direct action of the fish-ins placed Warrior and the NIYC directly in the middle of the civil rights movement, as did the Cherokee Village protest, as agitators and community organizers, rather than intellectual elites as they have sometimes been labeled. Warrior's calls for an end to well-meaning but paternalistic outsiders creating and overseeing programs for American Indian communities coincided with similar calls from Stokely Carmichael and the Black Power movement. The sheer force of will of Warrior and others in the NIYC to create social change saw them invited to presidential forums on poverty and asked for their advice on how to change the status quo. That the movement and leaders who came after Warrior would overshadow his and the NIYC's achievements should not be used as evidence of their ineffectiveness. Rather, it is as tribute to the ground he and they broke and the solid, unshakeable foundations of American Indian intertribal protest that they built.[30]

Red Power had many facets, not just those of direct action and militant protest. Warrior's ideal scenario was for a system that would recognize the integrity of the traditional tribal structure by validating the cultural knowledge and power of traditional elders rather than appointed leaders. The most pertinent connection he saw with the wider civil rights movement in the United States, and across the world, was the commonality of poverty among the oppressed. He had marched with Martin Luther King in 1963 and had planned to do so again. He was happy to reach across the ethnic divide if and when it suited tribal causes to do so, but only if the integrity of his and his cohorts' message remained intact. To Warrior and others in the NIYC, the tribal and intertribal fight for self-determination had begun in 1492 and superseded the struggles of other minorities, free speech activists, and antiwar protesters. As protesters around the world looked to Martin Luther King, Jr., Malcolm X, and Gandhi as role models for revolution and independence, Warrior looked to Tecumseh, the early-nineteenth-century Shawnee leader, and other American Indian historical figures. Warrior never called for the abolition of the BIA, the colonial overseer of Indian lands and peoples, but for a restructuring of the system so that the BIA served Indian communities rather than controlled them.[31]

As fast as Warrior's legend as the most militant of his generation of activists was growing in Indian Country—the "Stokely Carmichael of the Indians"—a chain of events he had long predicted overshadowed it.[32] In November 1969, a time in San Francisco when, according to scholar Tom Findley, stories of Warrior were almost legendary, a group calling itself "Indians of All Tribes" occupied Alcatraz Island in a bid to reclaim federally abandoned land for Indians.[33] This occupation, led by Richard Oakes (Mohawk), began a surge in militant activism from urban Indians who had been hitherto largely marginalized in federal Indian affairs. Although this was the second such attempt at occupying the island, in many ways, the occupation followed, and built upon, the fish-ins of 1964 and the Cherokee Village blockade in 1967.[34] The propaganda success of the occupation and the worldwide publicity it garnered over the course of nineteen months encouraged the fledgling American Indian Movement (AIM) to adopt similar inflammatory rhetoric and later militant activism.

Originally named Concerned Indian Americans, AIM was formed in 1968, the year Warrior died. AIM's original purpose was to fight racism and police abuse in the Twin Cities of Minneapolis and St. Paul. Building upon the momentum of the Alcatraz occupation and the media attention it garnered, AIM cut a swath across America from 1971 to 1973 and burned their way into the public, even international, consciousness. From "protests and picketing in Minneapolis, Albuquerque, Sacramento, Cleveland, and Chicago" in 1970, the group's confrontational tactics escalated to include the 1972 occupation of BIA headquarters in Washington, D.C., and the seventy-three-day armed siege at Wounded Knee, South Dakota, in 1973. These were two examples of the system being smashed—as Warrior had predicted to Stan Steiner.[35] As AIM forced itself into the public eye, the massive publicity it generated allowed its leaders to rewrite history in their own image and cast the NIYC as ineffectual intellectuals.

AIM leader Russell Means asserted, "Before AIM, Indians were dispirited, defeated and culturally dissolving. People were ashamed to be Indian. You didn't see the young people wearing braids or chokers or ribbon shirts in those days."[36] Such a view of history stood unchallenged until recently. Despite this dismissal of the role of the NIYC and the foundations it had built, AIM leaders actively sought NIYC advice and counsel in the early years of the organization. Although overtures from AIM regarding an official alliance were rejected by the NIYC in the year following Pipestem's coup, Gerald Wilkinson's "new" NIYC and AIM shared a common ideology. From 1970 until the BIA takeover in 1972, the NIYC and AIM were allies, having come together in Norman, Oklahoma, to create the American Indian Task Force. The two groups eventually parted ways over tactical differences, when the NIYC refused to join AIM at Wounded Knee and sent only "words of support" instead.[37]

Claims such as that of Means dismissed Warrior and the NIYC, their work, and their legacy. Red Power, a slogan created by Warrior and Thom, was acknowledged as having started with Alcatraz rather than the NIYC. It is unfortunate that AIM did not acknowledge the debt of advice and example it owed to the NIYC, whose foundations of direct action the movement built upon. Della remembered AIM activist Dennis Banks's private admission to her, that "Clyde really was a big part of getting him to get involved" in American Indian activism, because "Clyde's speeches were everywhere and it was picked up and these guys began to read them," but he neglected to do so publicly.[38]

Members of the previous NIYC board had fought against the two groups joining forces because of vastly different ideologies, which suggests the scale of changes Wilkinson brought to the NIYC. At the Norman, Oklahoma, meeting, Charlie Cambridge voted against joining forces with AIM for reasons that Warrior would have understood and supported. To Cambridge, as with others on the board, "The basic philosophy of the American Indian Movement was to establish an 'Indian.' I got into a lot of trouble with the American Indian Movement because I told them that you guys are trying to create an 'Indian.' The creation of a generic or pan-Indian is the same thing that the Bureau of Indian Affairs has been trying to do for centuries."[39] It was also what James Howard and Bob Thomas had created in their two essays on pan-Indianism. AIM's success in fostering this concept of a generic Indian identity allowed Thomas's theory of pan-Indianism to become the accepted norm, and pan-Indianism is often categorized as the driving ideology of Red Power. However, the tribally oriented, culturally focused, and community based identities of people like Warrior, Thom, Witt, and others defined Red Power in its original form. The NIYC, for many of the old guard at least, "was closer to reservations," Cambridge argued, which was where they insisted that true cultural identity, or at least history, existed. An alliance with the urban-based AIM, many of whose members had been educated at boarding schools, "was something that just could not work because the basic philosophies were entirely different."[40]

In contrast to AIM and its philosophy of loyalty to the collective Indian, Warrior's legacy of Red Power was born of his tribal identity and cultural upbringing. To Warrior and many of his cohorts, loyalty began first with family and then extended outward to clan, then tribe, then the NIYC, and only then "Indian" and "American." Warrior often questioned the validity of the terminology and asked, "What is an American Indian?" He proudly proclaimed himself to be a tribal person who was part of a collective, which, to borrow from the powwow world in which he was immersed, was intertribal.[41] The NIYC recognized community and tribal identity, and the protection of tribal knowledge and traditions, as the driving forces behind their activism. The NIYC was a movement based upon consensus, as were the communities from which its members came. Ironically, many of the original AIM leaders and proponents of Indianness, such as Clyde Bellecourt and Dennis Banks, are now respected community elders, having cast off the generic Indianness that Cambridge described in favor of embracing tribal identity and cultural traditions.

Many of Warrior's speeches, essays, or addresses began with the words "I am a full-blood Ponca Indian from Oklahoma." It was the community-centered nature of his Ponca culture that gave Warrior the self-knowledge upon which his version of Red Power was built. Despite the material deprivation that accompanied tribal life, the Ponca community in Bois D'Arc was his comfort zone.[42] As Warrior proclaimed in 1964, "I know who I am. I am me, tribe warrior."[43] This self-belief gave Warrior the conviction that his worldview, the Ponca worldview, was valuable and essential to the world. He was convinced that the communally focused cultures of American Indian nations were worth protecting and preserving. Each community had its own traditions, values, history, and culture, which identified it as distinct from the others. Warrior recognized this and elucidated upon it in many speeches when he rejected the concept of a single Indian identity. His fight for treaty rights recognized these cultural distinctions and was not rhetorical, or a method to castigate the federal government, but a crucial element of protecting

and preserving his cultural and his individual identity. This was
Red Power.

In 1953, D'Arcy McNickle, as leader of the NCAI, issued a clarion
call, proclaiming that "the fight for civil rights has not yet been won,
but the fight for the right to be culturally different has not even
started."[44] Warrior, more than many others, epitomized this quote.
For him, full-bloodedness entailed cultural identity and immersion
rather than federally stipulated blood quantum. Blood quantum
was a legal definition. If one was not a member of a federally recognized tribe, one had no access to a blood quantum card and was
therefore, at least to the federal government, not an American Indian. This invalidated hundreds of thousands of state-recognized
tribal members who were then, as many still are, fighting for federal
recognition. To Warrior, this was culturally irrelevant, especially in
terms of self-identity, as it made a person fully dependent upon the
federal government for one's identity. He had made this distinction
clear in the early days of the NIYC when he objected to the proposal
to only allow federally recognized Indians to become members.

To Warrior, true identity was tribal and cultural, federally recognized or not, and his worldview measured cultural identity by
participation in, and fidelity to, traditional cultural practices within
the framework of the tribal community. Federal recognition was
a political tool through which tribes regained or retained what he
viewed as limited sovereignty.[45] As distinct as each tribal community was, it only remained so while the people within that community retained its values and practices—including its language.
His grandfather's quarter-Irish blood was irrelevant to who he was
or how he identified himself. Warrior had been raised with Ponca
as his first language, with Ponca customs as his worldview, with
Ponca songs in his head and on his lips from morning until night,
and the sound of the drum beating every day. He was raised with
the history of injustice that the federal, and then state and city governments, had meted out to his people, from forced removal from
their ancestral homelands to stealing the legally owned land from
under them. He was raised with the principals of the clans of the
Ponca people being together and working together as one community, as represented by the seven eagle feathers and three teepees on

the tribal seal. His immersion and celebration of this heritage and knowledge meant to Warrior that he was a full-blood, a culturally participating Ponca Indian. This was Clyde Warrior's Red Power.

Warrior used this background and knowledge to fight for the protection and preservation of his culture, history, and identity. For Warrior, it was these three motifs that formed the cornerstone of Red Power, and his and his cohorts' fight for self-determination. His activism, rhetoric, and confidence stemmed from his culture, community, and identity. His was a proactive fight for Indian rights, from the grassroots of tribalism and community action, rather than a reactive fight against federal Indian policy from a political perspective. He was also far from the angry but ineffective intellectual that scholars have portrayed for many years, full of stirring rhetoric yet part of an organization that ultimately achieved little. In 1970, Richard Nixon's speech on Indian affairs carried clear echoes of Warrior's words, as had President Johnson's in 1968. Nixon's address, influenced by "several years of volatile Indian demonstrations and demands," was full of many of the same images and arguments that Warrior had been making throughout the previous decade.[46] The speech was also heavily influenced by the previous year's publication of the Kennedy Report on Indian Affairs, by Senators Robert and Ted Kennedy, for which Warrior had been interviewed on several occasions. Warrior and the NIYC had reached from the reservation and the classroom to directly influence federal Indian policy in a promising new direction for American Indian tribes and individuals.

On the issue of self-determination, Nixon told the Congress, "The Indian community is almost entirely run by outsiders who are responsible and responsive to Federal officials in Washington, D.C., rather than to the communities they are supposed to be serving." The result of this bureaucratic inequality was an "erosion of Indian initiative and moral." He also tackled the issue of community as a collective with the tribe as its focus, rather than a geographic location irrespective of the people within it. He argued that his policy was "to strengthen the Indian's sense of autonomy without threatening . . . sense of community." We must ensure, he urged, that Indians can assume control of their own lives "without being separated involuntarily from the tribal group." To do this, Nixon proposed passing laws that would enable "a tribe or a group of tribes or any other Indian community to take control or operation of any federally funded and administered programs in the Department of the Interior and the Department of Health, Education and Welfare whenever the tribal council or comparable community governing group voted to do so."[47]

While Nixon's self-determination policy was far from perfect, never removing the yoke of federal supervision of tribal laws, it was dramatically more far-reaching that Johnson's Community Action Program (CAP) had been for Indian nations. It also answered Warrior's 1967 demand: "junking the present structure and creating another."[48] CAP may have allowed for tribes to begin working toward economic independence and community control of tribal programs, but Nixon's self-determination policy built upon these foundations and went further. His guarantee that Indians could "assume control" over their own lives was ultimately enshrined in law under the Self-Determination and Education Assistance Act of 1975. The act answered many of the complaints that Warrior, his cohorts, and later activists such as Richard Oakes and AIM had leveled against the federal government in their years of campaigning.

There was a refrain to Nixon's proposed Indian Education policy that echoed, almost exactly, the rhetoric of many of Warrior's speeches, and many of the ideas that had sprung from the NIYC collaboration with the Far West Laboratory in Berkeley. The "Far Out Lab," as scholar Steve Talbot recalled the nickname, was where the likes of Thom and Warrior met with Jack Forbes and members of United Native Americans (UNA).[49] It was hardly a place associated with conservative politicians, but Nixon, as Warrior had done, tied education to self-determination, explaining that, "consistent with our policy that the Indian community should have the right to take over the control and operation of federally funded programs, we believe every Indian community wishing to do so should be able to control his own Indian schools." Nixon asserted that this control ought to be exercised by school boards selected by Indians.[50]

Nixon's address answered the call for change that the Warriors and Martha Grass had fought for in White Eagle, that the NIYC and Far West Laboratory had attempted to implement in their ten-school project, that the Navajo created at the much-vaunted Rough Rock Demonstration School, and later campaigners such as Richard Oakes called for in San Francisco. Furthermore, Nixon promised that technical help would be provided to Indian communities wishing to establish school boards, while a nationwide review would be conducted on the educational status of all Indian schoolchildren, followed by an annual report on "the status of Indian education, including the extent of local control."[51] Unfortunately, Nixon's timing was too late for White Eagle School, which had closed in 1969. When the proposals became law in 1975, the Ponca Tribal Council did not take the president up on his offer, and Ponca children today continue to be schooled within the Ponca City system.

This situation, with Warrior's ideas adopted after it was too late for his own people, was typical of a man who represented so many paradoxes in his writing, activism, and lifestyle. He argued bitterly against federal control of Indian affairs and Indian lives and frequently lambasted the bureaucratic system as it stood, but his ideas were later used by reform-minded politicians. He was one of the most forthright and militant activists of his generation yet never, unlike many militant leaders of previous and subsequent generations, called for the abolition of the BIA. Instead, he recognized the value of the BIA, if it could be reformed to provide services to Indian communities on an individual basis rather than impose monolithic and immutable bureaucratic oversight of those communities. He often predicted that the generation that followed his would dismiss his as ineffectual and strive to be bigger, bolder, and louder than he ever was, and he was proven right. That a coup in the NIYC led the organization he helped create to be complicit in this rejection of his legacy, albeit temporarily, is ironic. The irony doubles when one considers that his best friend orchestrated the coup in an effort to preserve his legacy. Warrior would have found this highly amusing.[52]

Warrior would have understood and agreed with the idea that, for many, his alcoholism taints his legacy. He had described the addiction as "unconscious suicide," with people thinking, "Life ain't worth it. Best we should stay drunk and die or . . . kill each

other than have to live the life we have."[53] Although he instilled
hope and pride in many of those around him, he never managed
to shake that despair personally. Perhaps he would have agreed
with his friend Mel Thom, who, discussing Warrior's death with
journalists, tragically described drinking as "almost an honorable
way for an Indian to die. Because when an Indian [man] drinks he
is a free man."[54]

Now, generations later, Warrior's words are as pertinent and vi-
brant as they were in the 1960s, and they deserve a much larger
audience. Warrior's legacy and his contribution to Red Power
and the civil rights movement is slowly being recognized, as can
be seen in Steve Newcomb's November 2013 article "Clyde Warrior and the American Indian Fight to Be Free" in *Indian Country
Today*. As Gus Palmer, Jr., remembered finding people he knew that
fit Warrior's "five types of American Indian," so do people today.
As Warrior argued that tribal sovereignty was a sham as long as
it required oversight by the secretary of the interior, so do people
recognize his argument now. And at a time when the federal government is proposing to return control of Johnson-O'Malley funds
to public school districts rather than Indian education boards, Warrior's fears for the education of Native students are again vibrantly
pertinent. A new generation of American Indian students are reading Warrior's words and identifying with them in the same way
that their grandparent's generation did. This too is Clyde Warrior's
Red Power.[55]

As his words are now reaching a new generation, Warrior's
memory is still cherished by family and friends. Four decades after
his death, Della, now a well-respected elder who achieved personal
professional success as tribal chairwoman of the Otoe-Missouria
and president of the Institute of American Indian Arts, still dis-
plays the pain of loss that only a widow can know. Warrior's sister,
Charmain Billy, faithfully presents a slideshow of his words and
achievements to Ponca tribal elders every March 3, or Clyde Warrior Day as she calls it, in honor of his making that date historic for
Native Americans in the 1964 Washington fish-ins. This is not to be
confused with the NIYC's annual Clyde Warrior Day on August 31,
a paid vacation day for NIYC staffers in memory of their founding

Commemorative stone in front of the Clyde Warrior Memorial Building, White Eagle, Oklahoma, sitting atop a Ponca time capsule.

member. Along with Kathryn Red Corn, she is also striving to resurrect summer workshops to help educate the newest generation of American Indian college students and in the process honor his name and memory.

Shirley Hill Witt, one of the last surviving founding members of the NIYC, describes Warrior's energy, intellect, spirit, and great humor as if she spoke with him just yesterday. Gerald Brown, Charlie Cambridge, Al Wahrhaftig, and Gus Palmer, Jr., still remain in awe of Warrior's intellect and powerful rhetoric as well as his ability to touch people, see their strength, and galvanize them into action. His brother Steve Pensoneau and sisters Charmain Billy, Darlene Harjo, Betty Pensoneau, and Vernice Willis fondly remember a loving and playful older brother who teased them incessantly. Before his own untimely death, Mel Thom remembered that Warrior "would tell Indians to learn their tribe's language and history, especially the treaties, teach the young people the value of Indian life, what makes tribes unique; make the young practice the values, customs and culture; maintain a close relationship with God; and work together to bring about a better life for Indian people."[56] His college roommates, Garrick Bailey and Tony Isaacs, remember long and intense conversations about politics and Indian music respectively, Warrior catering to each of their tastes effortlessly, while his old hobbyist buddy Frank Turley still claims, as have Isaacs and others, that Warrior was the only person who ever whistled "49" songs. Turley counts the piece of Warrior's Straight Dance regalia that the family gifted to him as one of his most treasured possessions.[57] Hank Adams, whose determination to fight for his community's way of life led to Warrior and the NIYC organizing the Red Power movement's first intertribal direct action protest—the fish-ins, remembered Warrior's commitment to traditionalism as being so strong that "his life was in the song."[58] Every one of them also remembers the most graceful, fluid, and elegant dancer they have ever seen.

The story of Clyde Warrior's life and legacy is long overdue, especially given his and the NIYC's influence on federal Indian policy during the civil rights movement era. He demanded social and political change, which government administrators first resisted but then began to initiate years after his tragic death. He also framed and created an ideology of intertribal Red Power, in which the future for American Indian communities is rooted in tribal traditionalism. This ideology is as strong now as it was then.

EPILOGUE

On December 19, 2007, Ponca Tribal Chairman Dan Jones and Della Warrior hosted the grand opening ceremony of the Clyde Warrior Memorial Building in White Eagle, Oklahoma. The multipurpose building, which houses a library, conference center, child protection services office, and meeting areas for tribal members, is shaped like a traditional Ponca roundhouse and rests on the former site of the BIA's Ponca Boarding School, which closed in 1924, after which the post-elementary level children of White Eagle were sent to Chilocco Indian School near the Kansas border. Elementary school children were educated on a day school inside the tribal complex. By the time Chilocco closed in 1980 the vast majority of Ponca schoolchildren were educated in the Ponca City public school system. The construction of the Warrior Building was described by HUD's Office of Native Americans Programs (ONAP) as a key element of the strategic plan for the Ponca Tribe to strengthen the ability of the Tribal government to provide for the safety, health, social, cultural, and economic needs of its members."[1] Long-standing friends of Clyde joined family members, tribal officials, and the head of the construction firm responsible for building the memorial in paying tribute to Warrior's memory and legacy. Chief Jones was presented with an official commendation on behalf of the people of Oklahoma, signed by Governor Brad Henry, State Senator David Myers, and State Representative Ken Luttrell. On a typically cold but surprisingly wind-free Oklahoma winter day, the ceremonial blankets

The Clyde Warrior Memorial Building, Ponca tribal complex, White Eagle, Oklahoma.

presented to honored guests were especially welcome, even though most attendees were appropriately dressed in heavy coats.

Buried in front of the building—and marked by a large boulder inscribed "The Warrior Memorial" during the one hundred thirtieth Ponca Powwow on August 26, 2006—is a time capsule scheduled to be opened in 2136. Among the artifacts inside the capsule are sets of men's, women's, and children's traditional regalia, personal mementos from numerous tribal members, a specially commissioned drum, and "35 CDs containing over 600 songs . . . and a 700 page detailed text about each song."[2] That a monument in his name proudly stands guard over the tribal time capsule is a fitting testimony to Clyde Warrior's "Red Power." His is a legacy of protecting and honoring the vitality and absolute necessity of tribal identity, traditions, values, sovereignty, and cultural integrity that lives on.

NOTES

INTRODUCTION

1. This short but effective denouncement of European heritage shocked many observers when Warrior uttered it in the presidential race for the SRIYC, but it also helped win him a landslide victory. Clyde Warrior, "Which One Are You?," *Americans Before Columbus* 2, no. 4, (December 1964), 1, 7.

2. Warrior's campaign also echoed the work of the Society of American Indians (SAI), an Indian rights organization formed by educated American Indians early in the twentieth century; however, while the SAI celebrated pan-Indian identity over tribal identity, Warrior championed the latter.

3. Donald Fixico, "Ethics in Writing American Indian History," in *Natives and Academics: Researching and Writing about American Indians*, ed. Devon A. Mihesuah (Lincoln: University of Nebraska Press, 1998), 86.

4. Ibid.

5. The model school program pioneered by the National Indian Youth Council and the Far West Laboratory broke new ground in educational thinking and was matched by a similar experimental, Rough Rock Demonstration School on the Navajo reservation, at the same time (the mid-sixties).

6. Interview with Della Warrior, February 17, 2010.

7. Letter from Stan Steiner to Della Warrior, October 24, 1969, Box 3, Folder 32, National Indian Youth Council Papers, University of New Mexico, Center for Southwest Research (hereafter: NIYC Papers).

PROLOGUE: A PONCA HISTORY

1. James H. Howard, *The Ponca Tribe* (1965; repr., Lincoln: University of Nebraska Press, 1995), 5.

2. Interview with Jimmy Duncan, March 7, 2013. I use the term "spirituality" to differentiate from more formally structured religious belief systems.

3. Further information on Ponca clans and language is found in Howard, *Ponca Tribe*, which is, to date, the most extensive published study of the Ponca people. There are a variety of ways to spell and pronounce "Hethuska," including

Haoshki, Hay-thu-schka, and Helocka, depending on sources and the era within which the society was discussed. I have used the most commonly used spelling in contemporary times: Hethuska.

4. Ibid., 92.

5. Stephen Dando-Collins, *Standing Bear Is a Person: The True Story of a Native America's Quest for Justice* (Cambridge, Mass.: Da Capo, 2004), 12.

6. Dennis Zotigh, "Moving History: The Evolution of the Powwow" (self-published essay, 1991). In author's possession.

7. "White Eagle Park," Ponca Tribe of Oklahoma (official website of the Ponca Nation), http://www.ponca.com/121626.html, accessed July 20, 2012.

8. "Ponca Tribe," Ponca Tribe of Oklahoma, http://www.poncacity.com/about/ponca_tribe.html, accessed September 2014.

9. Several texts discuss the Standing Bear case, including Stephen Dando-Collins's *Standing Bear Is a Person*.

10. Dando-Collins, *Standing Bear Is a Person*, 49.

11. For more details of this argument: ibid., 54.

12. Warrior's discussion of the conflicting worldviews within the Ponca Nation are discussed in more detail in chapter 2.

13. Dando-Collins, *Standing Bear is a Person*, 137.

14. Ibid., 223–24.

15. William T. Hagan, *Taking Indian Lands: The Cherokee (Jerome) Commission, 1889–1893* (Norman: University of Oklahoma Press, 2003), 223–24.

16. Ibid.

17. Ibid., 226.

18. Ibid., 227.

19. Indian Appropriation Act, April 1, 1904, Section 8. (33 Stats., 217)

20. "An Act Making appropriations for the current and contingent expenses of the Indian Department and for fulfilling treaty stipulations with various Indian tribes for the fiscal year ending June thirtieth, nineteen hundred and three, and for other purposes." May 27, 1902, 32 Stat., 245, in Kappler, *Kappler's Indian Affairs: Laws and Treaties*, chapter 888, 119.

21. Ibid.; Act of March 1, 1907, 34 Stat., 1015, in Kappler, *Kappler's Indian Affairs: Laws and Treaties*, chapter 2285, 270.

22. Mathes and Lowitt, *The Standing Bear Controversy*, 182.

23. Interview with William Collins, Sr., Ponca Oral History Material, Western History Collections, University of Oklahoma (hereafter: Ponca Oral History Collection).

24. "Ponca," in *Encyclopedia of Oklahoma Indian History and Culture*, Oklahoma Historical Society, http://digital.library.okstate.edu/encyclopedia/entries/p/p0007.html.

25. Howard, *The Ponca Tribe*, 73.

26. "History of the Marland Oil Company," Ponca City, Oklahoma, http://poncacity.com/history_tid-bits_marland_oil.htm.

27. Ibid.

28. Clyde Ellis, *A Dancing People: Powwow Culture on the Southern Plains* (University Press of Kansas, 2003), 72.

29. Interview with Sylvester Warrior, May 3, 1969, Oklahoma Federation of Labor Collection, M452, Box 5, Folder 2, Western History Collections, University of Oklahoma, Norman, Oklahoma.

30. William C. Sturtevant, and Raymond J. DeMallie, *Handbook of North American Indians, Volume 13, Part 1: Plains* (Washington, D.C.: Smithsonian Institute, 2001).

31. "History," Ponca Tribe of Oklahoma, http://www.ponca.com/history, accessed April 5, 2007; page discontinued September 3, 2014.

32. Ellis, *A Dancing People*, 127.

33. Interview with William Collins, Sr., Ponca Oral History Collection.

34. Ellis, *A Dancing People*, 157.

35. The society name is spelled a variety of ways in the Osage community. More contemporary members tend to use "Inloshka" or "Inlonshka," while others opt for "I-losh-ka." The tribal newspaper, the *Osage News*, favors "In-Lon-Shka." The word itself is an elision of two terms, which is common in Osage vocabulary—*ee-lon-pa* (eldest son) and *schka* (a place word indicating something like celebration grounds). The combination of the two is also intended to honor the origins of the society from the Ponca Hethuksa.

36. Stan Steiner interview with Clyde Warrior, September 1966, Stan Steiner Papers, Department of Special Collections, Stanford University (hereafter: Stan Steiner Collection).

37. Ibid.

38. Author's interview with Darlene Harjo, November 20, 2011.

1. A PONCA UPBRINGING

1. Clyde Warrior, "Poverty, Community, and Power," *New University Thought* 4, no. 2, (Summer 1965): 5.

2. Interviews with Darlene Harjo, November 20, 2011, and Charmain Billy, August 25, 2010.

3. Ibid.

4. Interview with Vernice Willis, June 12, 2013.

5. Warrior's self-confidence was one of the main personality traits sources such as Shirley Hill Witt, Della Warrior, and Hank Adams (from his interview with Robert Warrior) remembered about him.

6. Interview with Steve Pensoneau, August 25, 2010.

7. Warrior's worldview framed every aspect of his activism and was a vital ingredient in his later realization that the most likely path to success for tribal preservation was in culturally relevant education that would allow American Indian schoolchildren to maintain intellectual sovereignty.

8. Interview with Charmain Billy, August 25, 2010

9. Interview with Darlene Harjo, February 20, 2010.

10. Ibid.

11. Untitled, undated, autobiographical essay in Warrior's handwriting. Box 5, Folder 3, NIYC Papers.

12. "History," Ponca Tribe of Oklahoma, http://www.ponca.com/history, accessed April 5, 2007; page discontinued September 3, 2014; interview with Frank Turley, July 27, 2009.

13. Howard, *The Ponica Tribe*, 92; interview with Jimmy Duncan, March 7, 2013.

14. Interview with Darlene Harjo, November 20, 2011.

15. Aleta Lutz, "Drums for the Powwows," unattributed newspaper article clipping, Ohoyohoma Club Scrapbook, Boyce Timmons Collection, Box 3, Folder 4, Western History Collections, University of Oklahoma.

16. Interview with Betty Pensoneau, October 5, 2010; Aleta Lutz, "Drums for the Powwows," Ohoyohoma Club Scrapbook, Boyce Timmons Collection, Box 3, Folder 4, Western History Collections, University of Oklahoma.

17. Aleta Lutz, "Drums for the Powwows," Ohoyohoma Club Scrapbook, Boyce Timmons Collection, Box 3, Folder 4, Western History Collections, University of Oklahoma.

18. Herbert C. Stacker, "Intertribal Gathering at Crownpoint, New Mexico, in 1920 and 1921 and Intertribal Indian Ceremonial Held Annually in Gallup, N.M., Starting in 1922," 3, Stacker Family Papers, Box 1, Center for Southwest Research, University Libraries, University of New Mexico (hereafter the Stacker Family Papers).

19. Ibid.

20. Interview with Gus Palmer, Jr., August 27, 2009. Palmer and his grandfather often accompanied Warrior and his grandfather as part of a large group of friends who would travel to Gallup.

21. There are numerous stories surrounding the origin of the term "49," ranging from California Gold Rush references, to the Anadarko Exposition of 1949, to suggestions that the figure represents the number of surviving members of an unspecified tribe's warriors who returned alive from World War II. The two most common Oklahoma versions involve the Kiowa and Comanche tribes. The Kiowa version suggests that "49" reflects the number of Kiowa courtship songs created before the first federal dance ban, in 1883. The Comanche version suggests that the 49 was originally a war journey ceremony used against the Kiowas before they became allies in the 1830s.

22. Dennis Zotigh, "Moving History: The Evolution of the Powwow," self-published essay. In author's possession.

23. A more detailed overview of the evolution of powwow culture is presented in Clyde Ellis's *A Dancing People.*

24. Sylvester Warrior discussed the decline of the Hethuska Society in a 1969 interview with Leonard Maker at the Gives Water Service Club grounds. Interview with Sylvester Warrior, May 3, 1969, Oklahoma Federation of Labor Collection, M452, Box 5, Folder 2, Western History Collections, University of Oklahoma, Norman, Oklahoma.

25. William Collins, Sr., Ponca Oral History Material, Western History Collection, University of Oklahoma.

26. Interview with Tony Isaacs, July 30, 2009.

27. Interview with Shirley Hill Witt, March 9, 2010.

28. "Paying" for a child or relative to enter the arena is a modern variation of an old Plains tradition. The family paying for the privilege will "buy" a song from the drum, which usually entails paying the drum—the drummers and singers at one drum—to sing a family song. The family will also host a "special," in which gifts representing food and shelter are presented to head dancers and singers as well as the host powwow committee. This is a way of formally introducing children to traditional cultural practices, with the blessings of their ancestors and elders.

29. Tony Isaacs interview.

30. Honor beats are the moments in a song here the drum is struck hardest.

31. Gus Palmer, Jr., interview.

32. The switch in dance categories was due to Warrior's weight gain.

33. There are several texts that discuss the diffusion of the Ponca Hethuska. The two most reliable are Clyde Ellis's *A Dancing People* and William C. Meadows's *Kiowa, Comanche and Apache Military Societies.*

34. James Howard, "Pan-Indian Culture of Oklahoma," *Scientific Monthly*, November 1955, 220.

35. Interview with Metha Collins, Clyde Warrior Ponca Oral History Project, Doris Duke Collection, University of Oklahoma (hereafter: Ponca Oral History Project).

36. Interview with Bill Collins, Sr., Ponca Oral History Project.

37. Interview with Metha Collins, Ponca Oral History Project. More information on giveaways and specials is found in Clyde Ellis's *A Dancing People.*

38. Interview with Jimmy Duncan, March 5, 2013.

39. Charmain Billy interview, August 25, 2010.

40. Della Warrior interview, February 28, 2010.

41. Frank Turley interview, July 27, 2009.

42. Sources include Charmain Billy and Della Warrior interviews. One possibility is that the two became closer as Warrior got older, hence the differing viewpoints on their relationship.

43. Frank Turley, e-mail interview, February 27, 2009.

44. Philip L. Deloria, *Playing Indian* (New Haven, Conn: Yale University Press, 1998), 144.

45. Frank Turley interview, July 27, 2009.

46. Ibid.

47. Interview with Tony Isaacs, July 30, 2009. In author's possession; Frank Turley interview, July 27, 2009.

48. Tony Isaacs interview.

49. Ibid.

50. Charmain Billy interview, November 13, 2010.

51. Darlene Harjo interview, November 20, 2011.

52. Warrior essay, NIYC Papers; Charles T. Powers, "Bitter Look at Uses of Red Power," *Kansas City Star*, March 7, 1968.

53. Charles T. Powers, "Bitter Look at Uses of Red Power," *Kansas City Star*, March 7, 1968.

54. Della Warrior, "Education, Art, and Activism," in *Beyond Red Power*, edited by Daniel Cobb and Loretta Fowler (Santa Fe, N.M.: School for Advanced Research Press, 2007), 295.

55. Interview with Kathryn Red Corn, February 9, 2010.

56. Frank Turley interview, July 27, 2009.

57. Kathryn Red Corn interview.

58. Charles T. Powers, "Bitter Look at Uses of Red Power," *Kansas City Star*, March 7, 1968.

59. Untitled, undated, autobiographical essay in Warrior's handwriting. Box 5, Folder 3, NIYC Papers.

60. Interview with Steve Pensoneau.

61. Warrior used the experiences of high school to inform much of his early political rhetoric and also a prism for understanding the cultural clashes that existed between Americans and Indians.

62. Jimmy W. Duncan, *Hethuska Zani: An Ethnology of the War Dance Complex*, Master's thesis, Northeastern State University, 1997.

63. Ibid.

64. Interview with Sylvester Warrior, May 3, 1969, Oklahoma Federation of Labor Collection, M452, Box 5, Folder 2, Western History Collections, University of Oklahoma, Norman, Oklahoma.

65. Duncan, *Hethuska Zuni*, 24.

66. Ibid., 92–93.

67. Ibid., 95, 96.

68. Ibid.

69. Ibid.

70. Interview with Jimmy Duncan, March 7, 2013.

71. Duncan, *Hethuska Zuni*, 100.

72. Interview with Frank Turley, July 27, 2009.

73. Ellis, *A Dancing People*.

74. The government policies were designed to remove people from tribal communities and force them to integrate into the hegemonic society. As such, cultural revitalization on reservations and tribal communities across the country signified a firm rejection of these policies by Indian people. James Howard's 1945 article "Pan-Indian Culture of Oklahoma" described powwow culture as pan-Indianism and created the template for the contemporary interpretation of pan-Indianism as a result of cultural homogeneity among Indians and the shedding of tribal identity in favor of a more homogenous Indian identity.

75. Clyde Warrior CV, Box 2, Folder 4, Murray Wax Papers, Department of Special Collections, Newberry Library, Chicago (hereafter: Murray Wax Papers).

76. Howard, *The Ponca Tribe,* 126.

77. The cultural education Warrior received from his grandparents was as essential to his activism as the intellectual education he received as a young adult. It was the combination of the two that allowed Warrior's voice to emerge and gave him the tools with which to frame Red Power as an ideology.

2. LAYING THE FOUNDATIONS OF A MOVEMENT

1. The success that Warrior and his cohorts enjoyed integrating themselves into college life was an achievement in itself. Many of the discussions on the nascent youth conference then, as today, focused on ways of improving American Indian college retention numbers, as many Indian students found the social and cultural disconnect between college life and their traditional upbringing too harsh.

2. Della Warrior interview, Robert Warrior Papers.

3. The Minnehaha Club was a debate society at Chilocco, which suggests that Warrior's oratory skills may have come via his grandmother. The role of first sergeant was one that reflected the militaristic worldview of Indian boarding school administrators. Following the Carlisle School model, Chilocco students were divided into "companies" in imitation of the armed forces and received military ranks.

4. "Ittanaha Club Makes a Comeback," *Cameron University Collegian* 79, no. 4, September 19, 2005.

5. Sterling Fluharty, "'For a Greater Indian America'": The Origins of the National Indian Youth Council," Master's thesis, University of Oklahoma, 2003.

6. Mona Reed interview, November 13, 2010.

7. Robert Allen Warrior and Paul Chaat Smith, *Like a Hurricane* (New York: New Press, 1996), 41.

8. Tentative workshop program, American Indian Institute Papers, Western History Collections, University of Oklahoma.

9. Charles E. Minton, "The Place of the Indian Youth Council in Higher Education," *Journal of American Indian Education* 1, no. 1 (July 1961), 54–55.

10. Ibid.

11. Ibid.

12. Interview with Gerald Brown, April 1, 2010.

13. Ibid

14. Ibid.

15. Interview with Frank Turley, July 27, 2009.

16. Albert L. Wahrhaftig, "Looking Back to Tahlequah: Robert K. Thomas' Role Among the Oklahoma Cherokee, 1963–1967," in Pavlik, *A Good Cherokee, A Good Anthropologist,* 93.

17. For a more detailed discussion of the workshops and their educational and ideological impact, see Paul McKenzie-Jones, "Evolving Voices of Discontent: The

Workshops on American Indian Affairs, 1956–1972," *American Indian Quarterly* 38, no. 2 (2014): 221.

18. McNickle's role and influence as an Indian leader are well documented in Dorothy Parker, *Singing an Indian Song: A Biography of D'Arcy McNickle* (Lincoln: University of Nebraska Press, 1992).

19. "Education for Leadership," information factsheet on the 1961 Workshop of Native American Educational Services, Box 7, Folder 3, Robert Rietz Papers, Special Collections Research Center, University of Chicago Library (hereafter: Rietz Papers). There are many excellent articles written about the Chicago conference, with Nancy O. Lurie's being the most authoritative, as she was assistant coordinator under Sol Tax. Nancy Oestrich Lurie, "The Voice of the American Indian: Report on the American Indian Chicago Conference," *Current Anthropology* 2, no. 5 (December 1961): 495.

20. Paul McKenzie-Jones, "'We Are among the Poor, the Powerless, the Inexperienced and the Inarticulate': Clyde Warrior's Campaign for a 'Greater Indian America,'" *American Indian Quarterly* 34, no. 2 (2010), 246.

21. Clyde Warrior, "Social Movements," lecture, Wayne State University, February 4, 1966, Robert Warrior Papers.

22. "The Voice of the American Indian: Declaration of Indian Purpose," American Indian Chicago Conference, University of Chicago, June 13–20, 1961, p. 5, Box 4, Records of American Indian Charter Convention, Sol Tax Collection, National Anthropological Archives, Smithsonian Institute.

23. Clyde Warrior, "Social Movements," lecture, Wayne State University, February 4, 1966, Robert Warrior Papers.

24. Interview with Shirley Hill Witt, March 9, 2010. Although nine students founded the National Indian Youth Council, many more than that signed on to the idea at Chicago, and ten attended the first meeting.

25. Clyde Warrior, "Social Movements," lecture, Wayne State University, February 4, 1966, Robert Warrior Papers.

26. Letter from Herb Blatchford to Mel Thom, June 28, 1961, Box 1, Folder 11, NIYC Papers.

27. Interview with Shirley Hill Witt, September 29, 1010.

28. Rosalie Wax and Robert K. Thomas, "American Indians and White People," *Phylon* 22, no. 4 (1961): 307.

29. Interview with Della Warrior, February 17, 2010.

30. Bradley Shreve, *Red Power Rising: The National Indian Youth Council and the Origins of Native Activism* (Norman: University of Oklahoma Press, 2011), 93, 100.

31. Interview with Frank Turley, July 27, 2009.

32. *The Indian Progress,* July 10, 1961, 4.

33. *The Indian Progress,* July 17, 1961, 2.

34. The attendance at All American Indian Days reflects the growing popularity of the powwow circuit in the 1960s. For many tribes, powwows were a welcome economic boost to their people, especially artists who used the events to sell their handmade products to tourists and fellow Indians.

35. Minutes of the National Indian Youth Council, August 10, 11, 1961, 1–2, Box 1, Folder 11, NIYC Papers. A more detailed analysis of the inaugural meeting of the NIYC is available in Bradley Shreve's *Red Power Rising*.

36. Finding office space and sleeping accommodations for the youth caucus was something of a masterstroke for Blatchford given the number of visitors expected at the fortieth Ceremonial.

37. Minutes of the National Indian Youth Council, August 10, 11, 1961, 1–2, 6–11, Box 1, Folder 11, NIYC Papers.

38. Ibid.

39. Ibid.

40. Della Warrior interview, Robert Warrior Papers. Robert Warrior (Osage) is not related to Clyde and Della Warrior.

41. Letter from Herb Blatchford to Clyde Warrior, November 12, 1961, Box 1, Folder 11, NIYC Papers.

42. The presence of the NIYC drum, and the NIYC's insistence upon beginning and ending every meeting with a prayer, was the inspiration for the later American Indian Movement's creation of an AIM song to be sung before and after every meeting.

43. Letter from Clyde Warrior to D'Arcy McNickle, February 19, 1962, Box 24, Folder 212, D'Arcy McNickle Collection, Newberry Library (hereafter: McNickle Papers).

44. *The Indian Progress*, no. 5 (March 30, 1962), Box 9, Folder 5, Records of the American Indian Charter Convention, Sol Tax Collection, National Anthropological Archives, Smithsonian Institute.

45. Robert Rietz and Bob Thomas both commented upon there being a greater vibrancy among the 1962 class than there had been the previous year. Rosalie Wax credited this to the growing reputation of the workshops and the growing influence of previous students on their peers.

46. The description of the relationship as intense was made by Hank Adams (Interview with Hank Adams, Robert Warrior Papers). Della Warrior also mentioned the relationship in her February 17, 2010, interview.

47. Clyde Warrior, 1962 Final Exam, Box 7, Folder 3, Rietz Papers.

48. Letter from Clyde Warrior to Helen Peterson, December 2, 1962, Box 10, Folder 47, Peterson Papers. Interview with Della Warrior, February 17, 2010.

49. Interview with Della Warrior, February 17, 2010.

50. Letter from Clyde Warrior to Helen Peterson, December 2, 1962, Box 10, Folder 47, Peterson Papers.

51. *Indians for Indians Hour* was broadcast on the University of Oklahoma's student radio network and ran until the early 1970s. It began as a half-hour program created by Don Whistler, a Sac and Fox student at OU.

52. William C. Meadows, *Kiowa, Apache, and Comanche Military Societies* (Austin: University of Texas Press, 1999), 151.

53. *Indians for Indians Hour*, Broadcast #143, April 9, 1963, Western History Collections, University Libraries, University of Oklahoma.

54. Figures taken from a 1963 Arizona Indian Education Association conference speech by James C. Officer titled "Indian Unity." The speech was later published in *the Journal of American Indian Education* 3, no. 3 (October 1963): 15.

55. *Indians for Indians Hour,* Broadcast #143.

56. *Indians for Indians Hour,* Broadcasts #144 and 145.

57. Ibid.

58. Ibid. Mistrust and enmity between Kiowa and Comanche citizens is not universal but certainly exists in Oklahoma. Some say that part of the reason for this was self-protection: to insure separation during times that the federal government has sought to amalgamate the tribes.

59. Interview with Garrick Bailey, October 26, 2009.

60. Ibid.

61. Ibid.

62. Kathryn Red Corn interview.

63. Della Warrior interview, February 10, 2010

64. Warrior maintained an attachment to the Boulder workshops, and he would return regularly as a guest lecturer. Eventually he organized NIYC sponsorship of the workshops.

3. THE CULTURAL FOUNDATIONS OF RED POWER

1. Charles T. Powers, "Bitter Look at Uses of Red Power," *Kansas City Star,* March 7, 1968.

2. Clyde Warrior, "Social Movements," lecture, Wayne State University, February 4, 1966, Robert Warrior Papers.

3. Shreve, *Red Power Rising,* 159.

4. Interview with Hank Adams, Robert Warrior Papers.

5. Terry Anderson, *The Movement and the Sixties: Protest in America from Greensboro to Wounded Knee* (New York: Bantam Books, 1995), 155.

6. Stokely Carmichael and Charles V. Hamilton, *Black Power: The Politics of Liberation* (New York: Random House, 1967), 43.

7. The assertion that Red Power followed Black Power is based upon the long-held assumption that American Indian militant activism began with the 1969 occupation of Alcatraz rather than with the birth of the NIYC. No comparison of the roots of the movements has been made until the recent scholarship of historians such as Brad Shreve.

8. Steve Pensoneau interview.

9. Clyde Warrior, "Social Movements," lecture, Wayne State University, February 4, 1966, Robert Warrior Papers.

10. The argument in favor of pan-Indian homogeneity often overlooks the nuances between sacred and social mores within tribal life. For traditionalists such as Warrior, these nuances signpost clear distinctions between tribal and clan identities and lifestyles.

11. Robert Burnette, *The Tortured Americans* (Englewood Cliffs, N.J.: Prentice-Hall, 1971), 81.

12. Shirley Hill Witt interview, September 29, 2010.

13. Burnette, *The Tortured Americans*, 81.

14. Hank Adams, "Indian Fishing Rights," *ABC: Americans before Columbus* 1, no. 2 (December 1963): 4.

15. The chipmunks comments came from the September 29, 2010, interview with Shirley Hill Witt. The other quote comes from Marlon Brando, *Songs My Mother Taught Me* (New York: Random House, 1974), 378. Brando dedicated this autobiography to Clyde Warrior, among others.

16. Interview with Hank Adams, Robert Warrior Papers.

17. Hank Adams, "Indian Fishing Rights," *ABC: Americans before Columbus* 1, no. 2 (December 1963): 4.

18. Bradley Shreve offers an exhaustive and extremely informative analysis of the background to Public Law 280 and its impact upon the tribes of Washington State in "'From Time Immemorial': The Fish-In Movement and the Rise of Intertribal Activism," *Pacific Historical Review*, 78 no. 3 (2009): 403–34.

19. "Ponca Protests Treaty Making by Washington," *ABC: American before Columbus* 2, no. 2 (May 5, 1964): 3.

20. Brando, *Songs My Mother Taught Me*, 375; Blatchford quoted in Shreve, *Red Power Rising*, 126.

21. Home video by Rueben Wells. Copy in author's possession.

22. Shreve, *Red Power Rising*, 130. "Ebb Tide" was a song recorded by many artists in the 1950s and 1960s, including Frank Sinatra and the Platters. The Righteous Brothers recorded the most popular version in 1965.

23. "Ponca Protests Treaty Making by Washington," *ABC: American before Columbus* 2, no. 2 (May 5, 1964): 3.

24. Ibid. The Panama Canal crisis of 1964 flared up over the scarcity of Panamanian flags in the Canal Zone. The dispute led to almost two hundred Panamanian students storming the border, with thousands more joining the struggle after the protesters' flag was torn. This in turn led to an international crisis during which Panama revoked the terms of the Rio Treaty after accusing the United States of aggression. The dispute lasted for over a year and led to President Jonson threatening to build a new canal.

25. Bradley Shreve's "From Time Immemorial" examines the long and arduous road to victory that ultimately ended in the Boldt decision.

26. "Ponca Protests Treaty Making by Washington," *ABC: American before Columbus* 2, no. 2 (May 5, 1964): 3.

27. Ibid.

28. Ibid.; Shreve, *Red Power Rising*, 13.

29. Shirley Hill Witt interview, September 29, 2010.

30. Many of the reforms suggested by the Meriam Report (*The Problem of Indian Administration*, edited by Lewis Meriam) had been carried out under the

stewardship of John Collier as commissioner of Indian affairs, although the changes usually did not go far enough, or states did not uphold their part of the bargain in providing recommended services. A detailed discussion of Collier's tenure and the Meriam Report can be found in Kenneth Philp's *John Collier's Crusade for Indian Reform, 1920–1954* (Tucson: University of Arizona Press, 1977).

31. Clyde Warrior, 1962 Final Exam, Box 7, Folder 3, Rietz Papers.

32. Ibid.

33. Cohen's essays—"Colonialism: A Realistic Approach," *Ethics* 55, no. 3 (April 1945): 167–81; "Colonialism, US Style, *Progressive* 15, no. 4 (April 1951): 16–18—formed the bedrock of all future academic analysis of Indian reservations as being subject to internal colonial rule. They mapped out the many ways that the US government served as colonial master over Indian nations.

34. Clyde Warrior, "Time for Indian Action," presentation (Indian Leadership: Accent on Youth Conference, Wisconsin State University, Eau Claire, June 12, 1964), American Indian Mission and Ministry Collection, National Council of the Episcopal Church, New York.

35. Ibid. Italics mine.

36. Interview with Shirley Hill Witt, September 29, 2010.

37. Clyde Warrior, "Which One Are You?" *ABC: Americans before Columbus* 2, no. 4 (December 1964): 1.

38. Ibid.

39. Ibid.

40. Ibid.

41. Ibid.

42. Ibid. Mel Thom's address "A Greater Indian America" provided the de facto slogan for the NIYC, and numerous essays under this banner appeared in *ABC* throughout the years.

43. Vine Deloria, Jr., "Bob Thomas as Colleague," in Steve Pavlik, *A Good Cherokee, a Good Anthropologist.*

44. Gus Palmer, Jr., interview.

45. Ibid.

46. Paul C. Smith and Robert A. Warrior, *Like a Hurricane: The Indian Movement from Alcatraz to Wounded Knee* (New York: New Press, 1996), 76.

47. Gus Palmer, Jr., interview.

48. Clyde Warrior, "How Should an Indian Act?" *ABC: Americans before Columbus* 2, no. 5 (January 1965), 2.

49. Clyde Warrior, "How Should an Indian Act?"

50. Interview with Jimmy Duncan, May 7, 2013.

51. Ibid.

52. Clyde Warrior, "How Should an Indian Act?"

53. Ibid.

54. Ibid.

55. Interview with Mike Tucker, October 1, 2009. Tucker remembers the conversation becoming heated at times, before a relieved Warrior finally emerged with his role as tail dancer intact.

56. Clyde Warrior, "How Should An Indian Act?"

57. Quoted in Stan Steiner, *The New Indians,* 69. Italics are Steiner's.

58. Clyde Warrior, "Social Movements," lecture, Wayne State University, February 4, 1966, Robert Warrior Papers.

59. Ibid.

60. Clyde Warrior, classroom observations, March 25, 1966, Box 488, Folder 17, Murray Wax Papers.

61. Clyde Warrior, "Social Movements," lecture, Wayne State University, February 4, 1966, Robert Warrior Papers.

62. Several studies, including Fred Beauvais, "Spotlight on Special Populations: American Indians and Alcohol," *Alcohol Health and Research World* 22, no. 4 (1998): 253–59, have identified the Red Power movement as the turning point in American Indian drinking trends, as the push for self-determination included many calls for tribal treatment of alcoholism, and this began to reverse the steadily increasing numbers of casualties of alcohol addiction.

63. Warrior, "Poverty, Community, and Power," 5.

64. Ibid.

65. Letter from Bob Thomas to D'Arcy McNickle, April 22, 1964. Box 24, F 212, D'Arcy McNickle Papers.

66. Clyde Warrior, "Poverty, Community, and Power."

67. Ibid.

68. Interview with Al Wahrhaftig, September 16, 2010.

69. Ibid.

70. Stan Steiner interview with Clyde Warrior, September 1966, Stan Steiner Papers.

71. Ibid.

72. Ibid.

73. Steiner, *The New Indians,* 127.

74. For more on the Jerome commissioners' views on the Ponca, see Hagan, *Taking Indian Lands.*

75. Burnette, *The Tortured Americans,* 81; Stan Steiner interview with Clyde Warrior, September 1966, Stan Steiner Papers.

76. Stan Steiner interview with Clyde Warrior, September 1966, Stan Steiner Papers.

77. James Howard's *The Ponca Tribe* describes the Ponca clan system and its limited role in contemporary Ponca life.

78. Stan Steiner interview with Clyde Warrior, September 1966, Stan Steiner Papers.

79. Ibid.

80. Many on the New Left recognized these same issues in American society and denounced a condition that pervaded mass culture. Rather than corrupting mass society as those on the New Left feared, Warrior saw these conditions fragmenting and ultimately destroying tribal cultures, to the point where complete assimilation would occur. This created even more incentive within him to fight to retain and protect those cultures and traditions.

81. Clyde Warrior, "Social Movements," lecture, Wayne State University, February 4, 1966, Robert Warrior Papers.

82. Ibid.

4. MAKING THE CASE FOR SELF-DETERMINATION

1. Clyde Warrior, "On Current Indian Affairs," *ABC: Americans before Columbus* 2, no. 2 (May 5, 1964): 2.

2. The NCAI program, modeled after the Marshall Plan of foreign aid to European nations, is discussed at length in Thomas Cowger's *The National Congress of American Indians: The Founding Years.*

3. "On Current Indian Affairs."

4. Ibid.

5. Ibid.

6. Ibid.

7. Ibid.

8. Ibid.

9. Interview with Shirley Hill Witt, March 9, 2010. 10. Clyde Warrior, "Don't Take No for an Answer," *ABC: Americans before Columbus* 2, no. 6 (August 1965): 6.

11. Ibid

12. Ibid.

13. Ibid.

14. Gerald Brown interview.

15. The slogan came from Mel Thom's inaugural address as the first president of the NIYC.

16. Warrior's cultural pluralism is another reason why the NIYC and American Indians are often excluded from the grand narrative of the civil rights era. Their desire to retain and maintain cultural individuality did not fit the narrative's theme of inclusion and equality. Clyde Warrior, "We Are Not Free," *ABC: Americans before Columbus,* May 1967, 4.

17. Vine Deloria, Jr., "Bob Thomas as Colleague," in *A Good Cherokee, A Good Anthropologist: Papers in Honor of Robert K. Thomas,* ed. Steve Pavlik (Los Angeles: American Indian Studies Center, University of California, 1998), 27.

18. Ibid.

19. Interview with Hank Adams, Robert Warrior Papers.

20. Garrick Bailey interview.

21. Vine Deloria, Jr., "Bob Thomas as Colleague," 7–32.

22. Ibid., 28.

23. Vine Deloria, Jr., *Custer Died for Your Sins: An Indian Manifesto* (New York: Macmillan, 1969), 164–66.

24. Interview with Hank Adams, Robert Warrior Papers.

25. Vine Deloria, Jr., "Bob Thomas as Colleague," 29.

26. National Indian Youth Council press release, undated, Box 3, Folder 30, NIYC Papers.

27. "Warrior Replaces Brown as NIYC Chief," Box 3, Folder 30, NIYC Papers.

28. Clyde Warrior, "Social Movements," lecture, Wayne State University, February 4, 1966, Robert Warrior Papers.

29. Ibid.

30. Ibid. Warrior's framing of religious ties to the land was one that Vine Deloria, Jr., later extrapolated to contrast to Western religious traditions in his highly acclaimed *God Is Red.*

31. Clyde Warrior, "Social Movements," lecture, Wayne State University, February 4, 1966, Robert Warrior Papers.

32. Ibid.

33. Ibid.

34. Classification of American Indians primarily among the poverty statistics in US surveys meant that they were perceived as an economic concern rather than a civil rights concern. This perception permeated academia for several decades and led to the misconception that American Indians did not become involved in civil rights protests until the 1969 occupation of Alcatraz.

35. Stan Steiner interview with Clyde Warrior, September 1966, Stan Steiner Papers.

36. Lyndon B. Johnson, "Remarks at the Swearing in of Robert L. Bennett as Commissioner of Indian Affairs," April 27, 1966, American Presidency Project, University of California, Santa Barbara, http://www.presidency.ucsb.edu/ws/?pid=27563, accessed July 11, 2014.

37. Robert L. Hardesty, *The LBJ the Nation Seldom Saw* (Texas State University Digital Collections Repository), 18, https://digital.library.txstate.edu/handle/10877/3825. Originally published by Southwest Texas State University, 1983.

38. Johnson, "Remarks."

39. Stan Steiner interview with Clyde Warrior, September 1966, Stan Steiner Papers.

40. Similar proposals had been made previously to Congress as part of the NCAI's Point IX Program, but Warrior wanted tribes to be able to devise strategies themselves rather than have an imposed structure placed upon them. In his eyes, any other program simply extended paternalistic practices already in place. Warrior, "We Are Not Free," 4.

41. Ibid.

42. Ibid.

43. Ibid.

44. Warrior, "On Current Indian Affairs."

45. Warrior, "We Are Not Free."

46. Arthur C. Parker, "Arthur C. Parker Indicts the Government for Its Actions, 1915," in *Talking Back to Civilization: Indian Voices from the Progressive Era*, edited by Frederick E. Hoxie, 95–102 (Boston: Bedford/St. Martin's 2001).

47. Clyde Warrior, "We Are Not Free."

48. Ibid.

49. Ibid.

50. Ibid.

51. Alvin Josephy's *Red Power* gives excerpts of the tribal leaders' response to the proposed omnibus bill.

52. In *The Third Space of Sovereignty*, Kevin Bruyneel argues that Warrior's post-colonial rhetoric in "We Are Not Free" laid the groundwork for much of the political rhetoric of Vine Deloria, Jr., in *Custer Died for Your Sins*.

5. RISING TENSIONS IN CHEROKEE COUNTRY

1. Annual Report on Workshop of American Indian Affairs, Rietz Papers.

2. Della Warrior interview, Robert Warrior Papers.

3. The discussions and conference panels of regional youth councils were also a source of inspiration for Warrior and the NIYC as they sought to create and communicate an education plan that could be adopted and then adapted across Indian Country.

4. Daniel M. Cobb, "Devils in Disguise: The Carnegie Project, the Cherokee Nation, and the 1960s," *American Indian Quarterly* 31 no. 3 (2007): 470–71.

5. Ibid.

6. Ibid.

7. Quotes from letter inserted inside a letter from Sol Tax to Lloyd Morrisett of the Carnegie Corporation, January 14, 1966, Box 7, Folder 7, Rietz Papers.

8. Ibid.

9. Cobb, "Devils in Disguise," 470–71.

10. *Indian Voices*, July 1965, NIYC Papers.

11. Letter from Warrior to Wax, August 12, 1965, Box 488, Folder 17, Murray Wax Papers.

12. May 26, 1966, discussion between Warrior and Murray and Rosalie Wax about Sequoyah High School, Box 488, Folder 17, Murray Wax Papers.

13. Ibid.

14. Ibid

15. Ibid.

16. Interview with Della Warrior, February 17, 2010.

17. Warrior's responses to the schoolchildren and their education is detailed throughout his notes for Wax project, as cited above in note 11 and below in note 27. The Johnson-O'Malley Act was passed on April 16, 1934, to fund state education for American Indians. It was meant to also provide an equitable alternative

for Indian parents who did wish to send their children to BIA-operated boarding schools.

18. March 25, 1966, Clyde Warrior classroom observations, Box 488, Folder 17, Murray Wax Papers.

19. Ibid.

20. March 21, 1966, Clyde Warrior classroom observations, Box 488, Folder 17, Murray Wax Papers.

21. May 26, 1966, discussions between Warrior and the Waxes, Box 488, Folder 17, Murray Wax Papers.

22. Ibid.

23. March 21, 1966, Clyde Warrior classroom observations, Box 488, Folder 17, Murray Wax Papers.

24. James, William. "Upward Bound: Portrait of a Poverty Program, 1965–1985." *SAEOPP Journal* (Southeastern Association of Educational Opportunity) 5, 1986, 28–40.

25. "Report on Upward Bound—Indian Conference, April 18–19, 1966, Washington D.C." Native American Educational Services, Robert V. Dumont, Jr., Papers, Box 5, Folder 5, Special Collections Research Center, University of Chicago Library (hereafter: Dumont Papers)

26. Ibid.

27. Ibid.

28. Letter from Karen Rickard to Clyde Warrior, October 1966, Box 3, Folder 1, NIYC Papers.

29. Combined Evaluation of Upward Bound Projects. September 8, 1966, Box 488, Folder 17, Murray Wax Papers.

30. Ibid.

31. Letter from Murray Wax to Robert Bennett, June 1, 1966, Box 17, Folder 48, Murray Wax Papers.

32. Cherokee Education Project, September 19, 1966, Field Notes, Box 488, Folder 7, Murray Wax Papers.

33. Letter from Murray Wax to Bob Dumont, June 27, 1966, Box 1, Folder 1, Dumont Papers.

34. Cherokee Education Project. September 20, 1966, Field Notes, Box 488, Folder 7, Murray Wax Papers.

35. Ibid.

36. Ibid.

37. Interview with Kathryn Red Corn. Red Corn remembers a sense of confusion at their detainment but also feeling certain that this was part of the Boyd Pierce's campaign against them.

38. Interview with Al Wahrhaftig, September 16, 2010.

39. Cherokee Education Project. September 21, 1966, Field Notes, Box 488, Folder 7, Murray Wax Papers.

40. Letter from Murray Wax to Congressman Robert Ellsworth, September 29, 1966, Box 17, Folder 48, Murray Wax Papers.

41. Robert Dumont, "The Quality of Indian Education and the Search for Tradition," Box 1, Folder 9, Dumont Papers.

42. "Calling Agent Number 49," October 19, 1966, Box 488, Folder 7, Murray Wax Papers; letter from Bob Dumont to Murray Wax, November 7, 1966, and letter from Murray Wax to Bob Dumont, January 18, 1967, both from Box 1, Folder 8, Dumont Papers.

43. Letter from Bob Dumont to Murray Wax, November 7, 1966, Box 1, Folder 8, Dumont Papers.

44. Letter from Murray Wax to Bob Dumont, January 18, 1967, Box 1, Folder 8, Dumont Papers.

45. Letter from Murray Wax to Vine Deloria, Jr., October 20, 1966, Box 17, Folder 48, Murray Wax Papers.

46. The NCAI also viewed *Indian Voices* as a rival publication, and their own *Sentinel* newsletter, usually written by Deloria, often contained disparaging comments about Thomas's and Warrior's editing.

47. Letter from Murray Wax to Clyde Warrior, November 24, 1966, Box 17, Folder 483, Murray Wax Papers.

48. Ibid.

49. Letter from Murray Wax to Bob Dumont, January 4, 1967, Box 1, Folder 11, Dumont Papers.

50. Letter from Bob Dumont to Murray Wax, December 16, 1966. Box 1, Folder 11, Dumont Papers.

51. Della Warrior interview, Robert Warrior Papers.

52. Letter from Wax to Dumont, January 18, 1967, Box 1, Folder 11, Dumont Papers.

53. Letter from Mildred Dickeman to Murray Wax, February 7, 1967, Box 17, Folder 481, Murray Wax Papers.

54. Letter from Mildred Dickeman to Murray Wax, undated, Box 17, Folder 48, Murray Wax Papers.

55. Letter from Murray Wax to Mildred Dickeman, April 20, 1967, Box 17, Folder 481, Murray Wax Papers.

56. Rosalie Wax, *Doing Fieldwork: Warnings and Advice* (Chicago: University of Chicago Press, 1971), 301–3. The code names of the subjects were revealed to me in an e-mail conversation with Al Wahrhaftig, who is named in the text as Rudy Nimmermehr.

57. Letter from D'Arcy McNickle to Florence Dickerson, John Whitney Foundation, January 21, 1967, Box 9, Folder 123, D'Arcy McNickle Collection.

58. Letter from Millie Dickeman to Murray Wax, undated, Box 17, Folder 481, Murray Wax Papers. "Indian anti-intellectualism" meant being automatically suspicious of any attempt to define one's identity and culture within an academic framework.

59. Letter from Murray Wax to Millie Dickeman, April 20, 1967, Box 17, Folder 481, Murray Wax Papers.

60. Ibid.

61. Clyde Warrior, Application for Admission to the Graduate School, University of Kansas, Box 17, Folder 43, Murray Wax Papers.

62. Letter from Murray Wax to Industrial Areas Foundation, February 20, 1967, Box 17, Folder 482, Murray Wax Papers. Industrial Areas Foundation is a community organizing network for social change set up in 1940, which specializes in working among the poor and working-class communities.

63. Letter from Murray Wax to Clyde Warrior, April 12, 1967, Box 17, Folder 482, Murray Wax Papers.

64. Letter from Stuart Levine to Clyde Warrior, May 15, 1967, Box 17, Folder 482, Murray Wax Papers.

65. Warrior viewed the Ponca Powwow and NIYC conference as a victorious homecoming and exerted a great amount of effort into ensuring that all aspects of the joint event succeeded.

6. CREATING A CULTURALLY RELEVANT CURRICULUM

1. Interview with Hank Adams, Robert Warrior Papers.

2. The concept of culturally relevant education was groundbreaking at this time, and Hispanic and African Americans also began to demand schooling relevant to their ethnic history and worldviews. Among American Indians, Warrior and the NIYC were forerunners, building upon discussions with leading indigenous scholars such as Jack Forbes about the possibilities of creating holistic cultural curricula that helped paved the way for American Indian studies to break free from the intellectual constraints of American history and anthropology and embrace multiple disciplinary interactions.

3. The role of the NIYC moving toward an educational reform movement is discussed at length in Brad Shreve's *Red Power Rising*.

4. Interview with Della Warrior, February 28, 2011.

5. Ford Proposal, July 26, 1967, Box 2, Folder 7, Dumont Papers.

6. Clyde Warrior, "We Are Not Free."

7. Ford Proposal, July 26, 1967, Box 2, Folder 7, Dumont Papers.

8. Interview with Hank Adams, Robert Warrior Papers. Adams was impressed, as were many other people, with the ease with which Warrior could negotiate moving between Indian and white worlds, hence the phrase "cultural carrier."

9. Ford Proposal, July 26, 1967, Box 2, Folder 7, Dumont Papers.

10. Ibid.

11. Due to its less vigorous movement and its origins as the war dance of the southern powwow, the Straight Dance category in the sixties typically had far more entrants than the Fancy Dance that Warrior had previously contested. Now both categories are probably equally contested, although the Fancy Dance is seen as the more glamorous category.

12. "Bennett Keynotes Conference, Warrior Re-Elected Proxy," *ABC: Americans before Columbus*, November 1967, 1–4.

13. Jim Jackson, "Look to Future, Indians Urged," *Daily Oklahoman,* undated clipping, Box 5, Folder 8, Dumont Papers. According to Warrior's cousin Vernice Willis, the family still maintains the same campsite each year during the Ponca powwow, with the space reserved for them as per traditions dating back to the original Hethuska Society. Willis interview.

14. Jim Jackson, "Look to Future, Indians Urged," *Daily Oklahoman,* undated clipping, Box 5, Folder 8, Dumont Papers.

15. "Bennett Keynotes Conference, Warrior Re-Elected Proxy," *ABC: Americans before Columbus,* November 1967, 1–4.

16. Warrior, "On Current Indian Affairs."

17. Robert V. Dumont, "The Quality of Indian Education and the Search for Tradition," speech given at the annual meeting of the NIYC at the 90th annual Ponca Powwow, Box 12, Folder 482, Murray Wax Papers. Dumont's speech became a template for the NIYC model of culturally relevant education projects aimed at removing the cultural barriers that blocked many American Indian children from advancing academically.

18. Ibid.

19. Ibid.

20. Ibid.

21. Ibid.

22. Figures taken from a selection of NIYC papers discussed in the chapter, namely correspondence between NIYC members and Far West Laboratory, confirming acceptance of grant monies received.

23. President's National Advisory Commission on Rural Poverty, *The People Left Behind* (Washington, D.C.: US Department of Health, Education, and Welfare, 1967), 12, 121.

24. Warrior, "Poverty, Community, and Power."

25. President's National Advisory Commission on Rural Poverty, *The People Left Behind* (Washington, D.C.: US Department of Health, Education, and Welfare, 1967), 12, 121.

26. Warrior, "Poverty, Community, and Power."

27. President's National Advisory Commission on Rural Poverty, *The People Left Behind,* 121, 126–27.

28. Della Warrior interview, February 28, 2011.

29. Steve Pensoneau interview. Steve's comment was not made in relation to Warrior's alcoholism but to the scale of achievement that Warrior made in crossing back and forth between the Ponca and Western worlds.

30. Della Warrior interview, Robert Warrior Papers.

31. Letter from Murray Wax to Millie Dickeman, October 15, 1967, Box 17, Folder 483, Murray Wax Papers.

32. Della Warrior interview, Robert Warrior Papers.

33. Letter from Murray Wax to Millie Dickeman, undated, Box 17, Folder 483 Murray Wax Papers.

34. Interview with Thomasine Grass, November 13, 2010.

35. Ibid.

36. Ibid.

37. Proposal of Programs for American Indian College Students, December 11, 1967, Box 17, Folder 485, Murray Wax Papers.

38. Letter from Bob Dumont to Clyde Warrior, November 27, 1967 Box 1, Folder 6, Robert Dumont Papers.

39. Ibid.

40. Proposal of Programs for American Indian College Students, December 11, 1967, Box 17, Folder 485, Murray Wax Papers, 7.

41. Ibid.

42. Ibid.

43. Ibid.

44. "Remarks on Indian Education," by Mrs. Martha Grass, Ponca, White Eagle, Oklahoma, Box 5, Folder 38, NIYC Papers.

45. Ibid.

46. Ibid.

47. Letter from Bob Dumont to Iola Hayden, January 26, 1968, Box 5, Folder 38, NIYC Papers.

48. Brief Resume of White Eagle School, Box 5, Folder 38, NIYC Papers.

49. Ibid.

50. Ibid.

51. Ibid.

52. Ibid.

53. Ibid.

54. Letter from Della Warrior to Robert Dumont, May 1, 1968, Box 5, Folder 38, NIYC Papers.

55. Charles T. Powers, "Bitter Look at Uses of Red Power," *Kansas City Star,* March 7, 1968.

56. "Indian Problem More Complex Than Just Question of Food," *Ponca City News,* Box 5, Folder 38, NIYC Papers.

57. Lyndon B. Johnson, "Special Message to the Congress on the Problems of the American Indian: 'The Forgotten American,'" March 6, 1968, American Presidency Project, University of California, Santa Barbara, http://www.presidency.ucsb.edu/ws/?pid=28709, accessed July 11, 2014.

58. Ibid.

59. Ibid.

60. Letter from Della Warrior to Glenn Nimnicht, May 1, 1968, Box 5, Folder 28, NIYC Papers.

61. Proposed Tutorial Program, Box 5, Folder 38, NIYC Papers.

62. Abstract of the Program and Budget, sent with June 11 letter from Della Warrior to Glenn Nimnicht, Box 5, Folder 38, NIYC Papers.

63. "Educational Lab Official Visits White Eagle Tutoring program," *Ponca City News,* June 28, 1968, Box 5, Folder 38, NIYC Papers.

64. Abstract of the Program and Budget, sent with June 11 letter from Della Warrior to Glenn Nimnicht, Box 5, Folder 38, NIYC Papers.

65. "Educational Lab Official Visits White Eagle Tutoring program," *Ponca City News,* June 28, 1968, Box 5, Folder 38, NIYC Papers.

66. "School History," Dilcon Community School, http://www.dilconeagles .com, accessed September 8, 2014.

65. An analysis of the role and contribution of the Boulder workshops and the NIYC to this vision of cultural retention and self-determination can be found in Paul McKenzie-Jones, "Evolving Voices of Discontent: The Workshops on American Indian Affairs, 1956–1972," *American Indian Quarterly* 38, no. 2 (2014): 224–57.

7. LEGACY

1. Della Warrior interview, Robert Warrior Papers.

2. Ibid.

3. Mel Thom, "A Tribute to Clyde Warrior," Box, 17, Folder, 483, Murray Wax Papers.

4. Interview with Shirley Hill Witt, March 9, 2010.

5. Interview with Della Warrior, February 17, 2010.

6. Interview with Betty Pensoneau, November 8, 2013.

7. Della Warrior interview, Robert Warrior Papers.

8. Interview with Frank Turley, July 27, 2009.

9. Della Warrior interview, Robert Warrior Papers.

10. Interview with Frank Turley, July 27, 2009.

11. Interview with Betty Pensoneau.

12. Interview with Frank Turley, July 27, 2009.

13. Teller quote: extract from the *Annual Report of the Secretary of the Interior,* November 1, 1883, House Executive Document, no. 1, 48th Congress, 1st session, serial 2190.

14. Della Warrior interview, Robert Warrior Papers.

15. Thomas A. Billings, July 9, 1968, "Eulogy for Clyde Warrior," "Indians" folder, Box 481, Records of the Indian Division Relating to Public Relations, 1965–1970, Records of the Office of Operations, Records of the Office of Economic Opportunity, Record Group 381, National Archives and Records Administration, College Park, Maryland.

16. Charles E. Heerman, "The Ponca: A People in the Process of Becoming," *Journal of American Indian Education* 13, no. 3 (May 1975): 25.

17. "A Tribute To Clyde Warrior," Box 17, Folder 483, Murray Wax Papers.

18. Letter from Mel Thom to "Friends of the Late Clyde Warrior," July 30, 1968, Box 17, Folder 483, Murray Wax Papers.

19. Della Warrior interview, Robert Warrior Papers.

20. "Proposal to the Carnegie Corporation for Funding Continuation of the Indian Education Survey Project," Box 1, Folder 7, Dumont Papers.

21. Ibid.

22. Ibid.

23. Heerman, "The Ponca."

24. Della Warrior interview, Robert Warrior Papers.

25. Letter from Stan Steiner to Della Warrior, October 24, 1969, Box 3, Folder 32, NIYC Records.

26. More on this coup and its repercussions can be found in Shreve, *Red Power Rising*, 178, 188.

27. National Indian Youth Council, "Third Quarter Report," July 1–September 30, 1968, Box 1, Folder 38, NIYC Papers.

28. National Indian Youth Council Press Release, December 22, 1969, Box 2, Folder 29, NIYC Papers.

29. Warrior's focus was always upon community uplift and cultural retention. He found Cold War rhetoric, however, an occasionally useful tool.

30. Stan Steiner interview with Clyde Warrior, September 1966, Stan Steiner Papers.

31. Seeing Tecumseh as Warrior's role model points to how Warrior's rhetoric and cause were internally focused on creating collaborative unions between distinct nations rather part of an international indigenous movement.

32. Burnette, *The Tortured Americans*, 81.

33. Tim Findley, "Alcatraz Recollections," in *American Indian Activism: Alcatraz to the Longest Walk*, ed. Troy Johnson, Joanne Nagel, and Duane Champagne (Urbana: University of Illinois Press, 1997), 78.

34. Paul Chaat Smith and Robert Warrior's *Like a Hurricane* gives a thorough treatise on the reasons behind, and reactions to, the occupation of Alcatraz and all that followed.

35. Smith and Warrior's *Like a Hurricane* is an excellent study of AIM and the momentum of the movement from Alcatraz to Wounded Knee.

36. Quoted in "Indian Activism," *Alcatraz Is Not an Island*, PBS, 2002, http://www.pbs.org/itvs/alcatrazisnotanisland/activism.html, accessed September 8, 2014.

37. Shreve, *Red Power Rising*, 192. Shreve cites the Wilkinson era as marking a sea change in strategic thinking for the NIYC and a new approach to activism and Indian affairs.

38. Interview with Charlie Cambridge, February 25, 2010.

39. Ibid.

40. Ibid.

41. Clyde Warrior, "Social Movements," lecture, Wayne State University, February 4, 1966, Robert Warrior Papers.

42. Clyde Warrior, "Poverty, Community, and Power," 6.

43. Clyde Warrior, "Social Movements," lecture, Wayne State University, February 4, 1966, Robert Warrior Papers.

44. Quoted in Cowger, *The National Congress of American Indians*, 113.

45. Cowger, *The National Congress of American Indians*, 113.

46. Jack Forbes, *Native Americans and Nixon*, 3.

47. Richard Nixon, "Special Message to the Congress on Indian Affairs," July 8, 1970, http://www.presidency.ucsb.edu/ws/?pid=2573, accessed September 6, 2014.

48. Clyde Warrior, "We Are Not Free." Jack Forbes's *Native Americans and Nixon* discusses the relationship between activists and the Nixon administration, including the various influences on his Indian policy.

49. Steve Talbot, "Indian Students and Reminiscences of Alcatraz," in *American Indian Activism,* edited by Johnson, Nagel, and Champagne. The UNA was an urban Indian group formed by Jack Forbes and others in 1968 after he began working at the Far West Laboratory in Berkeley, California. Initially they focused their activism on pushing for greater recognition in higher education before branching out into more militant acts of protest such as the occupation of Mount Rushmore in 1970.

50. Nixon, "Special Message to the Congress."

51. Ibid.

52. The lack of recognition of Warrior's legacy testifies to his reticence to accept accolades as a leader during his life.

53. Clyde Warrior, "Social Movements," lecture, Wayne State University, February 4, 1966, Robert Warrior Papers; "Memorial Rites Recognize Indian Leader," *Gallup Independent,* July 10, 1968.

54. "Memorial Rites Recognize Indian Leader," *Gallup Independent,* July 10, 1968.

55. The chord that Warrior's words strike so long after his death also serves as a reminder of how much work there is still to be done.

56. Quoted in "Fancy Dance Contest Honors World Champion Fancy Dancer," *Ponca City News,* Friday September 1, 1996.

57. Interview with Frank Turley. July 27, 2009.

58. Interview with Hank Adams, Robert Warrior Papers.

EPILOGUE

1. "Office of Native American Programs—Success Stories 2007," US Department of Housing and Urban Development, December 19, 2007, http://portal.hud.gov/hudportal/, accessed September 8, 2014.

2. Judie Aitken, "A Celebration—a Piece of History," http://www.judieaitken.com/a-celebration-a-piece-of-history, accessed September 8, 2014.

BIBLIOGRAPHY

MANUSCRIPT AND ARCHIVAL COLLECTIONS

Center for Southwest Research, University of New Mexico, Albuquerque
    National Indian Youth Council Papers
    Stacker Family Papers
National Anthropological Archives, Smithsonian Institute, Washington, D.C.
    Sol Tax Collection, Records of the American Indian Charter Convention
National Archives and Records Administration, College Park, Maryland
    Records of the Office of Economic Opportunity
National Council of the Episcopal Church, New York City
    American Indian Mission and Ministry Collection
National Museum of the American Indian Archive Center, Suitland, Maryland
    Helen Peterson Papers
Newberry Library, Department of Special Collections, Chicago
    D'Arcy McNickle Papers
    Murray Wax Papers
Princeton University, Seeley G. Mudd Manuscript Library, Princeton, New Jersey
    Hank Adams Papers
Stanford University, Department of Special Collections, Stanford, California
    Stan Steiner Papers
Tucker (Mike) Papers, personal collection, Sacramento, California
University of Chicago, Special Collections Research Center
    Native American Education Services, Robert Dumont Papers
    Native American Education Services, Robert Rietz Papers
Warrior (Robert) Papers, personal collection, Urbana, Illinois
Western History Collections, University of Oklahoma
    American Indian Institute Collection
    Boyce Timmons Collection
    Doris Duke Oral History Collections

Indians for Indians Hour Recordings
Oklahoma Federation of Labor Collection
Ponca Oral History Material
Wisconsin Historical Society, Library-Archives Division, Eau Claire Area Research Center
Veda W. Stone American Indian Reference Collection

BOOKS, ARTICLES, THESES, DISSERTATIONS, AND MANUSCRIPTS

Adams, Hank. "Indian Fishing Rights." *ABC: Americans before Columbus* 1, no. 2 (December 1963): 3–5.

Anderson, Gary C. *Little Crow: Spokesman for the Sioux*. St. Paul: Minnesota Historical Society, 1986.

Anderson, Terry H. *The Movement and the Sixties: Protest in America from Greensboro to Wounded Knee*. New York: Bantam Books, 1995.

Beauvais, Fred. "Spotlight on Special Populations: American Indians and Alcohol." *Alcohol Health and Research World* 22, no. 4 (1998): 253–59.

Brando, Marlon. *Songs My Mother Taught Me*. New York: Random House, 1974.

Brophy, William A., Sophie D. Aberle, et al. *The Indian: America's Unfinished Business*. Norman: University of Oklahoma Press, 1966.

Bruyneel, Kevin. *The Third Space of Sovereignty: The Post-Colonial Politics of US–Indigenous Relations*, Minneapolis: University of Minnesota Press, 2007.

Burnette, Robert. *The Tortured Americans*. Englewood Cliffs, N.J.: Prentice-Hall, 1971.

Cahn, Edgar S., ed. *Our Brother's Keeper: The Indian in White America*. New York: New Community Press, 1969.

Callahan, Alice Anne. *The Osage Ceremonial Dance I'n-Lon-Schka*. Norman: University of Oklahoma Press, 1990.

Carmichael, Stokely, and Charles V. Hamilton. *Black Power: The Politics of Liberation*. New York: Random House, 1967.

Churchill, Winston. *My Early Life: A Roving Commission*, New York: Simon & Schuster, 1930

Clarkin, Tom. *Federal Indian Policy in the Kennedy and Johnson Administrations*. Albuquerque: University of New Mexico Press, 2001.

Cobb, Daniel M . "Devils in Disguise: The Carnegie Project, the Cherokee Nation, and the 1960s." *Western Historical Quarterly* 33, no. 1 (2007): 465–90.

———. *Native Activism in Cold War America: The Struggle for Sovereignty*. Lawrence: University of Kansas Press, 2008.

Cobb, Daniel M., and Loretta Fowler, eds. *Beyond Red Power*. Santa Fe, N.M.: School for Advanced Research Press, 2007.

Cohen, Felix S. "Colonialism: A Realistic Approach," *Ethics* 55, no. 3 (April 1945): 167–81.

———. "Colonialism, US Style," *Progressive* 15, no. 4 (April 1951): 16–18.

————. *Handbook of Federal Indian Law*. Washington, D.C., Lexis Law Publishers, 1982.

————. "Indian Self-Government," *ABC: Americans before Columbus* 2, no. 5 (June 1965): 8.

Collier, John. *The Indians of the Americas*. New York: W. W. Norton, 1947.

Collings, Ellsworth, and Alma M. England. *The 101 Ranch*. Norman: University of Oklahoma Press, 1971.

Cornell, Stephen. *The Return of the Native: American Indian Political Resurgence*. New York: Oxford University Press, 1988.

Cornell, Stephen, and Joseph Kalt. "American Indian Self-Determination: The Political Economy of a Successful Policy." Conference presentation, Harvard Project on American Indian Economic Development, October 2010.

Cowger, Thomas W. *The National Congress of American Indians: The Founding Years*. Lincoln: University of Nebraska Press, 1999.

Dando-Collins, Stephen. *Standing Bear Is a Person*. New York: Perseus Books, 2004.

Davis, Julie, L. *Survival Schools: The American Indian Movement and Community Education in the Twin Cities,* Minneapolis, University of Minnesota Press, 2013.

Deloria, Philip. *Playing Indian*. New Haven, Conn.: Yale University Press, 1998.

Deloria, Vine, Jr. "Bob Thomas as Colleague." In *A Good Cherokee, a Good Anthropologist*, edited by Steve Pavlik, 27–38. Los Angeles: American Indian Studies Center, University of California, 1998.

————. *Custer Died for Your Sins: An Indian Manifesto*. New York: Macmillan, 1969.

Dinnerstein, Leonard, Roger L. Nichols, and David M. Reimers. *Natives and Strangers: A History of Ethnic Americans*, 5th ed. New York: Oxford University Press, 2010.

Duncan, Jimmy W. "Hethuska Zani: An Ethnology of the War Dance Complex." Master's thesis, Northeastern State University, 1997.

Ellis, Clyde. *A Dancing People: Powwow Culture on the Southern Plains*. Lawrence: University Press of Kansas, 2003.

————. "'More Real than the Indians Themselves': The Early Years of the Indian Lore Movement in the United States." *Montana: The Magazine of Western History* 58, no. 3 (Autumn 2008), 3–22, 92–94.

Ellis, Clyde, Luke E. Lassiter, and Gary H. Dunham, eds. *Powwow*. Lincoln: University of Nebraska Press, 2005.

Findley, Tim. "Alcatraz Recollections." In Johnson, Nagel, and Champagne, *American Indian Activism, Alcatraz to the Longest Walk*, 74–88.

Fixico, Donald. "Ethics in Writing American Indian History." In *Natives and Academics: Researching and Writing about American Indians*, edited by Devon A. Mihesuah, 84–100. Lincoln: University of Nebraska Press, 1998.

————. *Termination and Relocation: Federal Indian Policy, 1945–1960*. Albuquerque: University of New Mexico Press, 1990.

Fletcher, Alice C., and Francis La Flesche. *The Omaha Tribe*. Lincoln: University of Nebraska Press, 1992.

Fluharty, Sterling. "'For a Greater Indian America': The Origins of the National Youth Council." Master's thesis, University of Oklahoma, 2003.

Forbes, Jack. *Native Americans and Nixon: Presidential Politics and Minority Self-Determination, 1969–1972.* Los Angeles: American Indian Studies Center, 1981.

Gitlin, Todd. *The Sixties: Years of Hope, Years of Rage.* New York: Bantam Books, 1987.

Graham, Hugh D. *Civil Rights and the Presidency: Race and Gender in American Politics, 1960–1972.* New York: Oxford University Press, 1992.

Hagan, William T. *American Indians.* Chicago: University of Chicago Press, 1961.

———. *Taking Indian Lands: The Cherokee (Jerome) Commission, 1889–1893.* Norman: University of Oklahoma Press, 2003.

Hardesty, Robert L. *The LBJ the Nation Seldom Saw.* Texas State University Digital Collections Repository, https://digital.library.txstate.edu/handle/10877/3825. Originally published by Southwest Texas State University, 1983.

Hauptman, Laurence M., and Jack Campisi. "The Voice of Eastern Indians: The American Indian Chicago Conference of 1961 and the Movement for Federal Recognition." *Proceedings of the American Philosophical Society* 132, no. 4 (December 1988): 316–29.

Heerman, Charles E. "The Ponca: A People in the Process of Becoming." *Journal of American Indian Education* 14, no. 3 (May 1975): 23–31.

Hertzberg, Hazel. *The Search for an American Indian Identity: Modern Pan-Indian Movements.* Syracuse: Syracuse University Press, 1971.

Howard, James H. "Pan-Indian Culture of Oklahoma." *Scientific Monthly* 81, no. 5 (November 1955): 215–20.

———. *The Ponca Tribe.* Lincoln: University of Nebraska Press, 1995.

Hoxie, Frederick E., ed. *Talking Back to Civilization: Indian Voices from the Progressive Era.* New York: Bedford/St. Martin's, 2001.

Hurtado, Albert L., and Peter Iverson, eds. *Major Problems in American Indian History.* 2nd ed. Boston: Houghton Mifflin, 2001.

James, William. "Upward Bound: Portrait of a Poverty Program, 1965–1985." *SAEOPP (Southeastern Association of Educational Opportunity) Journal* 5 (1986), 28–40.

Johnson, Lyndon B. "Remarks at the Swearing in of Robert L. Bennett as Commissioner of Indian Affairs," April 27, 1966, American Presidency Project, University of California, Santa Barbara, http://www.presidency.ucsb.edu/ws/?pid=27563, accessed September 6, 2014.

———. Johnson, Lyndon, "Remarks at the University of Michigan, May 22, 1964," American Presidency Project, University of California, Santa Barbara, http://www.presidency.ucsb.edu/ws/index.php?pid=26262&st=&st1=, accessed September 6, 2014.

———. "Special Message to the Congress on the Problems of the American Indian: 'The Forgotten American,'" March 6, 1968, American Presidency Project, University of California, Santa Barbara, http://www.presidency.ucsb.edu/ws/?pid=28709, accessed September 6, 2014.

Johnson, Troy, Joanne Nagel, and Duane Champagne. *American Indian Activism: Alcatraz to the Longest Walk*. Urbana: University of Illinois Press, 1997.

Josephy, Alvin M. *Now That the Buffalo's Gone: A Study of Today's American Indians*. Norman: University of Oklahoma Press, 1982.

———. *Red Power: The American Indians' Fight for Freedom*. New York: American Heritage Press, 1971.

Josephy, Alvin M., Joane Nagel, and Troy Johnson. *Red Power*. 2nd ed. Lincoln: University of Nebraska Press, 1999.

Kappler, Charles Joseph. *Kappler's Indian Affairs: Laws and Treaties*. Vol. II, *Treaties*. Washington, D.C.: Government Printing Office, 1904.

Kennedy, John F. "Radio and Television Report to the American People on Civil Rights," June 11, 1963. American Presidency Project, University of California, Santa Barbara, http://www.presidency.ucsb.edu/ws/index.php?pid =9271&st =&st1=, accessed September 3, 2014.

Lurie, Nancy Oestrich. "The Voice of the American Indian: Report on the American Indian Chicago Conference." *Current Anthropology* 2, no. 5 (December 1961): 478–500.

Mails, Thomas. *Dog Soldier Societies of the Plains*. New York: Marlowe, 1973.

Mathes, Valerie Sherer, and Richard Lowitt. *The Standing Bear Controversy: Prelude to Indian Reform*. Urbana-Champaign: University of Illinois Press, 2003.

McKenzie-Jones, Paul. "Evolving Voices of Discontent: The Workshops on American Indian Affairs, 1956–1972." *American Indian Quarterly* 38, no. 2 (2014): 207–36.

———. "'We Are among the Poor, the Powerless, the Inexperienced and the Inarticulate': Clyde Warrior's Campaign for a 'Greater Indian America.'" *American Indian Quarterly* 34, no. 2 (2010): 224–57.

McNickle, D'Arcy. *Native American Tribalism*. Oxford, UK: Oxford University Press, 1973.

Meadows, William C. *Kiowa, Apache, and Comanche Military Societies*. Austin: University of Texas Press, 1999.

Meyer, Gerald. "The Cultural Pluralist Response to Americanization: Horace Kallen, Randolph Bourne, Louis Adamic, and Leonard Covello." *Socialism and Democracy* 25, no. 3 (Nov. 2011): 19–51.

Mihesuah, Devon A., ed. *Natives and Academics: Researching and Writing about American Indians*. Lincoln: University of Nebraska Press, 1998.

Minton, Charles E. "The Place of the Indian Youth Council in Higher Education." *Journal of American Indian Education* 1, no. 1 (July 1961): 29–32.

Nagel, Joane. *American Indian Ethnic Renewal: Red Power and the Resurgence of Identity and Culture*. New York: Oxford University Press, 1996.

Newcomb, Steve. "Clyde Warrior and the American Indian Fight to Be Free." *Indian Country Today*, November 20, 2013, http://indiancountrytodaymedia network.com, accessed September 6, 2014.

Nixon, Richard. "Special Message to the Congress on Indian Affairs," July 8, 1970, American Presidency Project, University of California, Santa Barbara, http://www.presidency.ucsb.edu/ws/?pid=2573, accessed September 6, 2014.

Officer, James C. "Indian Unity." *Journal of American Indian Education* 3, no. 3 (1963): 1–18.

Parker, Dorothy. *Singing an Indian Song: A Biography of D'Arcy McNickle*. Lincoln: University of Nebraska Press, 1992.

Pavlik, Steve, ed. *A Good Cherokee, a Good Anthropologist: Papers in Honor of Robert K. Thomas*. Los Angeles: American Indian Studies Center, University of California, 1998.

Philp, Kenneth. *Termination Revisited: American Indians on the Trail to Self-Determination, 1933–1953*. Lincoln: University of Nebraska Press, 2002.

President's National Advisory Commission on Rural Poverty. *The People Left Behind: A Report*. Washington, D.C.: Government Printing Office, 1967.

Riesman, David, *The Lonely Crowd: A Study of the Changing American Character*. New Haven: Yale University Press, 1950.

Rosier, Paul C. *Serving Their Country: American Indian Politics and Patriotism in the Twentieth Century*. Cambridge, Mass.: Harvard University Press, 2009.

Rydell, Robert, W. *All the World's a Fair*. Chicago: University of Chicago Press, 1984.

Scott, Erica A. *Chilocco Survivors: Contested Discourses in Narrative Responses to Ponca Alcohol Abuse*. Master's thesis, University of North Carolina at Chapel Hill, 2009.

Seaman, Muriel Belle. "History of the Ponca Agency in Oklahoma." Master's thesis, University of Oklahoma, 1931.

Shreve, Bradley. "'From Time Immemorial': The Fish-In Movement and the Rise of Intertribal Activism." *Pacific Historical Review* 78, no. 3 (2009): 403–34.

———. "Red Power Rising: The National Indian Youth Council and the Origins of Intertribal Activism." PhD diss., University of New Mexico, 2007.

———. *Red Power Rising: The National Indian Youth Council and the Origins of Native Activism*. Norman: University of Oklahoma Press, 2011.

Smith, Paul C., and Robert A. Warrior. *Like a Hurricane: The Indian Movement from Alcatraz to Wounded Knee*. New York: New Press, 1996.

Starita, Joe. *"I Am A Man": Chief Standing Bear's Journey for Justice*. New York: St. Martin's Griffin, 2008.

Steiner, Stan. *The New Indians*. New York: Dell, 1968.

Sturtevant, William C., and Raymond J. DeMallie. *Handbook of North American Indians, Volume 13, Part 1: Plains*. Washington, D.C.: Smithsonian Institute, 2001.

Talbot, Steve. "Indian Students and Reminiscences of Alcatraz." In Johnson, Nagel, and Champagne, *American Indian Activism: Alcatraz to the Longest Walk*, 104–13.

Thomas, Robert K. "Pan Indianism." *Midcontinent American Studies Journal* 2 (1965), 75–83.

Tibbles, Thomas H. *The Ponca Chiefs: An Account of the Trial of Standing Bear*. Lincoln: University of Nebraska Press, 1972.

Trafzer, Charles, Jean A. Keller, and Lorene Sisquoc, eds. *Boarding School Blues*. Lincoln: University of Nebraska Press, 2006.

Troutman, John, W. *Indian Blues: American Indians and the Politics of Music, 1879–1934*. Norman: University of Oklahoma Press, 2009.

Wahrhaftig, Albert L. "Looking Back to Tahlequah: Robert K. Thomas' Role Among the Oklahoma Cherokee, 1963–1967." In Pavlik, *A Good Cherokee, A Good Anthropologist*, 93.

Warrior, Clyde. "Don't Take No for an Answer." *ABC: Americans before Columbus* 2, no. 6 (August 1965): 6.

———. "How Should An Indian Act?" *ABC: Americans before Columbus* 2, no. 4 (December 1964): 1.

———. "On Current Indian Affairs." *ABC: Americans before Columbus* 2, no. 2 (May 5, 1964): 2.

———. "Poverty, Community, and Power." *New University Thought* 4, no. 2 (Summer 1965): 5–10.

———. "Time For Indian Action." *ABC: Americans Before Columbus* 2, no. 4 (December 1964): 3.

———. "We Are Not Free." *ABC: Americans before Columbus,*= May 1967, 4. This piece represents Warrior's address to the President's National Advisory Commission on Poverty in Memphis, Tennessee, February 2, 1967.

———. "Which One Are You?," *ABC: Americans before Columbus* 2, no. 4 (December 1964), 1, 7.

Wax, Rosalie. *A Brief History and Analysis of the Workshops on American Indian Affairs Conducted for American Indian College Students, 1956–1960*. Coral Gables, Fla.: Dept. of Anthropology, University of Miami, 1961.

———. *Doing Fieldwork: Warnings and Advice*. Chicago: University of Chicago Press, 1971.

Wax, Rosalie, and Robert K. Thomas. "American Indians and White People." *Phylon* 22, no. 4, 305–17.

Westad, Odd Arne. *The Global Cold War: Third World Interventions and the Making of Our Times*. New York: Cambridge University Press, 2005.

Wishart, David J. *An Unspeakable Sadness: The Dispossession of the Nebraska Indians*. Lincoln: University of Nebraska Press, 1994.

Zotigh, Dennis. "Moving History: The Evolution of the Powwow." Self-published essay, 1991.

INTERVIEWS BY AUTHOR

Garrick Bailey, telephone interview, October 26, 2009

Charmain Billy, Ponca City, Oklahoma, February 20, 2010

———, White Eagle, Oklahoma, August 25, 2010

———, White Eagle, Oklahoma, November 13, 2010

Gerald Brown, telephone interview, April 1, 2010

Charlie Cambridge, telephone interview, February 25, 2010

Jimmy Duncan, Broken Arrow, Oklahoma, March 5, 2013

———, e-mail interview, March 7, 2013

Thomasine Grass, White Eagle, Oklahoma, November 13, 2010

Darlene Harjo, Ponca City, Oklahoma, February 20, 2010

———, email interview, November 20, 2011

Tony Isaacs, Taos, New Mexico, July 30, 2009

Gus Palmer, Jr., Norman, Oklahoma, August 27, 2009

Betty Pensoneau, telephone interview October 5, 2010

———, e-mail interview, November 8, 2013

Steve Pensoneau, Ponca City, Oklahoma, August 25, 2010

Jeri Redcorn, Norman, Oklahoma, September 24, 2010.

Kathryn Red Corn, telephone interview, September 2, 2010

Mona Reed, White Eagle, Oklahoma, November 13, 2010

Mike Tucker, telephone interview, October 1, 2009

Frank Turley, e-mail interview, February 27, 2009

———, Santa Fe, New Mexico, July 27, 2009

Al Wahrhaftig, telephone interview, September 16, 2010

Della Warrior, Sacramento, California, February 17, 2010

———, telephone interview, February 28, 2011

Vernice Willis, Tulsa, Oklahoma, June 12, 2013

Shirley Hill Witt, Skype interview, March 9, 2010

———, Skype interview, September 29, 2010

PERIODICALS

ABC: Americans before Columbus

Aborigine (National Indian Youth Council)

Albuquerque Tribune

Cameron University Collegian

Daily Oklahoman

Gallup Independent

Indian Country Today

The Indian Progress

Indian Voices

Kansas City Star

Navajo Times

New Mexico Association on Indian Affairs Newsletter

Ponca City News

Index